International Economics

International Economics

Theory, Policy, and Practice

BY

John Charles Pool
St. John Fisher College

AND

Stephen C. Stamos, Jr.
Bucknell University

Lexington Books

D.C. Heath and Company/Lexington, Massachusetts/Toronto

Library of Congress Cataloging-in-Publication Data

Pool, John Charles.
International economics: theory, policy, and practice / John Charles Pool,
Stephen C. Stamos, Jr.
p. cm.
ISBN 0-669-17150-6 (alk. paper)
1. International economic relations. I. Stamos, Steve, 1947-   .
II. Title.
HF1359.P67 1990
337—dc20
87-45996
CIP

Published simultaneously in Canada
Printed in the United States of America
Casebound International Standard Book Number: 0-669-17150-6
Library of Congress Catalog Card Number: 87-45996

The paper used in this publication meets
the minimum requirements of American National Standard
for Information Sciences—Permanence of Paper
for Printed Library Materials, ANSI Z39.48-1984. ∞™

Year and number of this printing:

91 92 93 94 8 7 6 5 4 3 2

Contents

Figures

Tables

Preface and Acknowledgments

This is a time when interest in business and economics seems to be growing at an increasing rate. Economics classes are oversubscribed. Everyone, it seems, wants to learn how to make money.

It is also a time of general optimism in the business world. By the fall of 1989 the United States had entered its eighth year of sustained growth. The stock market was booming, inflation seemed under control, interest rates were low, and unemployment—while still high by historical standards—seemed to have stabilized. There was calmness and optimism in the air.

Yet it was an uneasy calm. Students and businesspeople were perplexed by news of record high trade deficits and the concomitant loss of the U.S. industrial sector to foreign competition, and by the very real possibility that Third World underdeveloped countries would be unable to pay their debts. *Default* had become a household world.

Most of the economics textbooks don't have an explanation for all this. There is, in our view, a void in the literature on international economics that can be used in the classroom. We hope to fill that void by providing an up-to-date analysis of the international sector in a historical context—the twentieth century—and by using basic microeconomic principles and relevant examples to develop the essential concepts and principles of international trade and finance.

In this book we examine the issues in both historical and current context and, especially, analyze the myriad of proposed solutions in an orderly and, we hope, understandable fashion that will be accessible to both the lay reader and college students, who have the largest stake in it all.

We think these problems could be resolved if there were enlightened leadership that understood the necessity of coordinated worldwide economic policy and the need for all players to sacrifice the short-run illusion of prosperity to the longer-run goals of stability. But chances are that will not happen until the external forces that are now destabilizing the world economy impose a solution on us that will be painful for everyone.

We owe a great debt to the many writers who have had the courage and prescience to point out that the emperor has no clothes. Among them are Michael Blumenthal, Irving Friedman, Ben Friedman, Harry Magdoff, Alfred Malabre, Morris Miller, Michael Moffit, Peter Peterson, Robert Reich, Felix Rohatyn, Alan Sinai, and Paul Sweezy. And there are many more.

Among those who contributed more directly to this particular project are professors James Crotty of the University of Massachusetts-Amherst, Patrice Franko-Jones of Colby College, Victor Kaspar of the Rochester Institute of Technology, Ross M. LaRoe of Denison University, Norris C. Clement, San Diego State University, and Tom Riddell of Smith College, who reviewed the manuscript in its earlier stages and who agreed with at least some of our analysis.

In this computerized world it is hard to remember what it was like to write a book without word processors, computer-generated graphics, and that wonderful invention, the spell-check. But that aside, Linda Vollmer processed the words with a diligence and patience far beyond what anyone could reasonably expect.

Last, but hardly least, we have to acknowledge our debt to our families: Betty, Mike, and Laura Linda; Lucie, Barry, and Lisanna, who, as always, are our most enthusiastic supporters.

We believe this book is suitable for students in a variety of courses. While international economics is the most obvious, it should be quite appropriate for courses such as Contemporary International Economic Problems, International Studies, and International Business Policy. The book is written in simple, nontechnical language, but it neither trivializes the international sector, as introductory textbooks usually do, nor does it mathematize the subject, which is the approach of most advanced texts. Therefore, the book is appropriate for students at many levels. We hope it helps them understand how, in the real world of the 1990s, there will be no such thing as a national economy any more—virtually everything will depend on the smooth functioning of the international economy.

Part I

The Theory of
International Trade

1
The Setting

I f there is any single word that describes the world economy in
the postwar period it is *change*. It is easy to forget that at the
turn of the second half of this century, in 1950, no one really
knew what was on the moon, jet airplanes and television were just
being developed, stereo sound systems didn't exist, nor did
personal computers, and no one had traveled in space. Now we
take all those things for granted. They are a routine part of our
personal lives. But by far the most important change to come
along—indeed, sneak up on us—in the past few decades is the
internationalization of the world economy—the globalization of
the production process.

In 1989 the international sector accounted for about 20 percent of the U.S. Gross National Product. Counting both imports
and exports, one out of five jobs in the United States is, in one
way or another, dependent on producing goods and services for
sale abroad, and the United States is relatively self-sufficient
compared to many nations of the world. Some 25 percent of the
economies of Western Europe depend on international trade and
50 percent of the Japanese economy functions solely in the international sector.

It is now virtually impossible to buy *anything* in the United
States that is not at least partially produced abroad. Just about the
only part of an IBM computer that is made in the United States is
the cover. Congresswoman Louise Slaughter (D–N.Y.) once asked
the Xerox Corporation to supply her with a copying machine that
was completely produced in the United States. They couldn't. It is

not possible to purchase even one videocassette recorder made in the United States—all are made abroad, as are virtually all color television sets. And automobiles, once produced in Detroit, are now an amalgamation of parts produced around the world. The Ford Escort—the "world" car—in the United States is assembled from parts produced in fifteen different countries. Only the valves, wheel nuts, tappets, and windows are produced in the United States (see figure 1–1).

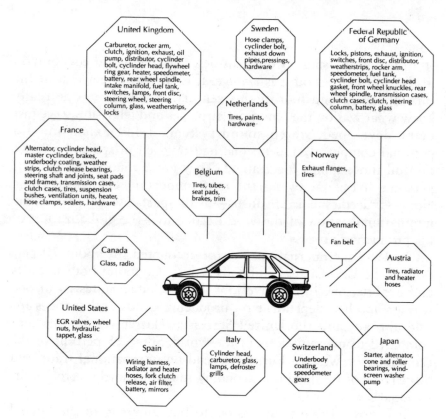

Source: World Bank, *World Development Report, 1986* (New York: Oxford University Press, 1986), p. 47.

Figure 1–1. *Global Manufacturing: The Component Network for the Ford Escort (Europe)*

But to imply that these developments, however startling they may be, are "bad," is at the least, ridiculous, and at the worst, naive. World standards of living *have* improved dramatically from the globalization of the production process and everyone, even the most myopic members of Congress who get reelected on protectionist campaigns that appeal to a misplaced sense of patriotism, know it. The world has become internationalized and, even if we wanted to, there is no way to stop it. If you are one who thinks we should, consider what life would be like without imports. Transportation would virtually grind to a halt—44 percent of U.S. oil is imported. Gasoline prices would more than triple and probably would be rationed. Prices of petroleum-based products, which is everything from Frisbees to office equipment, would skyrocket. But even if you could afford gasoline you probably couldn't buy a car after the one you have stopped running for lack of replacement parts. Imports are 30 percent of the U.S. auto market and, for one example, imported parts make up 30 percent of domestically produced General Motors cars. You would have to give up coffee (99.9 percent imported) and chocolate (80 percent imported), and virtually anything electronic in your life. After your TV broke down you wouldn't be able to watch the World Series but that wouldn't matter because it wouldn't be happening—all the baseballs are made in Haiti and the Dominican Republic, and 90 percent of the athletic shoes are imported.

The list goes on and on. The issue, of course, is that everyone—or at least almost everyone—benefits from international trade. The theory behind that, which is the topic of the first part of this book, is both simple and complex. The theory of comparative advantage, which has been around since the early 1800s, posits that every country gains by "putting its best foot forward," specializing and trading, and in theory it is easy to demonstrate that is true. But as we shall attempt to demonstrate, it is often more true for some than others, which leads to a myriad of problems, not the least of which is that the United States is rapidly losing many of the comparative advantages it once enjoyed. That's the complicated part.

Baseball gloves	Only the most expensive models made here.
Cars	Imports make up 29% of the United States market. Domestic cars contain up to 30% foreign parts.
Chocolate	80% of all cocoa is imported.
Coffee	99.9% is imported.
Gasoline	44% of all oil is imported.
Liquor	One-fourth of all liquor is made overseas.
Personal computers	Even IBM and Apple PCs couldn't be made without foreign parts.
Running shoes	Tough to find any made in the United States.
Toys	Most toys—even Barbie dolls—are made overseas.
VCRs	All are made overseas.

Source: *USA Today*, Nov. 14, 1988, B–1.

Figure 1–2. *What Life Would Be Like without Imported Goods*

Beyond that the theory of international finance, which doesn't have a simple version, has become increasingly complicated. Trade is facilitated by a complex system of exchange rates and payment mechanisms, which depends largely on good faith and the general acceptance of some common unit of account to settle international transactions. That unit of account was once gold, but gold has long since been replaced by key currencies that are used by nearly all countries to settle accounts. The simple fact that the U.S. dollar is the world's key international currency has led to problems that would not have been imaginable to those who set up the current international financial system at Bretton Woods, New Hampshire, in 1944. The theory behind that system completes the first part of this book. Then we take up the problems.

It is well known, if not universally recognized, that the international economy has reached a level of imbalance that approaches crisis proportions. The steady erosion of the once dominant position of the United States in the world economic arena, coupled with the rapid rise of Japan, West Germany, and the Newly Industrialized Countries (NICs) of the Pacific Rim to a position of unparalleled economic power, means that the international economic system will be drastically reordered in the 1990s. The problems can be ignored, but they won't go away. Adjustments will have to be made. The pressing question facing the policy makers and the monetary authorities is: Will the adjustments be planned and orderly or will they be chaotic? Currently, for most people, they are chaotic.

By August 1986, the unemployment rate in the United States was 6.8 percent, but, in Aliquippa, Pennsylvania, just north of Pittsburgh, over 13 percent were unemployed. The economic recovery that spread across the nation between 1983 and 1986 missed Aliquippa completely. Its steel plant, which had employed more than twelve thousand workers several years previously, employed only eight hundred in 1986. What happened in Aliquippa happened throughout Pennsylvania. In 1976, there were more than two hundred thousand jobs in the steel and primary metals industry in the state, but by 1986, fewer than one hundred thousand remained.

To protect himself against a sharply devalued currency, Venezuelan businessman Jose-Manuel Sanchez sold 20 million bolivars worth of stock in Venezuelan companies and with the proceeds bought $1 million worth of certificates of deposit from Chemical Bank in New York, depositing the rest in a West German bank.

In 1981, petroleum was selling for $32.50 a barrel. U.S. oil fields were crowded with geologists and drilling rigs. But by August 1986, petroleum prices had collapsed to $12.50 a barrel and the oil fields had become symbols of debt, bankruptcy, and unemployment. Texas alone faced a $3.2 billion state budget deficit and an unemployment rate of almost 12 percent.

In 1986 a USX steel worker on strike complained that after accepting a $3-per-hour reduction in wages and benefits two years previously, the company was now demanding another cut of $5.50 per hour in wages and benefits. Without this concession from the union workers, the company claimed, it could not compete against foreign steel producers and would be forced to shut down.

A formerly unemployed machinist from Chicopee, Massachusetts, is now working in a new high-tech industry off Route 128 outside Boston. While he is delighted to be working, he made $4.85 an hour in 1986 in his new job, compared to $9.75 an hour in his former job. To make ends meet, his wife is working at a fast-food restaurant for $3.35 an hour.

Just off Interstate 90 in the middle of Minnesota, in a small breakfast diner, a poster tacked to the wall above the cash register reads, "Future Farmers of America: Who Needs Them?"

An Iowa farmer who has just lost his farm wearily contemplates the irony of his misfortune: his overproduction of corn contributed to declining grain prices and eventually the foreclosure of his farm. As he reads the evening newspaper, he sees that so much grain was produced over the past year that there is no place to store it. On another page is a story about famine and starvation in East Africa, and below that story he reads that the president has offered to sell wheat to the Soviet Union at a 30 percent discount. Even at that price, the Russians aren't buying. They can get it cheaper elsewhere. Unable to comprehend the interdependence of these seemingly unrelated stories, he reflects on his new job in a service station, owned by his wife's brother.

Mexican peasant Maria Nuñez, a mother of eleven children, discovered one morning that tortillas, the main staple of her family's diet, had doubled in price during the past six months. She was informed that the government had further reduced its food subsidy. The reduction had something to do with deficits, debt, and a loan from the International Monetary Fund in Washington, D.C., which is a long way from her small farm in Santa Cruz just outside of Guadalajara.

In Rochester, New York, a Kodak production line worker with twenty-two years of seniority is laid off. Competition from the Japanese, he is told, is the reason. What, he wonders, as he drives his Toyota to the unemployment office, has become of the American dream?

The problem revolves around three major developments, all of which were unexpected and none of which are—we shall argue—sustainable. Each development is a story in itself, but each is interrelated. The first and probably least understood development is the staggering Third World foreign debt, which dates back to the early 1970s. That debt, which now approaches *$1.5 trillion,* is becoming a more and more serious threat to the stability of the international financial system as it compounds to astronomical levels. Many solutions have been proposed, but none has been implemented in a way that alleviates the problem. As a consequence of mounting debt, service obligations standards of living in the underdeveloped world have been pushed back to levels lower than they were twenty-five years ago.

The second development, better understood but just as serious, is the unprecedented recent explosion of the U.S. federal budget and balance of payments deficit—the twin deficits, as they are called. As a consequence of record-high federal deficits beginning in 1981, the U.S. national debt more than doubled in only five years. Interest payments on this debt are the third largest category in the federal budget—after defense and social security—and are causing a massive transfer of wealth from the tax-paying middle class to the bond-owning upper class. If the debt were internally owned it would still be a problem, but not an unsustainable trend. But, increasingly, the debt is being purchased by foreign interests that are awash in dollars accumulated from the trade imbalance. This, in turn, has pushed the United States into a net foreign debtor position for the first time since 1914.

This third development, the U.S. foreign debt, which exceeded $600 billion at the end of 1989, represents the excess of foreign-held assets in the United States over the total of foreign assets held by U.S. citizens and corporations. For some time after World War II the buildup of U.S. assets abroad, which was mostly caused by the globalization of the production process spearheaded by U.S.–based multinational corporations, meant the United States could count on a net surplus of foreign investment income in its current account to offset, if need be, negative trade balances. This changed dramatically in 1985 as the ever-growing trade deficits overwhelmed declining net investment income. This reversed the once-dominant position of the United States in the international economy.

At the same time the United States was becoming the world's largest debtor nation, Japan became the world's largest creditor, followed closely by West Germany. A creditor nation has two options. One, it can invest the funds earned from its export surplus into its own development and toward raising its own standard of living or, two, it can invest the funds in the country with which it has a trade imbalance. Japan largely has chosen to recycle its export surpluses to the United States by purchasing U.S. Treasury bonds, corporate stock, and to a lesser—but rapidly increasing—extent by directly investing in U.S. plants and equipment or real estate. Thus a mutually dependent relationship between the two nations has evolved over a very short time.

Japanese investments have supplemented the now-feeble U.S. savings rate and served to finance U.S. federal budget deficits, thereby allowing American consumers to maintain the high standards of living to which they have become accustomed. This has meant that the U.S. economy has become almost completely dependent on the infusion of Japanese capital funds that can be withdrawn at will, pushing the financial markets into chaos, if not collapse, and the United States into a severe recession that would reverberate throughout the world. This has meant that the

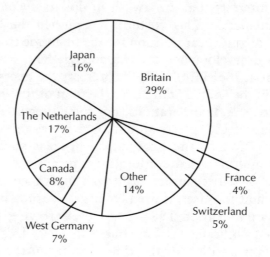

Total foreign direct investment in the United States at the end of 1988 was $304.2 billion.

Source: Commerce Department.

Figure 1–3a. *The Foreign Owners*

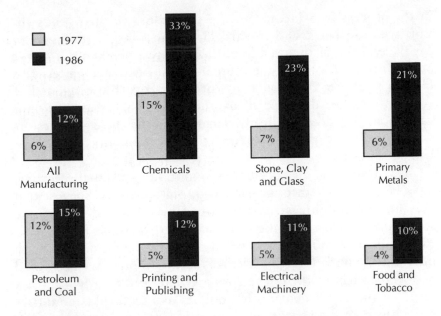

Dollar value of assets of U.S. affiliates of foreign manufacturing companies as a percent of all U.S. businesses in manufacturing in 1977 and 1986, the most recent year available.

Source: Commerce Department.

Figure 1–3b. *Growing Foreign Ownership of U.S. Industry*

traditional tools of monetary and fiscal policy have become obsolete. The United States has lost control of its own economic destiny.

Japan and the other trade surplus-creditor countries have little option but to recycle their surpluses back to the United States. The U.S. addiction to Japanese imports has provided the engine of growth for Japan. Without U.S. markets, which are far and away their largest, the Japanese would be forced to look elsewhere for outlets for levels of production that far exceed their own traditional consumption patterns. Since there are no comparable markets, the relationship has become almost totally symbiotic. But in the process it is Japan, not the United States, that holds the upper hand. The trend toward larger and larger amounts of Japanese direct, as opposed to portfolio, investments in the United States further reinforces the mutual interdependence patterns. A Honda plant in Ohio or a downtown office building in Los Angeles can't be disposed of overnight as U.S. Treasury bonds can. Soon, if it doesn't already, Japan and other foreign investors will have almost as big a stake in the U.S. economy as does the United States itself.

Traditional theories of international trade and finance, which have been around since the early eighteenth century, suggest that this uncomfortable situation could be adjusted into some semblance of balance either automatically, through free-market exchange rate movements, or in a planned manner through intervention in the foreign exchange markets. Both have been tried and neither has worked. The strong dollar of the early 1980s, a result of increased demand for dollars as the surplus countries sought to reap the benefits of artificially high interest rates in the United States, exacerbated the trade imbalance to crisis proportions. The coordinated intervention that began in the fall of 1985—and resulted in a 50 percent depreciation in the value of the dollar against the currencies of the major U.S. trading partners—did little to ameliorate the situation. By 1989 the U.S. trade *and* current account balances were still near record highs.

It has become clear that something must be done to reorder the international economy toward a cooperative system that accounts for the rapid role reversal we have witnessed over the past few years. It is not realistic to continue acting as if the United States, and particularly the U.S. dollar, can continue to play the key dominant role in the world economy that it has for the past forty years. No nation can act as police force of the world, buyer of last resort, creditor of last resort, and keeper of the key currency while at the same time becoming the world's largest debtor. The arithmetic just doesn't add up, and everyone knows it. Rethinking that simple reality is the theme of this book. There are, we shall argue, ways in which the system can be brought back into balance without undue harm to the key players and, especially, to the innocent but interested bystanders in the Third

World who have already paid their dues but received nothing in return. They, more than anyone, hold the power to bring down the house of cards.

Understanding this ironic turn of events requires an understanding of the theoretical principles, subtleties, and realities of international trade, the functioning of the international financial system in its many variations, and the mechanics of international lending. These issues are the subject of this book. After they have been examined in some detail, we then take up the question of why previous policy prescriptions have failed, and suggest some possible solutions to this increasingly pressing problem.

Chapter 2 takes up the question of international trade and examines its history and theory in some detail in a mostly nonmathematical presentation. It essentially demonstrates why it is that everyone is supposed to gain from specialization and trade and why this doesn't always happen. The adjustments and refinements to this venerable theory are also treated and critiqued.

Chapter 3 examines the real-world roadblock to the free functioning of international trade: protectionist commercial policies that pervade most nations' trade strategies.

Chapter 4 then takes up the enigmatic world of international finance. Balance of payments accounting systems are examined as are the various systems of exchange rate determination in the context of both theory and practice. That sets the stage to begin introducing the reader to emerging problems in the international arena.

Chapter 5 treats what may well be the most important development of all: the globalization of production that has resulted from the relatively recent arrival of the multinational corporations, which now dominate all international trade transactions. Their role in the process of economic development has become pervasive; yet they remain a controversial dilemma for most underdeveloped countries.

Then, in chapter 6, we step back and attempt to put all this in a historical context, which, we feel strongly, is required to understand why international economic policy has become the number-one issue facing the world economy today. We trace the history of these unprecedented developments from the demise of the gold standard and the dollar-based Bretton Woods system to the oil price shock of the 1970s and the concomitant development of the Third World debt crisis. Efforts to ameliorate the increasing trade balances through exchange rate manipulation are then analyzed, with some emphasis on the role of the U.S. dollar as a faltering key currency.

Chapter 7 then analyzes the buildup of the triple debt crisis—the U.S. internal and external debts and the Third World debt—in historical and current context, again with some emphasis on the role of the United States in the process.

The question of why the current international financial system is not up to the task of bringing the system back into balance is then taken up in chapter 8, which analyzes in some detail the many schemes that have been proposed to correct the situation. We argue that none of the proposals is adequate unless taken in the broader context of a new system of international economic coordination. For such a system to be implemented, an international conference on the order of Bretton Woods will be necessary, this time with Japan, West Germany, the NICs, and especially, the Third World debtor countries at the table.

No fundamental changes can take place without the cooperation and, indeed, insistence of the largest player in the game: the United States, which still has an economy more than twice as large as Japan and West Germany put together. Chapter 9 takes up the question of how the United States could creatively face up to its dilemma and take the lead in instituting changes before it is compelled to by forces that may soon be beyond its control.

Then chapter 10 focuses on the rapid changes taking place in the other industrialized countries, with emphasis on Japan and West Germany, and tries to explain why it is that even though they both hold most of the cards, neither seems willing or able to take the mantle of world economic leadership.

Finally, in chapter 11 we consider the various policy options that must be implemented if this increasingly serious situation is to ever be resolved.

2
International Trade Theory

International trade has a long and illustrious history. As far back as classical antiquity nations have traded. There are several reasons. One is of course that everyone gains or, at least perceives that they gain, from the process. Otherwise it wouldn't happen. Another, perhaps more important, reason is that all nations are interdependent. No nation can be self-sufficient—independent from international trade—without great sacrifices.

The United States, for example, is one of the more self-sufficient countries in the world, yet it depends on imports for the large majority of its bauxite, diamonds, tin, coffee, nickel, manganese, rubber, tungsten, bananas, gold, platinum, and chromium. The latter two—crucial in the production of jet engines and many other industrial processes—are nonexistent in the United States and come almost exclusively from South Africa.

So every nation needs imports, some more than others. It follows, then, that if a nation needs imports it also needs exports, because other than borrowing the money there is no other way to pay for imports. All nations, therefore, need imports *and* exports, which is to say, they need international trade.

In one sense international trade is very simple: countries specialize in whatever they can produce the most efficiently and trade the resulting product to others for whatever they do best. Given that the distribution of skills and national resources throughout the world is not the same everywhere, everyone gains from the process. But in another sense the process is quite complicated. That's because everyone's self-interest is involved.

Gains from international trade are the same as gains from any kind of trade. When people specialize, productivity is increased; when they trade, their income and their overall consumption is higher.

All this is easier to understand if you just put it in your own personal context. Chances are you don't make your own shoes or clothing. Instead you specialize in doing whatever you can do best and you sell your services (your labor) or products in the marketplace. So either directly or indirectly you trade with others and both you and they presumably are better off. Just as no one is self-sufficient, no nation these days tries to get along without international trade. You can understand this better if you try to build an automobile in your garage, or to grow some bananas in your garden.

This process of specializing and trading was first elaborated on in detail by Adam Smith in 1776 in the classic book *The Wealth of Nations*. Smith's work still provides the theoretical foundation and rationale for free-market capitalism.

In some twelve hundred pages Smith elaborated on the fact that people gain by pursuing their own self-interest. A private vice—selfishness—becomes a public virtue when people selfishly specialize in doing whatever they can do best, "truck" the result off somewhere, and "barter" it, that is, exchange it, for something else. Free competition (the theory says) between buyers and sellers assures that the whole process works out to everyone's best interest, and it is a normal and important part of the capitalist system. This is the rationale of the theory of capitalism.

Historical Context

What is often overlooked is that Smith wrote *The Wealth of Nations* not only as an explanation of how capitalism works; much of his motive was to debunk the mercantilist trading policies of the eighteenth-century nation–states.

In the earlier days of recorded history nations traded to obtain more goods, which seems a logical enough motive. But by the fifteenth century, with the coming of the commercial revolution, this motive for trade gradually eroded as the accumulation of goods was replaced by the desire to accumulate gold instead. This seemingly irrational motive for international trade, which came to be called *mercantilism,* still colors most nations' economic policy to this day.

The mercantilists felt that gold (as opposed to goods) represented wealth, that it provided security (to pay for armies) in times of war, and that it stimulated trade in the sense that money encouraged economic activity. Thus, by the eighteenth century it was generally acknowledged that a "favorable" balance of trade meant exporting more than was imported and accumulating a surplus of gold in the process.

The mercantilists felt that the primary objective of trading internationally was to export as much as possible and accumulate gold in return. But, Smith argued, nations, as well as individuals, gain from specializing and trading. Not goods for gold but goods for goods. "The revenue," he said, "of the person to whom it is paid, does not so properly consist in the piece of gold, as in what he can get for it, or in what he can exchange it for."[1] This set the stage for a controversy that has persisted for more than two hundred years now. If Smith was right, as most economists nowadays believe he was, then there is no place in a rational world for protectionist, self-interested measures to restrict trade through artificial barriers such as tariffs and import quotas. By 1988 total world exports had reached an astounding volume, more than *$2 trillion,* so clearly international trade is no small issue. (See figure 2–1.)

Theoretical Rationale for Trade

Refined by Smith's follower, David Ricardo, and dressed up in modern terminology, the theoretical rationale for international trade is usually couched in terms of the advantages involved for both parties. With rare exceptions almost any nation can produce any two given products. Steel *and* wheat, bananas *and*

$ trillions

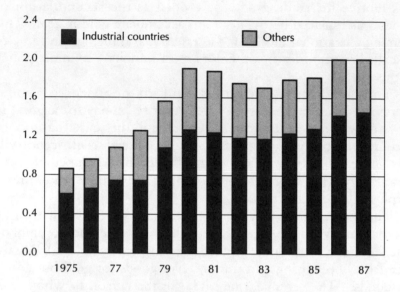

Source: OECD, *Economic Indicators,* July 1985, p. x.

Figure 2–1. *Trends in World Trade, 1975–1987*

refrigerators, guns *and* butter being but a few of the more obvious examples. The same nation can also chose to produce steel *or* wheat, bananas *or* refrigerators, guns *or* butter. The problem comes in deciding on what combination to produce, since the possibilities are infinite.

To understand this one must first understand production possibility curves. This concept can be illustrated graphically as shown in figure 2–2. The vertical axis represents the use of all resources available for producing civilian goods and services (food, clothing, shelter, education, and so on). On the horizontal axis the country's resources are being used to produce only military goods (tanks, airplanes, missiles, and so on). Thus, the farther out on the vertical axis the more civilian goods are being produced, while the farther out on the horizontal axis the more the available resources are being used for the production of military goods.

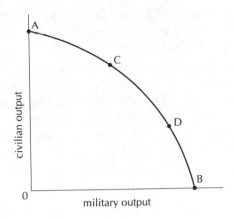

Figure 2–2. *Production Possibilities Frontier I*

The curved line, ACDB, represents what economists call the *production possibilities frontier*, and shows the various combinations of civilian and military goods (and services) that could be produced if all the country's resources were fully utilized. Point A, therefore, represents the use of all the country's resources for civilian output while point B represents using all of its resources in military production. Obviously, finding a country at either of these extremes is very unlikely; a more likely position might be point C or D. Point C would, for example, represent a situation where our hypothetical country is producing a lot of civilian goods and relatively few military goods, while D represents more military and few civilian goods.

The main concept to be considered here, however, is that as long as its resources are fully employed to produce more military goods—to move from C to D, for example—this country would have to give up (sacrifice) some civilian production. In other words, in this case, where we have classified all types of goods and services into two categories, the opportunity cost of producing more of one good is the amount of the other that cannot be produced.

An important point to understand about the production possibilities frontier is its *shape*. Why is it curved and not a straight line? The shape illustrates an important concept in economics, *the principle of increasing costs,* which simply states that as the production of one good expands, the opportunity cost of producing more of another good increases.

Note that in figure 2–3, instead of illustrating the production possibilities frontier with the examples of military and civilian goods, we have relabeled the two axes "agricultural output" and "industrial output." Now, let's begin by assuming that our economy is producing a lot of agricultural output and only a little industrial output, as represented by point A. Now what would happen if our economy decides to allocate more resources to industrial output and therefore moves along the production possibility frontier to point B? Note that by reallocating resources from agriculture to industry the economy has lost some agricultural output (equal to an amount illustrated by the vertical distance AA'), but gained some industrial output (equal to an amount illustrated by the horizontal distance A'B). If, however, our economy is already producing a lot of industrial output, then to increase industrial output by the same amount (C'D, which is equal to A'B) our economy will have to give up a much larger amount of agricultural output than it did before. In other words, as more industrial goods are produced, the opportunity cost in terms of agricultural output sacrificed becomes greater and greater. This occurs because the first resources transferred from agriculture to industry tend to be those resources most adaptable to producing industrial goods. But, as more and more industrial goods are produced, resources are transferred from agriculture to industry that are less and less capable of adapting to industrial production. Thus, the cost of producing higher and higher levels of industrial output increases in terms of how much agricultural output is sacrificed and in terms of how many resources must be reallocated to reach a given level of industrial output.

Before we proceed, this point is worth elaborating on a bit; there are many useful concepts that can be illustrated with it. First, let's ask ourselves what point on figure 2–4 would represent this country if its resources were not fully utilized? Since line ACDB represents the various combinations of agricultural and industrial goods (and services) that could be produced if all the

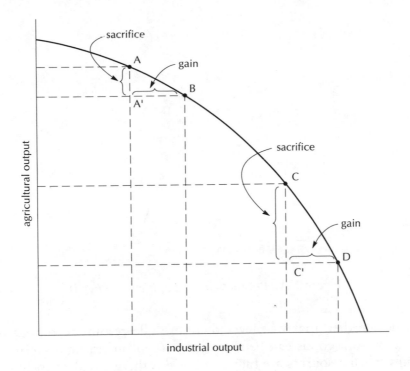

Figure 2–3. *Principle of Increasing Costs*

country's resources were fully utilized, any point inside that line represents some lesser combination of agricultural and industrial output if some of the country's resources are idle. Thus, either point E or point F could represent the country with underused or idle resources. Obviously, there are more idle resources at point F than at point E. Similarly, the output of both agricultural and industrial goods and services is lower at F than at E.

At point F, for example, the country can increase agricultural/industrial output without having to give up industrial/agricultural output. Thus, a movement from F to E represents an increase in agricultural output while the quantity of industrial production remains constant. In fact, given the existence of idle resources, the country could move from F to D, or F to C, implying that output of both types of goods rises. We can

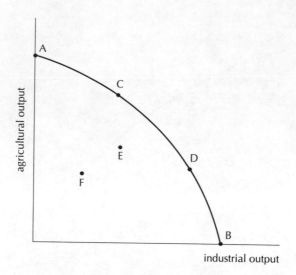

Figure 2–4. *Production Possibilities Frontier II*

conclude then that whenever there are idle resources, output of one or both goods can be increased without incurring a sacrifice; only when resources are fully employed is there a real opportunity cost.

Finally, let's look at one more use of this concept. In figure 2–5 we have drawn the curve AB, but notice that then we have shown a *shift—change in the location—*of the curve out and to the right, to A'B'. This signifies an expansion of the production possibilities for our hypothetical country. How might this come about?

Let's assume that our country is operating under the constraints imposed by the production possibilities curve AB. But for some reason—perhaps a global recession reduces the country's exports—the country finds itself operating at less than full employment, say, at point F, where most countries have been operating in recent years. However, at some point the global economy recovers and the country's exports surge. Increased exports stimulate greater use of all resources and higher output of both agricultural and industrial goods. As a result the economy is now operating at point E, and there is no way to increase output

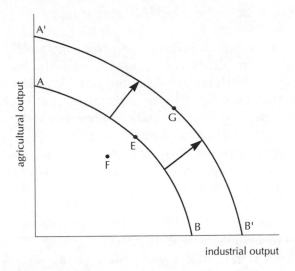

Figure 2–5. *Shifting the Production Possibilities Frontier*

any further as long as we have the same quantity and quality of resources. However, given the strong demand for its exports, our hypothetical country is able to finance and import greater quantities of capital equipment that makes workers more productive. We illustrate this by shifting the curve AB outward and to the right, to A'B'. This means that over time, and because of the introduction of more and better capital equipment, our economy is able to expand output and move to a point on the new curve, say, point G. Note, however, that once the economy has increased its output to any point on the new production possibilities curve, A'B', and all resources are once again fully employed, then to increase agricultural or industrial output, output of the other type of good must be sacrificed, unless the curve can be shifted outward. Again, understanding the concept of production-possibility alternatives, tradeoffs, and opportunity costs is crucial to understanding almost all economic problems and issues. And, as we shall see later, it has many applications to problems of maximizing efficiency and allocating resources to achieve social goals. One of its most common uses is illustrating the theory of absolute and comparative advantage.

Theory of Absolute Advantage

Obviously if a country is efficient at producing steel and needs wheat, like, for example, West Germany, Japan, and South Korea, then the thing to do is produce steel and trade it to some country, like the United States, Canada, or Argentina, that is efficient at producing wheat. Or if you are efficient at producing bananas but need refrigerators, like Central America, then you'll certainly want to leave the production of refrigerators to someone else, like the United States, which is pretty good at it, and put your efforts into producing bananas. These examples are what is called *absolute advantage*. In such a case everyone clearly gains from specializing and trading internationally. This is demonstrated in figure 2–6, derived from the data in table 2–1.

Using some simplifying assumptions (like the fact that all present U.S. copper miners would have to become wheat farmers

Table 2–1
Production Possibilities of United States and Chile
with and without Trade

Without trade:

	Wheat	or	Copper
United States	12	or	3
Chile	3	or	12

In isolation trying to produce both:

	Wheat	and	Copper
United States	6	and	1.5
Chile	1.5	and	6
total production	7.5	and	7.5

Total possible production with trade and complete specialization:

	Wheat	and	Copper
United States	12		0
Chile	0		12
total	12		12

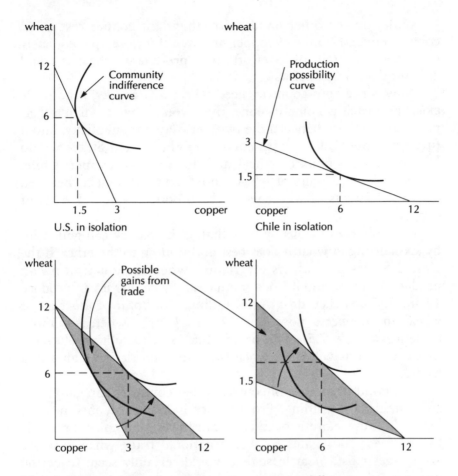

Note: In international economic theory "community indifference curves" are derived from the somewhat similar concept used in the microeconomic theory of consumption. A higher indifference curve is better than a lower one. The same logic is applied to production possibility curves, which are analogous to the consumer's budget constraint line, and are shown here as linear for simplicity, although as we have just seen, they are convex.

Figure 2–6. *Gains from Trade with Absolute Advantage*

for this to work), we can easily see that the United States has a clear absolute advantage over Chile in wheat production. If all U.S. resources went into wheat production then it could produce 12 units of wheat, whereas Chile could only produce 3 units.

Chile, on the other hand, with abundant copper resources, could produce 12 units of copper but even if it gave up completely on copper and put all its efforts into producing wheat it could only produce 3 units of wheat.

Now, since both countries need wheat *and* copper, if no trade exists and each is going it alone, they would have to divide their production efforts between the two, let's say, for simplicity, into a fifty-fifty split. Under those conditions the United States would be producing 6 units of wheat and 1.5 units of copper; Chile, the opposite: 1.5 units of wheat and 6 units of copper. Between the two 7.5 units of wheat would be produced, and 7.5 units of copper.

It's probably obvious by now that each country can gain a lot by specializing in what it does best and trading to the other. If the United States puts all its effort into wheat production it can produce 12 units, and if Chile produces only copper it can produce 12 units. Then they do a little trading. The *total* production of wheat and copper is now 12 + 12, or 24 units, whereas without trade it was only 7.5 + 7.5, or 15 units. So clearly it would seem that everyone is better off when the two countries specialize and trade.

The point of all this, of course, is that countries can gain from specializing and trading. Productivity is increased, incomes are higher because more is sold, costs are lower, and consumption is higher. Everybody gains from international trade when absolute advantages exist, or at least that would certainly seem to be the case.

Theory of Comparative Advantage

A more complicated problem comes up if one country is more efficient at producing both products. What if the United States is more efficient at producing both wheat and copper? Is there then any reason why the United States should trade with Chile? Offhand, common sense would tell us there's not. But, as David

Ricardo demonstrated in the early 1800s, both countries can still gain from trade so long as even only a comparative advantage exists. This is demonstrated in figure 2–7.

Let's think, for example, about trade between the United States and Argentina. Both are pretty good at producing beef and wheat, yet the two countries still trade. The United States and Argentina trade beef and wheat, even though the United States is

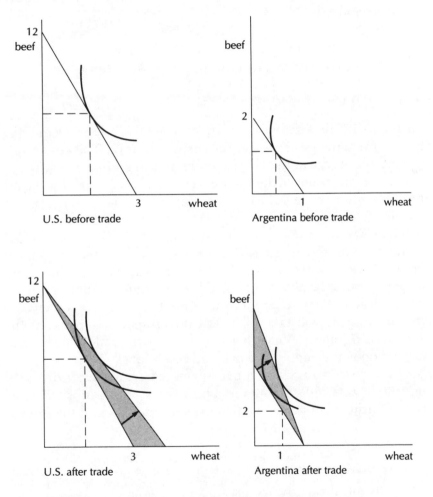

Figure 2–7. *Gains from Trade with Comparative Advantage*

more efficient at producing both. Why? Because with specialization there are still advantages in trading, otherwise trade obviously wouldn't occur.

In figure 2–4 we saw that the United States can produce 12 units of beef *or* 3 units of wheat. Argentina, however, can produce 2 units of beef or 1 unit of wheat. So if the United States specializes in beef and sells it to Argentina, and Argentina specializes in wheat and sells some to the United States both countries still gain.*

Assumptions of Comparative Advantage

Terms of Trade

Put in a slightly different context, what we have been examining here is the terms of trade between two countries. The cost ratios of beef and wheat in the United States and Argentina are different and therefore trade makes sense. The cost ratios are the terms under which trade takes place. In the earlier comparative advantage example, beef and wheat in the United States are 4:1, while in Argentina they are 2:1. So to gain from trade the United States must be able to get wheat for a cost of less than 1/4 unit of beef, which is what it would cost to produce it at home, and Argentina must be able to get beef for less than 1/2 unit of wheat, which it would pay to produce it domestically. So trade between the two nations will take place at ratios somewhere between the 4:1 and 2:1 range. What the actual terms of trade will be will depend on world supply and demand conditions.

In a more practical sense terms of trade are normally measured by comparing import and export price ratios—that is, by measuring the price a country pays for imports and the price it

---

*Note that in this oversimplified model (of bilateral trade), a large country like the United States cannot in reality gain from this exchange as much as is theoretically possible. Why? In this case Argentina does not have the capacity to produce enough beef to supply all the needs of the United States. Nevertheless, in the real world both countries trade with a large number of other countries so the principle still holds, and most economists agree that free trade—because of the theory of comparative advantage—brings about the most efficient possible allocation of resources.

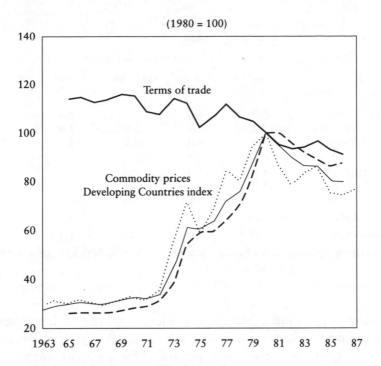

(1980 = 100)

Source: OECD, *Economic Indicators,* July 1989, p. x.

Figure 2–8. *Non-Oil Developing Countries' Trade Indexes*

receives for exports. This, then, can conveniently be expressed as an index number, as in:

$$\text{Terms of Trade} = \frac{\text{index of X prices}}{\text{index of M prices}} \times 100$$

If, for example, on a base year of 1980 the U.S. export price index was 113 in 1986 and the import price index was 95, then the terms of trade over the 1980–86 period have improved from 100 to 119.*

---

*TOT = $\frac{113}{95}$ x 100 = 119

Table 2–2
Terms of Trade, 1965–1987
(average annual percentage change)

Country group	1965–73	1973–80	1980–84	1985	1986[a]	1987[b]
Terms of trade						
Developing countries	0.7	1.6	−0.9	−2.3	−7.3	0.6
Low-income countries	1.7	−2.5	0.0	−3.6	−2.0	0.5
Middle-income countries	0.6	2.2	−1.0	−2.1	−7.9	0.4
Oil exporters	0.0	10.0	−1.8	−3.1	−38.7	9.3
Exporters of manufactures	1.8	−2.7	0.3	−0.4	3.9	−2.4
Highly indebted countries	1.4	3.5	−0.7	−2.3	−14.3	−0.5
Sub-Saharan Africa	−8.4	4.8	−1.4	−5.9	−23.5	1.1
High-income oil exporters	0.3	13.4	−2.3	−2.2	−49.1	7.6
Industrial countries	−1.0	−3.0	0.1	1.7	9.5	−0.1

Source: World Bank, *World Development Report, 1988* (New York: Oxford University Press, 1988), p. 192.

[a] Estimated.
[b] Projected.

That is a considerable improvement, unless one compares it to, say, Japan, which experienced a 55 percent improvement in its terms of trade over the same period. That means compared to 1980, Japan with a 15 percent increase in its export price index and a 26 percent decrease in its import price index had to give up 55 percent less exports to obtain the same amount of imports.

This, as we shall see in more detail later, is a significant issue in the underdeveloped Third World as the terms of trade for their exports (mostly primary products) have consistently deteriorated since 1970, while First World terms of trade for industrial products have improved (see table 2–2).

Thanks to the simplicity and theoretical elegance of the model it is clear enough that international trade benefits everyone. So a theory developed in the early 1800s has become the rationale for most economists' belief that free trade is good and anything that interferes with it, such as tariffs, quotas, and other protectionist measures is, by definition, bad. But there are, in the theory itself, some serious problems that must be considered. They involve, as is often the case in economic analysis, the assumptions of the model.

Ricardo assumed that costs remain constant no matter what the level of production, so that it would be possible for a nation to increase its production to satisfy the needs of other nations without increasing its own cost levels. But modern economics has documented to the satisfaction of most that since production is subject to diminishing returns, it is also subject to increasing costs sooner or later, depending on what is being produced. In such a case the increased costs may cancel out much if not all the benefits of comparative advantage.

Ricardo also did not take into consideration the heavy transportation costs that may be involved in international trade. These often considerably raise the costs of imported goods over domestically produced.

Finally, Ricardo assumed that the factors of production that may be generally mobile within a country may be immobile internationally. These days capital may be mobile internationally, labor less so, and certainly land is not. It is not so easy, as modern times have demonstrated all too clearly, for a country to abandon production of one product and move the factors into the production of another without serious reallocation problems, many of which can cause serious political difficulties beyond just the practical economic realities. The loss of more than 2 million jobs to foreign competition in the United States since 1980 is but one example of many.

So, in general, while the theory of comparative advantage does provide a certain useful perspective by which the trading process can be viewed, it is not a panacea that can be expected to explain the much more complicated process of the internationalization of world production.

Heckscher-Ohlin Refinements

Problems of oversimplification and unrealistic assumptions aside, if one can agree that the basic idea that nations can gain from trading when cost differences exist then the relevant question becomes: What will, or should, be traded? Modern refinement and elaborations of the theory of comparative advantage have at once clarified this issue and opened up a Pandora's box of controversy.

The best-known extension of Ricardo's work was done by Swedish economist Eli Heckscher and his student Bertil Ohlin. In an extensive study carried out over a number of years they concluded that the simplistic notions of comparative advantage did not explain sufficiently *why* it is that there are production cost differences between nations.

The reason, they argued, is that different countries have different proportions and intensities of the factors of production, that is, land, labor, capital, and technical know-how. Countries with large relative proportions of one factor, for example, fertile land, will tend to produce those things that use that resource more intensively. Thus the seemingly obvious conclusion is that a land-rich country like the United States would tend to focus on agricultural production and trade the surplus to a country with more intensive proportions of, for example, labor. Consequently, one might expect that the United States would gain from trading wheat to China in exchange for silk—a relatively labor-intensive product. This seems an obvious verification and elaboration of the theory of comparative advantage, and it is, but, carried one step farther, there are some interesting implications.

In the first place, putting such a theory into practice means that as trade increases so does interdependence between trading partners. If a labor-intensive–land-scarce country abandons agricultural production in favor of producing some labor-intensive product, then it becomes dependent on the benevolence of the food supplier. As a practical political reality this has problems that have been demonstrated many times in history. The most dramatic recent example is probably the growing U.S. dependence on imported oil.

Beyond that, however, the more interesting—and more relevant to modern-day economic policy—conclusion of the Heckscher-Ohlin thesis is that putting comparative advantage into practice tends over time to equalize prices of the factors of production worldwide. Put in cost terms, as one country begins to use its plentiful factor it becomes more scarce, and more expensive, while its less abundant factors become cheaper. As the opposite occurs in the other country, similar price changes occur. The result is that factor prices tend to equalize. In recent times the

United States has been moving toward shifting production abroad to "take advantage of" cheaper labor abroad. One result has been lower-priced imports of labor-intensive products. The other result has been a gradual lowering of wages in the United States and increasing wages in many of the developing countries. In the 1960s, U.S. average wages were more than double wages for comparable jobs in Japan. By the 1980s, however, wages in Japan had *surpassed* wage levels in the United States. So it is important to remember that for comparative advantage to work out to *everyone's* advantage the gains from trade must exceed the losses from reallocation of resources.

Leontief Paradox

Concerned about this seeming inconsistency, Nobel laureate economist Wassily Leontief used input–output analysis to analyze a small sample of U.S. imports and exports and apparently contradicted the Heckscher-Ohlin thesis. Since the United States is a capital-intensive economy it was commonly assumed that it exported capital goods in exchange for labor-intensive products. His research, however, showed *just the opposite:* the United States was exporting products that contained less capital and *more* labor than the goods it was importing.

This forced international economists to return to the drawing boards. To be sure, there were problems with Leontief's analysis. Land had not been included as a factor, and there was the problem of separating skilled from unskilled labor, but the basic problem lingered. In the case of the United States the capital–labor mix was the opposite of what the theory said it should have been.

Later research by Raymond Vernon and others partially explained the seeming paradox. The use of advanced technological production techniques and, especially, the investments in the research and development to develop them, had not been incorporated into the model. From this it became clear that the real comparative advantage the United States had over the rest of the world (in the 1950s and 1960s) was its ability to develop and use technical know-how. Indeed, Vernon argues that the technological requirements of the product better explain patterns of trade. Thus new products are produced in countries with large research and development capabilities while older, more "mature" products can be replicated in the less industrialized nations.

Nowadays it is generally agreed that the theory of comparative advantage and especially the Heckscher-Ohlin elaboration of it only explain trade in sectors heavily dependent on abundance in land and other natural resources, that is, agriculture and primary products. Other trade exchanges—the vast majority of which take place between industrialized countries—depend on differences in levels of technology and the ability to use it.

The irony here is that what was once a huge comparative advantage for the United States in world markets has now become a distinct *disadvantage*. First Japan, but now increasingly the Newly Industrialized Countries, have been able to rapidly adopt the new technologies and combine them with abundant labor resources to out-compete the United States in nearly all manu-facturing areas. Much of the other trade that does occur takes place between *already* industrialized areas where the comparative advantages are small but the taste for diversity is great, mostly in luxury goods such as expensive automobiles and wines. So comparative advantage, while still theoretically attractive, doesn't tell us much about international trade in an increasingly techno-logically oriented world. Therefore, while virtually all economists and all but the most myopic politicians agree that international trade benefits everyone, it is becoming clear that the issues are not as simple as the theory of comparative advantage would seem to imply.

Further Complications

What complicates the issue is the apparently obvious fact that for a system of trading goods internationally to work there has to be at least some semblance of balance between what is traded—that is, between what is imported and what is exported. Otherwise, someone gains more of the gains than is fair and, someone else loses.

Again the analogy of individuals trading in the market is relevant. The idea of trading is to come out on top. The winners in the exchange process are those who are good "horse traders" or good bargainers. Everyone tries to buy cheap and sell dear. If you win at this game you can become wealthy; if you lose you'll be poor. The point is that there are always winners and losers.

Now if we extend this logic to the international arena a similar process occurs. Everyone wants to be a winner, which in this case means every country wants to export more than it imports. In one sense, as we have seen, this is a curious kind of logic because by exporting more than it is importing a country is sending more of its goods out of the country than it is getting back. This seems a strange way to interpret the general welfare, and it was, as we saw, why Adam Smith railed against the mercantilists: all you accumulate when you have an export surplus is gold or, more likely, other countries' currency, which is, in the final analysis, just paper.

But what's at issue here is the more emotional question of jobs. These days almost 20 percent of the U.S. economy is involved in and dependent on the international sector, that is, exports and imports. For most other countries, especially Japan and Western Europe, that figure is much higher. For example, more than 50 percent of the Japanese economy depends on exports, which means half of its jobs depend on international trade.

Since every country wants to provide more jobs for its people, everyone tries to increase exports as much as possible, while at the same time limiting imports, which, of course, costs jobs. The problem, however, is that since one country's exports are another's imports *it is clearly not possible for everyone to have an export surplus.* Nonetheless, everyone tries. This is why international trade is often called a "beggar-thy-neighbor" game. The object is to make yourself better off at your neighbor's expense.

One result of this is export fetish protectionism. It seems logical enough that if your objective is to maximize exports and minimize imports then one simple way to do it is to put a tax on imports, a *tariff*, or to limit by law the quantity of them, a *quota*. Tariffs and quotas have the effect of increasing prices in the domestic industries by protecting them from foreign competition. This, of course, saves jobs at home. However, it also raises a host of problems, and is one of the most controversial issues in economics, as we shall see in the following chapter.

Key Concepts

Mercantilism
Absolute Advantage
Comparative Advantage
Heckscher-Ohlin Refinements
Leontief Paradox

Discussion Questions

1. Can you name any case where trade between two countries fits the theory of comparative advantage?

2. In 1988 the Canadian national election was a hotly contested referendum over the question of free trade with the United States. Free trade won. Do you think Canada will gain or lose? Why?

3. Why is it, if comparative advantage exists, that the United States has consistently run balance of trade deficits with the rest of the world?

4. Japan in recent years has been pursuing a policy many call mercantilistic. Can you explain what this means and why they feel they benefit from it?

5. How, in your own life, do you "specialize and trade"? What do you gain from it? Can you name some specific examples?

3
International Commercial Policy

The Theory and Reality of Protectionism

Given the apparent logic of the argument for free trade it would seem that by now all protectionist measures, such as tariffs and quotas, would be ancient history and that the world would be enjoying the benefits of free, unfettered, trade. But that has not been the case, although in the postwar period there has been a general reduction in the overall level of trade restriction, negotiated mostly in the series of discussions that have taken place under the auspices of the General Agreement on Tariffs and Trade, more commonly known as the GATT. GATT was established in 1948 in general recognition that tariffs, quotas, and other restrictions of trade are largely self-defeating. In some ways it has been successful, in others not.

More than one hundred countries belong to the GATT or are associated with it in one way or another. The GATT is both a set of rules to which member countries agree to adhere and a forum in which negotiations and trade discussions take place. One of its most important functions is to mediate and settle trade disagreements between nations.

The basic principles of GATT, which are spelled out in a long and complicated document, are:

1. All trade must be conducted on the basis of nondiscrimination between members. Special trade agreements between members are not permitted except under particular circumstances.

In essence, this means that all members of GATT agree to give "most favored nation," that is, trade preference, treatment to each other. Nonmembers, meaning primarily the Soviet Union and communist bloc countries, do not receive such concessions.

2. Members of the GATT agree, in principle, that trade protection measures are only appropriate in the case of domestic industries that would be severely damaged by free trade, and that in such cases, customs tariffs are the only mechanism that will be employed.

3. Finally, import quotas (qualitative restrictions on trade) are, in principle, prohibited. However, in practice, many exceptions are made and quotas remain common especially in areas such as textiles, steel, and automobiles.

Over the years there have been seven major multilateral trade negotiations held by the GATT, each of which has resulted in some overall liberalization of trade. The most extensive of these was the Tokyo Round, completed in 1979. In addition to some tariff reductions, the Tokyo Round produced some agreement on trade conduct in nontariff areas. Some progress was made, for example, in establishing codes on subsidies, reducing unrealistic technical barriers, and prohibiting antidumping (selling products abroad at cheaper prices than they are sold domestically).

The latest round—the Uruguay Round, which began in Punta del Este in 1986—has not, in the face of a rising protectionist sentiment in most countries, been very successful in further reducing trade barriers. Unresolved issues include trade guidelines in services such as banking and information industries, as well as opening heavily protected agricultural markets, all of which reflect U.S. interests.

The Rise of Neoprotectionism

The 1980s have been tumultuous times in the area of international trade. On the one hand, trade has increased dramatically and nations have become much more interdependent than before. But, on the other hand, we have seen the rise of a neoprotectionist movement that is historically unprecedented.

On the positive side, major bilateral trade agreements have been concluded between a number of countries, most notably the historic agreement between the United States and Canada, to eliminate all trade restrictions between the two countries by the year 2000.

Another positive development is the increasing recognition on the part of the industrialized countries that the developing countries should receive trade restriction concessions as they attempt to expand their export markets. As an example, in the 1970s the United States, Japan, and the European Economic Community (EEC) implemented a system of trade preferences (the Generalized System of Preferences, or GSP) that eliminates import duties on a wide range of products from over one hundred selected countries. In the United States the trade preferences cover almost $20 billion worth of U.S. imports—about 4 percent of total U.S. imports. These programs are in theory designed to help the developing countries increase their export opportunities and stimulate economic growth, employment, and economic growth. As a secondary, but not to be overlooked goal, they also help heavily indebted countries earn the foreign exchange necessary to service their staggering foreign debts. While the GSP is an impressive step in the right direction, it has not, in practice, had a significant effect on trade patterns. Only about 20 percent of developing countries' exports have been affected.

On the negative side, protectionist sentiments in the United States resulted in the passage of the Omnibus Trade Bill of 1988, which put into place a number of protectionist measures designed to restrict imports. This, coupled with an increasing protectionist movement in Western Europe, could be the first step in a trade war that could well reverse any gains achieved during the 1980s.

Theory of Protectionism

The theory of tariffs, quotas, and other protectionist measures is fairly simple, but the reality is extremely complicated. Virtually all economists agree that (with only a few exceptions) tariffs don't make economic sense. The reason is demonstrated in figure 3–1.

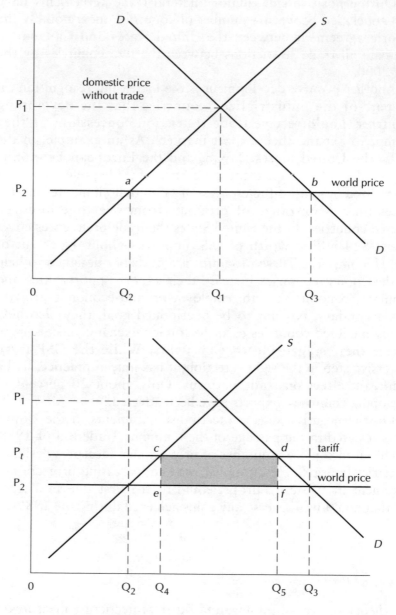

Figure 3–1. *The Effect of a Tariff on a Domestic Economy*

In the top graph a standard supply and demand diagram shows the conditions that would prevail if a country were in isolation and not trading internationally some product, say, steel. In isolation the price would be P1 and the quantity sold Q1. Now (assuming this is a small country) if it entered world trade it would be facing a horizontal (perfectly elastic) demand curve and could sell or buy all the steel it wanted to at the world price P2. Note, however, who gains and who loses.

Consumers gain, since they now can buy steel products at the new lower world price P2. Also, since the law of demand tells us that consumers will buy more at a lower price we know they probably will; they'll now buy Q3 at the lower price P2.

But, in this scenario domestic producers lose. They were producing and selling quantity Q1 at price P1, but now it will only be profitable for them to produce up to quantity Q2. The additional supply of steel (Q2 to Q3) will be imported. And the net result is that a lot of jobs in the domestic steel industry are lost to foreign competition.

So now protectionism enters the picture. The steel industry lobby puts pressure on the Congress to place a tariff, a tax, on steel imports. The effects of this are demonstrated in the lower graph in figure 3–1.

The tariff has the effect of raising the domestic price of steel from P2 to Pt. Consumers lose because they have to pay a higher price and will accordingly buy less, Q5Q3 less, to be specific. Producers, on the other hand, gain. At the higher price Pt will find it profitable to produce up to quantity Q4, or a gain of Q2Q4. The rectangle *cdef* represents the tariff-tax collected by the government.

So the net effect of the protectionist tariff is to increase domestic production, to increase steel producers' profits, and to increase employment in the steel industry. The government also gains tax revenues. The losers, of course, are consumers who are subsidizing the steel industry by paying the higher prices, which means to put it another way, that the effect of a tariff is to redistribute income from consumers in general to the steel producers and their employees and, to a lesser extent, to the government.

Nontariff Barriers: Quotas

Some economists (and many lobbyists) argue that quotas are a more efficient and equitable method of restricting trade. This, however, is usually not the case. Refer to figure 3–1. If a quota (a limit on the quantity of imports allowed to enter the country) were placed on the import of steel (as it has been) at a level of Q4Q5, then the net effect is to shift income to those who are able to obtain import licenses. They are able to procure steel at the world price P2 and sell it in the U.S. market for Pt, netting a nice profit. Domestic production is not any higher and consumers still pay the higher price—Pt. Thus, the only difference between a tariff and a quota is that the income goes to importers rather than to the government.

Moreover, quotas often yield strange and unexpected results. For example, for several years now Japan has agreed to voluntarily restrict its exports of automobiles to the United States. This gives the appearance that the U.S. auto industry gains sales and employment from the restricted supply of Japanese autos in the U.S. market. However, the quotas apply only to the number of autos imported, not the total value of them. So the Japanese merely began restricting exports of inexpensive autos, while increasing exports of luxury cars. The gap left at the low end of the market was filled by inexpensive West German, Korean, and Yugoslavian cars, and U.S. producers found themselves in the same competitive position they were in before. For these and other reasons tariffs are considered by most economists to be a preferable trade restriction mechanism to quotas.

Problems of Trade and Tariff Theory

As we have seen, the theory of international trade seems logical enough. Certainly it is pedagogically attractive and convincing. But, as is often the case in economics, there is one minor problem: it doesn't work very well. International trade does, of course, take place but the theory doesn't explain what actually happens.

The theory of comparative advantage (and the refinements of it that we reviewed in the previous chapter), says that if each nation specializes in what it can do best, everyone will produce and consume more when they trade *and* everyone will have higher incomes as a result.

The example David Ricardo used when he first proposed this idea was the relationship between Great Britain and Portugal, wherein Britain produced wool and Portugal produced wine, and they traded. Both, according to Ricardo, would gain. However, as one writer has pointed out, that didn't quite happen.

> Britain and Portugal began their partnership in 1373, when they formed an alliance against Castile, the Spanish empire. In 1580, Castile expanded into Portugal. Sixty years later, Britain began to offer Portugal military support against Spain in exchange for a series of economic concessions. A critical concession was made in the Treaty of Methuen, signed in 1703.
>
> According to this treaty, the Portuguese agreed to impose no tariffs on wool cloth and other woolen goods from Britain on the condition that the British lower duties on wine imported from Portugal to two-thirds of those currently imposed on imported French wine. Since the British had already lowered the duties on Portuguese wine in 1690, they clearly stood to gain more from the treaty than the Portuguese.
>
> The impact of the Treaty of Methuen on the Portuguese economy was tremendous. British wool exports to Portugal jumped by 120 percent between 1700 and 1710. During the same period, the Portuguese sold 40 percent more wine to the British and wine production expanded fivefold. But the group of small-time Portuguese artisans who made woolen products could hardly compete with the cheap imports of British wool, and were eventually forced to abandon their enterprise.
>
> By the 1850s, Portuguese economic growth had stagnated, and Portugal had become economically dependent on Britain. While the development of the textile industry had laid the foundation for the British Empire, specialization in wine had succeeded in transforming Portugal into what looked like a small South American republic that just happened to be attached to Europe.[1]

Another interesting and commonly cited case attempts to explain the theory of comparative advantage by using the now fabled example of the secretary and the lawyer. The lawyer can type faster than the secretary, yet the lawyer does the legal work

and leaves the typing to the secretary. Why? Because of comparative advantage. The lawyer can earn more doing the legal work
and (theoretically) between them, according to this arrangement,
their total product is greater as is, theoretically, their income.

But it is the lawyer's income that is higher, not the secretary's.
The arrangement is clearly to the lawyer's advantage. However, if
the secretary were encouraged to learn a new skill—such as legal
work—it would increase the comparative advantage, and income.
But this doesn't often happen with lawyers and their secretaries
and it doesn't often happen between countries.

So when we compare two countries trading under conditions
of comparative advantage, a similar process usually (but not
always) occurs. Most of the time smaller and/or underdeveloped
countries have a comparative advantage in one of two things:
abundant, cheap labor, as in most underdeveloped countries, or
abundant, cheap raw materials like, for example, tin in Bolivia,
copper in Chile, oil in Mexico.

If it is the abundant labor that is being traded, then specializing in labor-intensive products requires that labor will remain
cheap and incomes low. If incomes rise the rationale for trade is
gone.

The case of raw materials is somewhat more complicated.
Generally speaking it seems to make sense for resource-rich,
underdeveloped countries to export raw materials and get them
back in the form of processed capital goods, such as tractors, to
develop their agricultural sector, which should eventually make
them more self-sufficient. But there is a catch here. For specialization to be mutually beneficial the products have to be traded at
constant cost ratios—that is, the terms of trade have to remain
relatively constant. If they don't the smaller country—now totally
dependent on income from the exportation of a primary
product—is also totally dependent on world prices remaining
constant, which they almost never do.

Recently in the Philippines there was a rather dramatic
example.

Sugarcane was first produced on the archipelago as a snack
food. Not until the mid-1800s did the colony's Spanish rulers

decide to explore the possibilities of large-scale sugar production for export.

The island of Negros, which had an ideal environment for sugar production, was converted into a monocrop zone. By the late 1800s, half of the nation's sugar was being harvested in Negros. In the years of U.S. colonial rule, the United States encouraged the sugar industry by enacting a series of tariffs and import quotas that gave Philippine sugar a competitive advantage over sugar from other countries. When the United States cut off trade with Cuba, the U.S. government increased the quotas for the Philippines. The new quotas increased the country's dependence on U.S. markets, and propelled further increases in sugar production at the expense of diversification. Land that had produced food was increasingly used to produce sugar.

The fate of Negros became tied to the ups and downs of world sugar prices. In the spring of 1985, a 40 percent drop in the expected sugar harvest, combined with historical lows in the world price of sugar, wreaked a famine of alarming proportions on the island of Negros. Yet, according to Roberto Ortaliz, the president of the National Federation of Sugar Workers, proper use of the arable land on Negros could feed up to fifty times the total Filipino population of 55 million.[2]

There are thousands of similar examples. In recent years the terms of trade between primary product exports from the underdeveloped countries to the more industrialized countries have deteriorated by some 30 percent. This loss of income is primarily responsible for the huge foreign debt buildup and much of the international financial imbalance.

To say that nations shouldn't trade because the theory of comparative advantage doesn't always work out the way Ricardo envisioned it would be spurious and irresponsible. Nations *do* gain from trade. It's just that often some gain more than others. And this is a problem with serious implications.

Effects of Protectionism

One result of self-interested nations' trying to get more than their "fair" share of comparative advantage is protectionism, which, as we have seen, usually takes the form of tariffs and quotas.

It is interesting to note that, in general, during the postwar period, there has been a trend toward reducing tariffs and promoting free trade. President Reagan has been quoted as saying, "I remember well the antitrade frenzy in the late twenties that produced the Smoot-Hawley tariffs, greasing the skids for our descent into the Great Depression and the most destructive war this world has ever seen. That's one episode I'm determined we will never repeat."[3]

Indeed, the United States has been a vocal and active participant in the General Agreement on Trade and Tariffs and subsequent negotiations and efforts to reduce tariffs. The United States, in fact, has one of the most open economies in the world. Most other countries have much tougher restrictions on imports. For example, Brazil charges a 200 percent tariff on imported passenger cars; France limits Japanese auto imports to 3 percent of its domestic market; Mexico allows no Japanese cars to be sold in the country; and South Korea allows no auto imports whatsoever. But, still, roughly 25 percent of the U.S. economy is protected in one way or another by tariffs and quotas.

Even though there is virtually no logical argument in favor of protectionism, it prevails and is becoming an increasingly serious problem. In 1988 the U.S. Congress in an attempt to correct the huge U.S. trade deficit passed a very restrictive protectionist trade bill. The bill, among other things, requires the president to take actions that would cut the trade deficit with Japan, Taiwan, and West Germany by 10 percent annually, to impose U.S. labor standards on our trading partners, and to intervene in the foreign exchange markets to keep the dollar "weak" and make the United States more competitive internationally.

The problem is that protectionist measures have much broader implications than simply protecting jobs and domestic industries. There are at least three larger issues involved. The first is protection of special interest groups at the expense of the general welfare; second is the question of retaliation neutralizing any perceived benefits, however attractive they may appear on the surface, and, finally, there is the more serious question of the shifting patterns of trade and the concomitant deindustrialization of America.

Protecting Special Interest Groups

Let's take these issues one at a time. It is clear that protectionism does save jobs. In the United States alone almost 3 million jobs were lost to foreign competition over the 1980–1986 period, but many more were saved by tariffs and other trade restrictions—at a very high cost.

There are many different interpretations and estimates of the costs of protectionism. One study showed that tariffs and quotas raise the cost of imported goods by $50 million a year. Another study showed that because of trade restrictions U.S. citizens pay twice as much for imported clothing than they would without them, and the United States pays $2 billion more for goods made with steel, $500 million more for books, and $104 million more for motorcycles. Moreover, in 1985, American consumers paid $2,500 extra for each imported car and $1,000 extra for each domestic automobile.[4] In 1986 one textile-quota bill passed Congress (but vetoed by the president) would alone have cost U.S. consumers $14 billion, and it would have saved 100,000 jobs—at a cost of $140,000 per job.[5]

So the protectionist issue is primarily one of deciding what is the appropriate price for society to pay for protecting special interest groups. Clearly, this is a complicated policy question, and it's not going to go away soon.

The Question of Retaliation

A somewhat less emotional issue is retaliation, which is, at least, more amenable to rational analysis. Given that, as we have seen, international trade is a beggar-thy-neighbor situation in which everyone "does to others as they would do to you," it is not surprising that the one thing almost everyone agrees upon is that protectionism begets protectionism—that is, tariffs and quotas imposed by one country almost always cause retaliation by others.

There are hundreds of thousands of examples. One is probably sufficient to illustrate the point. In 1986, under pressure from northern timber interests, President Reagan imposed a tariff on the import of Canadian shingles. The United States imported about $157 million worth of shingles from Canada in 1985, out of total imports from Canada of $69 *billion.* Almost immediately Canada retaliated by imposing new restrictions on U.S.-made books, computers, and semiconductors.

Because of the unexpected rapid retaliation, some senators who had sponsored the bill were forced to rethink their position. One, Senator Daniel Evans (R–Wash.) was quoted in *The Wall Street Journal* as saying, "[This is] a good case study of what can happen when nations unilaterally attempt to protect their own positions through trade restrictions. . . . It's a splendid example . . . if we're only wise enough to understand it."[6]

If trade restrictions simply result in retaliation by a nation's trading partners—as they almost always do—we are, at best, looking at a negative sum game. Everybody loses. Total trade is reduced, prices are higher, less is produced and sold, and jobs are lost on both sides. If there is any clear-cut, logical argument against protectionism, it is the inevitable reality of retaliation.

Shifting Patterns of International Trade

Finally, there is the question of shifting trade patterns and the effect of this somewhat unexpected new reality on American industry.

The United States was for many, many years the predominant industrial power in the world. Exports of U.S. industrial products, automobiles, capital goods, and agricultural products fueled the expansion of the world economy in the postwar period. But by the 1970s a series of unexpected shocks changed all that. High oil-import prices, rising wages, declining productivity, the overvalued dollar, and a host of other factors—to which we will return later—caused U.S. heavy industry to seek protection from increasingly efficient and aggressive foreign competition, most notably the Japanese and Western Europeans, who, with the help of U.S. postwar reconstruction aid, became formidable competitors in the world market. More recently the Newly Industrialized Countries (Brazil, South Korea, Taiwan, and others) learned that they, too, could produce and sell industrial products. The result has been a dramatic shift in the distribution of world economic power, and with it the rise of huge U.S. trade deficits.

U.S. Trade Deficit

From the early 1900s until 1971 the United States maintained a trade surplus. It sold many more goods and services abroad than it bought. As shown in figure 3–2, some small current account deficits began to occur in the early 1970s, but they were mostly caused by the higher cost of oil imports. Then in 1982 (figure 3–3) the bottom dropped out, the trade deficit plummeted, and the balance of world economic power began to shift away from the United States to Japan and Western Europe and, to a lesser extent, to the Newly Industrialized Countries, especially Brazil, South Korea, and Taiwan. As figure 3–4 illustrates, the U.S. share of total exports *dropped* from 56 percent in 1980 to 46 percent in 1985, while Japan and West Germany's shares grew rapidly.

Tables 3–1 and 3–2 illustrate the changing composition of U.S. international trade over the 1965–85 period. As late as 1975, agricultural, industrial products, and capital goods exports far outweighed imports. Automotive imports were roughly balanced by exports and agricultural exports were four times petroleum imports. So in the 1970s the United States was largely trading food and industrial products for oil and raw material imports.

Overall, U.S. merchandise exports grew from around $115 billion in 1976 to an estimated $215 billion in 1986. But over that decade U.S. imports grew from $124 billion to $329 billion.

Even more dramatic and relevant to this analysis is that over the same decade imports from the Newly Industrialized Countries began (in 1981) to exceed exports to them. By 1986 U.S. exports to the NICs ran at a constant rate of about $60 billion, but NIC imports had grown to almost $100 billion, or a $40 billion deficit. It is this trend, along with the changing composition of U.S. trade in general, that rewrote the history of international trade in the latter part of the 1970s.

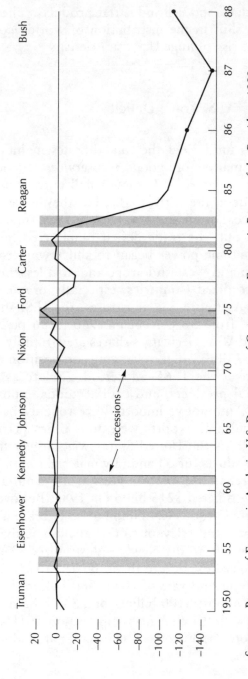

Source: Bureau of Economic Analysis, U.S. Department of Commerce, *Economic Report of the President,* 1989.

Note: Balance on current account in seasonally adjusted billions of $.

Figure 3–2. *U.S. International Accounts, 1950–1988*

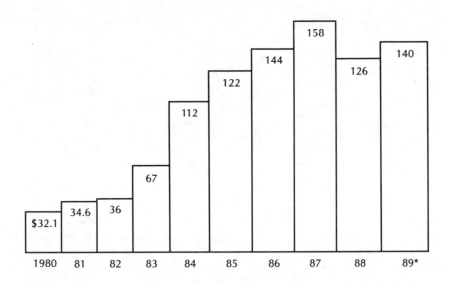

Source: International Monetary Fund, *International Financial Statistics*, Sept. 1989, p. 546.

Note: Billions of $.

*Estimate.

Figure 3–3. *U.S. Trade Deficit, 1980–1988*

But by the early 1980s this all began to change rapidly. Agricultural exports leveled off, as did petroleum imports (which actually declined) but industrial imports exceeded exports by 1985, capital goods imports (mostly machinery) doubled between 1980 and 1985, and automotive imports *more than doubled* during the same five-year period. This was the end of an era: the United States became a *net importer* of industrial products, with no corresponding increase in agricultural exports to make up the difference. U.S. employment in the manufacturing sector dropped from more than 21 million in 1979 to about 18 million in 1985. Roughly 3 million jobs were lost to foreign competition. A key factor in this strange scenario is that much of the problem is not just a question of "good old-fashioned" competition between the

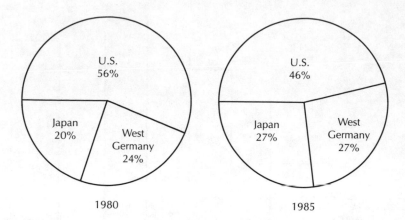

Source: Data Resources.

Note: Based on constant dollar values.

Figure 3–4. *Major Economic Powers' Relative Shares of World Exports, 1980, 1985*

United States and foreign manufacturers, but rather it is a result of U.S. multinational corporations' shifting their own production facilities abroad to take advantage of cheaper labor costs and less strict environmental protection regulations.

Nowadays the trade deficit takes two forms. First there are products in which the United States is simply no longer competitive: cameras, stereo components, videocassette recorders, television sets, and the like, which are almost all now produced in other countries. But the more important trend is that many intermediate products are now being produced abroad by American companies and *then* imported to the United States, thus exacerbating the trade deficit crisis. This process—called "outsourcing" or "export platforming"—is now a major part of the U.S. manufacturing process.

There are many examples. A *Business Week* study found that 75 percent of some IBM computers are produced abroad. More obvious are finished goods, like the Dodge Colt, which is produced in Japan by Mitsubishi and imported to the United

Table 3–1

*U.S. Merchandise **Exports** by End-use Category, 1965–1988*

(billions of $ U.S.)

	Total	Agricultural Products	Industrial Products	Capital Goods	Automotive Exports	Other Exports
1965	26.5	6.3	7.6	8.1	1.9	2.6
1970	42.5	7.4	12.3	14.7	3.9	4.3
1975	107.1	22.2	26.7	36.6	10.8	10.7
1980	224.3	42.2	64.9	74.2	17.5	25.4
1985	214.3	38.9	53.6	75.6	24.8	37.1
1986	227.2	36.5	57.3	75.8	21.7	35.9
1987	254.1	42.0	66.7	86.2	24.6	34.6
1988	322.4	55.4	85.1	109.2	29.3	43.4

Source: *Economic Indicators*, Aug. 1989; Council of Economic Advisors, U.S. Government Printing Office, Washington, D.C., 1989.

Note: Military shipments are excluded.

States by Chrysler. Such goods marketed by U.S. firms accounted for some $13 billion of the U.S. trade deficit (of $60 billion) with Japan in 1985. A Department of Commerce study concluded that imports of finished products produced abroad *by American firms* accounted for $50 billion of U.S. imports in 1983. That's 19 percent of total U.S. imports, or more than four times the U.S. merchandise trade deficit for that year.

Table 3–2

*U.S. Merchandise **Imports** by End-use Category, 1965–1988*

(billions of $ U.S.)

	Total	Petroleum Products	Industrial Products	Capital Goods	Automotive Imports	Other Imports
1965	21.5	2.0	9.1	1.5	0.9	8.0
1970	39.9	2.9	12.3	4.0	5.7	15.0
1975	98.2	27.0	23.6	10.2	12.1	25.3
1980	244.8	79.3	54.0	31.2	27.9	57.4
1985	328.7	48.8	62.7	61.4	62.2	93.4
1986	368.5	34.4	69.9	72.1	78.1	114.0
1987	406.2	42.9	71.2	84.8	85.2	125.8
1988	441.0	40.0	81.0	101.4	87.7	130.9

Source: *Economic Indicators*, Aug. 1989; Council of Economic Advisors, U.S. Government Printing Office, Washington, D.C., 1989.

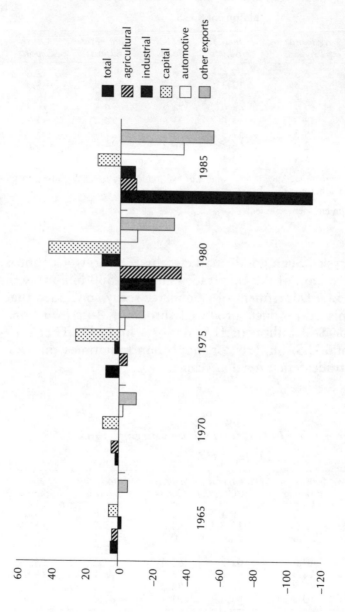

legend:
- ■ total
- ▨ agricultural
- ■ industrial
- ▨ capital
- ☐ automotive
- ▨ other exports

1965   1970   1975   1980   1985

60   40   20   0   −20   −40   −60   −80   −100   −120

Source: Department of Commerce.

Note: Net exports are exports minus imports.

Figure 3–5. *U.S. Net Exports by Product Group, 1965–1985*

Paradox of U.S. Deindustrialization

So international trade has become a complicated and paradoxical issue. As the rest of the world has become more developed and industrialized, the United States has lost its once-predominant position in the world economy. The old theories of comparative advantage and protectionism no longer seem as logical as they once did—at least from the U.S. perspective. The patterns of trade have shifted and the United States is rapidly becoming a deindustrialized nation. Services now account for 70 percent of the U.S. Gross National Product. The United States has become a nation of hamburger flippers, stock brokers, and insurance salesmen—services that are hard to export.

One result of all this is that the United States has now, for the first time since 1914, become a debtor nation. To understand the significance of that simple fact and how it relates to the present international financial situation, we will need to take an excursion into the world of international finance. It is a complex, perplexing, and precarious world, a world of exchange markets, "strong" and "weak" currencies, balance of payments, debts and defaults, gold, and arbitrage. It is a world understood by only a very few people. These days even the Gnomes of Zurich are perplexed.

Key Concepts

Tariffs
Import Quota
Protectionism
GATT
Terms of Trade
David Ricardo
Deindustrialization

Discussion Questions

1. Assume that the U.S. government places a tariff of $1 on each barrel of imported petroleum. What do you think would be the rationale for such a decision? What would be the predictable consequences of this policy?

2. The Japanese currently abide by a program of voluntary quotas on automobile exports to the United States. Assume that the United States decides to allow Japan to export 25 percent for autos to the United States. What would be the likely consequences of this policy? Why would the United States ever agree to such a policy? Would you support this policy?

3. Under what circumstances would it be possible to argue that "protectionism" is a rational and pragmatic policy?

4. What is the significance of a developing country's terms of trade declining?

5. Why do many economists think that the deindustrialization of the United States can be explained in terms of the shifting composition of trade and the globalization of production?

Part II

International Finance

4
The Mysterious World of International Finance

I t is relatively simple to understand how and why nations engage in international trade but, since direct barter exchanges are not generally practical, there has to be a system to pay for and account for international transactions. That means someone has to decide (and everyone has to agree) what will be acceptable to all nations as a medium of exchange to be used as the international currency. Then, since every nation has its own currency, there has to be some way to determine the exchange value of each currency in terms of some standard unit of account. This is the role of international finance.

Economists are fond of pointing out that it doesn't make sense to compare a household budget to the budget of a nation. The reason is that the flows of income are not the same. Since incomes flow in and expenditures out, households have to try to keep their flows of spending equal to their expenditures, i.e., they have to "live within their means." Governments, on the other hand, don't have that problem. Since they can always raise additional income by increasing taxes or by borrowing from their own citizens, governments can (and usually do) consistently run budget deficits.

However, when we begin to look at the economy from an international perspective, everything changes. As far as international transactions are concerned a nation's economy functions exactly like a household's. Expenditures have to roughly equal income or problems will soon follow. Internationally, budgets have to balance.

Balance of Payments Accounts

Nations keep track of their international financial position by
statistically analyzing their international expenditures and income
flows. The result is known as the *balance of payments* account,
which is a simple double entry accounting system involving debits
and credits—just like any household or business accounting
system. Since double entry bookkeeping requires that the debits
and credits must always balance, the issue is not one of "balance,"
because by definition, the balance of payments accounts must
always balance. Instead, the issue is one familiar to students of
economics: it is a question of trying to adjust to maintain
equilibrium.

Before we go on, take a look at table 4–1, which is a hypothetical, summarized version of the U.S. balance of payments
accounts.

First you can see that there are debits and credits—positive
and negative things—which can happen to the accounts in any
given year. Typical transactions that give rise to debits and credits
are shown here.

Second, you can see that the balance of payments accounts are
divided into five different categories, each of which tracks a
different type of transaction.

Table 4–1
Hypothetical Summary Balance of Payments for the United States
(in billions)

Category	Debit (–) (payments)	Credit (+) (receipts)	Net
Goods and services	$–350	+220	–130
Investment income	– 70	+ 90	+ 20
Current account balance	–420	+310	–110
Capital account	– 25	+125	+100
Reserve account	–	+ 8	+ 8
Statistical discrepancy	–	+ 2	+ 2
Total	–445	+445	0

Positive and Negative Effects on Balance of Payments Accounts

Positive (+) (Credits)	Negative (–) (Debits)
1. Any receipt of foreign money.	1. Any payment to a foreign country.
2. Any earning on an investment in a foreign country.	2. Any investment in a foreign country.
3. Any sale of goods or services abroad (export).	3. Any purchase of goods and services abroad (import).
4. Any gift or aid from a foreign country.	4. Any gift or aid given abroad.
5. Any sale of stocks or bonds.	5. Any purchase of stocks or bonds from abroad.

The first of these, the *current account,* shows the value of sales of merchandise and services, that is, imports and exports, and the flows of income from investments abroad and payments to foreign investors.

The current account data is what is generally referred to in the press because it reflects the *balance of trade,* which is simply the difference between exports and imports and is a large part of the current account. Overall balance of payments figures are often confused with balance of trade data. Actually the trade data are a relatively small, albeit important, part of the larger balance of payments picture.

Investment income is included in the current account because it is a *flow* of annual income payments. It includes, for example, interest and dividend payments on stocks and bonds, or profits from more direct investments, such as factories or companies' real estate.

The *capital account* measures annual additions to foreign investments and is, therefore, an addition to capital stock rather than a flow. The difference between flow and stock is a subtle but important part of understanding how the balance of payments accounting system works. In a household, budget flows are the paycheck, or other sources of income, while "stocks" are the accumulated assets, either financial or real. Flows of income add to the stock, that is, the net worth, if there is a surplus, and reduce it if there is a deficit.

The *reserve account* merely measures net additions to or deductions from a country's reserve assets that result from international transactions. Nations accumulate reserves in the form of foreign currencies if they sell more abroad than they buy, or in gold if they mine it or buy it, or in deposits with the International Monetary Fund, which serves as the central banks' bank. It is, theoretically, the account that makes the others balance.

Statistical discrepancies are included partly because the accounts must by definition balance, but more importantly, because the gathering of balance of payments data is, at best, an exercise in statistical fantasy and is not, in fact, very accurate. But, like most economic statistical data, it is useful not so much for the actual numbers involved but because such data allow us to discern trends that tell us a lot about how things are going, and where.*

Now, by looking again at table 4-1 we can begin to understand how balance of payments accounting works and why it is so important.

In this hypothetical year in its current account the United States exported some $220 billion worth of goods and services, and it imported $350 billion. So, obviously, it ran a balance of trade deficit of $130 billion. Since, in this household-like world, a country can't spend more than it earns unless the difference is borrowed or comes out of savings, something has to happen to balance the deficit.**

Also, in its current account for that year the United States earned more from its investments abroad ($90 billion) than foreigners earned from their investments here ($70 billion). The net difference of $20 billion paid for part of the trade deficit. The current account was, nonetheless, in deficit.

The rest of the deficit consisted of a considerable excess of net receipts from foreign investments made in the United States compared to U.S. foreign investments made abroad ($125 billion vs. $25 billion). This almost balanced the accounts, but not quite.

---

*In 1987 statistical discrepancy in the U.S. balance of payments accounts amounted to around $19 billion.

**There are some subtleties to this when it comes to the United States, which, because the U.S. dollar is the key international currency, has some special spending privileges.

A $10 billion deficit remained that had to in essence be paid by drawing down U.S. savings (by $8 billion); accumulations of foreign currencies were spent, or gold was sold, or funds were withdrawn from the U.S. "savings account" with the International Monetary Fund.

The rest was covered by some statistical discrepancy ($2 billion) in the U.S. favor. The net balance of payments is, of course, zero, which is what it must be according to the accounting rules.

Adjustments and Equilibrium in the Balance of Payments

As we have seen, since balance of payments accounts are set up in the standard "double entry" form common to business accounting, they always must balance. But, while this may be satisfactory for accountants, as economists we have to look further into the underlying trends of international economic relations. In this sense the concept of *equilibrium* interests us more than balance. Any household can keep its household accounts in balance from year to year if it can borrow one hundred thousand dollars from a rich uncle whenever needed, but the accounts (from the economist's viewpoint) are not in equilibrium unless one can be assured that the rich uncle will continue the loans forever—an unlikely possibility.

Any country can make its accounts balance, but maintaining international equilibrium is quite another thing. Microeconomics defines equilibrium as instantaneous or, at the most, a very short period of time. In macroeconomics we usually consider equilibrium over the period of one year. But in international economics equilibrium is generally considered to be at least a period of five or so years.

Thus, for our current purposes, international economic equilibrium can be defined as: a set of economic relationships between all inflow and outflow items in the balance of payments accounts, which can continue over a period of five or more years without governmental controls.

The simple practical test of equilibrium is whether, as we saw above, the balance of payments accounts show movement of reserves. If there is such movement we know immediately that the country in question is in either positive or negative disequilibrium. See, for example, table 4–2, which is the real-world (but still simplified) version of the U.S. balance of payments accounts for 1987.

The treatment of the problem of trying to maintain international economic equilibrium helps us focus upon the importance of the *macro*economic theory and, most importantly, to understand the powerful influence *international* economic relations have on *national* economic policy.

Clearly the accounts are not in equilibrium, as the current account is in deficit by $154 billion. Such a deficit must by

Table 4–2
The U.S. Balance of Payments, 1987

1. Exports of Goods and Services		+415
a. Exports of Merchandise	249	
b. Military Sales	10	
c. Sales of Services	52	
d. Foreign Investment Income	104	
2. Imports of Goods and Services		−555
a. Imports of Merchandise	−410	
b. Military Purchases	−12	
c. Purchases of Services	−50	
d. Income Paid to Foreign Investors	−83	
3. Net Unilateral Transfers		−14
a. Government Grants and Pensions	−13	
b. Private Remittances	−1	
4. Balance on Current Account		−154
Financed by:		
5. Net Capital Movements		+81
a. U.S. Capital Outflow	−86	
b. Foreign-capital Inflow	+167	
6. Official Reserve Assets		+54
a. Gold, Foreign Exchange, etc.	+9	
b. Foreign Government Investments	+45	
7. Statistical Discrepancy		+19
Balance		0

Source: *Economic Report of the President, 1989.*

definition (and practicality as well) be financed by some movement of funds into the United States, especially if foreign investment income is not large enough (as was the case during most of the past two decades) to finance the trade deficit. In this year net capital movements (new foreign investments) financed a large part of the deficit. The rest was financed by movement of reserve assets and especially official foreign government investments, which are generally counted as reserve movements. A statistical discrepancy conveniently covered the rest of the deficit. Thus any way you look at it, the U.S. international accounts are far from being in equilibrium as it is conventionally defined. How that can be corrected becomes the relevant question.

In the now traditional Keynesian framework, the national income (Y) is a function of the sum of consumption (C), investment (I), and government spending (G). Since the level of saving increases as income does, consumption is less than income at levels above equilibrium, thus creating a "savings gap" that can be (and usually must be to achieve full employment) filled by investment and/or government spending. Then the basic equilibrium equation becomes:

$$Y = C + I + G$$

$$Y = C + S + Tx, \text{ therefore: } I + G = S + Tx \text{ at equilibrium}$$

This is shown in the standard configuration in figure 4–1.

Savings are a leakage from the economy, as are taxes. Negative effects of savings can be offset by injections of investment, and taxes by government spending. In an open economy model, which is the only one with relevance these days, imports leak out of the system in the sense that payments for them flow abroad, while exports are considered injections because they create income. Given an assumption that the goal of economic policy is to achieve and maintain full employment, the problem becomes one of maintaining balance in each interrelated sector. The bathtub theorem illustrates this in simple form and is shown in figure 4–2.

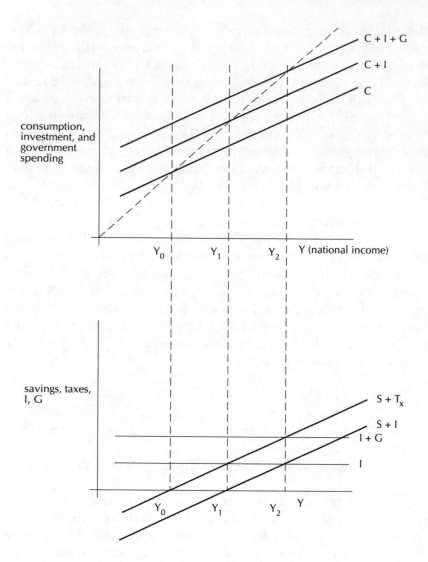

Figure 4–1. *The Keynesian Framework*

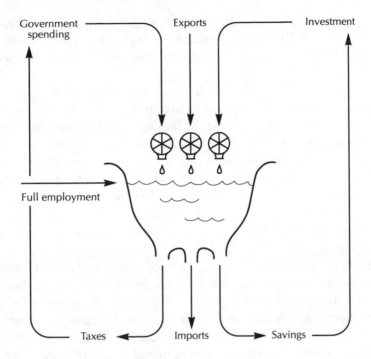

Figure 4–2. *Open Economy: Leakages and Injections*

The water level represents full employment. Leakages from any of the three drains will lower the water level, or the employment level. However, injections from any of the three faucets will raise the water level. The problem in the short run is to adjust the faucets so that the water—the employment level—remains the same.

If we focus only on the international sector and for convenience and simplicity assume away government and domestic investment, then

$$Y = C + (X - M) \text{ where X is exports and M imports.}$$

Exports can be assumed to be autonomous in the sense that, like investment, they do not vary significantly with the level of income. But imports do vary with income—partially because they are usually luxury goods, so the export–import relationship appears much like the standard savings–investment diagram familiar to introductory economics students. This is shown in figure 4–3.

Combining figure 4–3 with the lower portion of figure 4–1, we have an oversimplified but easily understandable model of an open economy in the context of leakages and injections. This is shown in figure 4–4. Keeping investment constant while increasing exports increases the level of income (from Y_0 to $Y(X–M)$) dampened, however, by a corresponding increase in imports. Now, to maintain equilibrium or attain positive disequilibrium, part of *national* policy becomes to *maximize* exports and *minimize* imports. This creates a number of interesting problems.

First, exports are, of course, sales of goods to another country. For every seller there must be a buyer. But it is clearly impossible for *all* nations to follow a policy of *maximizing* exports because when this policy is followed on a worldwide basis we have only sellers and no buyers. Thus, as a macro policy tool, trying to maximize exports *from an international point of view* leads us into an insoluble paradox.

Second, the policy of *minimizing imports,* which is forced upon every country by the present system of international finance,

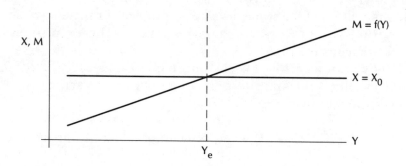

Figure 4–3. *International Sector: Leakages and Injections*

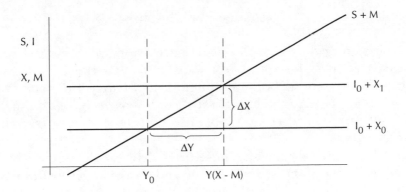

Figure 4–4. *Income Effect of Increasing Exports*

means that all nations, and especially the underdeveloped areas, must forgo imports that may be desperately needed to implement policies of national development.

Finally, because of the requirements of international finance, every nation is forced to pursue anti-inflationary monetary and fiscal policy to keep its prices competitive in world markets and therefore maximize exports.

Anti-inflationary policies mean in real terms that economic policy planners must purposely slow down their economy by cutting back on consumption (raising taxes), holding down investment (raising interest rates), and maintaining government expenditures on public services (education and other social infrastructure) at the lowest possible level. Pursuing this type of policy can hardly be construed as beneficial to any country, especially those nations struggling with the problems of poverty, general underdevelopment, and foreign debt.

This apparent paradox has led many economists to suggest that the present world monetary system *must* be changed to allow nations to deal with their own problems free from the restrictions of the present system of international finance. It is this problem that we address later in this chapter. But first we must understand the mechanics of the international financial structure in a current context.

Exchange Rate Systems

If you were a doctor of international economics looking at this chart (table 4–1 or 4–2) on your patient—the U.S. economy—what would be your diagnosis? Clearly the accounts balance, so the accountants are satisfied, but as we have seen there are serious equilibrium problems, so this won't satisfy the economists.

The country is running a huge trade deficit, covered only by a small net flow of investment income and a very large flow of new foreign investments, and it is even being forced to draw down its reserves.

Is this something that can continue forever? Maybe, maybe not. It all depends on the discipline of the international financial system. On the surface, with the limited data we have, it would appear that any country that is buying more than it is selling and depending on foreign investors to make up the difference is courting problems. What if, for some reason, foreign investors decide the United States is not such a good place to invest after all and withdraw their investments? What happens then? As you can probably imagine, economic theory has an answer to all of these questions: exchange rates should automatically adjust any balance of payment disequilibrium.

Every country in the world has a currency that has a rate at which it exchanges for another country's currency. (Look at table 4–3 for some examples.) These rates of exchange fluctuate every day depending on economic circumstances within, and transactions between, the two countries. And they affect all of us in a very direct way.

Exchange rates come to your attention a little more dramatically if you are on a vacation or a business trip in a foreign country. One day you cash a ten-dollar traveler's check in Japan and you get, say, two thousand yen for it, which is about enough to get you into a movie. Then the next day, the value of the dollar falls and you get only eighteen hundred yen for your ten dollars. Since prices have not changed in Japan, you have to come up with more money—in this case another dollar—if you want to see another movie. Exchange rate fluctuations like that happen all the time. What causes them?

Table 4-3
Major Foreign Currencies per U.S. Dollar

Period	Belgium (franc)	Canada (dollar)	France (franc)	Germany (mark)	Italy (lira)	Japan (yen)
March 1973	39.405	0.9967	4.5063	2.8131	568.87	261.83
1967	49.689	1.0789	4.9206	3.9865	624.09	362.13
1968	49.936	1.0776	4.9529	3.9920	623.38	360.55
1969	50.142	1.0769	5.1999	3.9251	627.32	358.36
1970	49.656	1.0444	5.5288	3.6465	627.12	358.16
1971	48.597	1.0099	5.5098	3.4829	618.32	347.78
1972	44.019	.9907	5.0443	3.1885	583.68	303.12
1973	38.954	1.0002	4.4534	2.6714	582.39	271.30
1974	38.959	.9780	4.8106	2.5867	650.80	291.84
1975	36.799	1.0175	4.2876	2.4613	653.09	296.78
1976	38.608	.9863	4.7824	2.5184	833.55	296.45
1977	35.848	1.0633	4.9160	2.3236	882.76	268.62
1978	31.493	1.1405	4.5090	2.0096	849.12	210.38
1979	29.342	1.1713	4.2567	1.8342	831.10	219.02
1980	29.237	1.1693	4.2250	1.8175	856.20	226.63
1981	37.194	1.1990	5.4396	2.2631	1138.58	220.63
1982	45.780	1.2344	6.5793	2.4280	1354.00	249.06
1983	51.121	1.2325	7.6203	2.5539	1519.32	237.55
1984	57.749	1.2963	8.7355	2.8454	1756.11	237.45
1985	59.336	1.3658	8.9799	2.9419	1908.88	238.47
1986	44.662	1.3896	6.9256	2.1704	1491.16	168.35
1987	37.357	1.3259	6.0121	1.7981	1297.03	144.60
1988	36.790	1.2306	5.9595	1.7570	1302.40	128.17

Source: *Economic Report of the President,* Jan. 1989, p. 431.

Within the country, when we make purchases of goods or services there is only one currency involved so the process is fairly simple. You hand over the money to someone and they will sell you what you want. The price you pay is, generally speaking, determined by the supply of the product that is available at the time and consumers' demand for it. But when you buy an imported product a much more complicated exchange process is triggered. If, for example, you buy a Japanese automobile, you pay for it in dollars, and that's all you have to think about. However, the Japanese auto producer can't pay his bills in dollars; he needs yen. So somewhere along the line your dollars have to be changed into yen so the Japanese auto producer can be paid in his own currency.

This exchange takes place in the foreign exchange market, which is why foreign money is called foreign exchange. The amount of yen a dollar will buy depends on a number of factors, but mostly it's a matter of how many yen Americans in general are wanting compared to how many dollars the Japanese are wanting. In 1987 the United States wanted (imported) $84 billion worth of Japanese products, but the Japanese wanted (imported) only $27 billion worth of U.S. goods. So, the U.S. trade deficit with them was $57 billion dollars.

Now, when the Japanese are selling more in the United States than we are there (as has been the case since 1973), we also are wanting more of their yen than they will want of our dollars. And, because of this excess demand for yen, it would seem to follow that the price of yen is going to go up, which is another way of saying that we will get fewer yen per dollar, or that the value of the dollar will fall.

When the dollar is down against the yen, U.S. imports from Japan are costing more, but U.S. exports to Japan are costing them less. So the United States sells Japan more at lower prices; Japan sells less to the United States at higher prices. The United States both loses and gains in this process. It pays higher prices for the Hondas and the Sonys, but the fact the Japanese goods are becoming more expensive means that U.S. consumers should switch to domestically produced goods and that more jobs will be created here. For the Japanese it's the opposite; lower prices for the American blue jeans or airplanes at the expense of less employment. So exchange rate fluctuations affect everybody in a very direct way and, as shown in figure 4–5, historically they are very volatile.

Determination of Exchange Rates

As we have seen, the price of one country's goods in relation to another's depends on the rate of exchange between their currencies. If rates of exchange are left to fluctuate freely according to the laws of supply and demand then they simply reflect the reciprocal demand for goods and services. This is because the

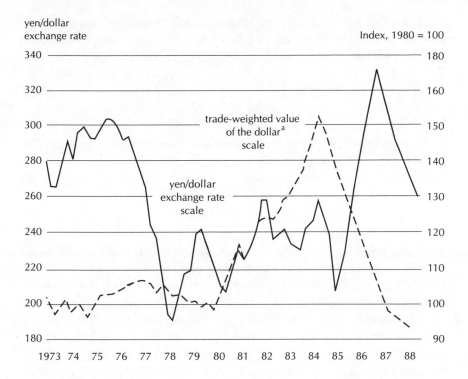

Source: International Monetary Fund, *International Financial Statistics*, 1989.

[a]Trade-weighted exchange value of the dollar vis-à-vis eleven industrial countries, excluding Japan.

Figure 4–5. *Exchange Value of the Dollar, 1973–1988*

demand for foreign currencies (foreign exchange) is a *derived* demand, derived from the demand for imports and exports.

When two countries are trading there are really two markets involved: the *product market* and the *foreign exchange market*. This complicates the process considerably. The key to understanding all exchange systems is understanding that the demand for foreign exchange (that is, foreign money) is not, to repeat, a *direct* demand but a *derived* demand. It is derived from a nation's demand for imports.

Demand for imports, we know, is a function of the nation's income, its tastes, the price of foreign goods, the price of domestic goods, and the rate of exchange (the price of foreign currency). That is:

$$Dm = f\ (Y,\ T,\ Pf,\ Pd,\ and\ Rx)$$

If all other variables are held constant, the demand for imports can be said (at any given point in time), *ceteris paribus,* to be a function of the rate of exchange:

$$Dm = f\ (Rx)$$

To see why, let's examine a simple case of a trade between the United States and Japan. Since there are two countries involved, the process is doubly complicated, which is one of the reasons international economics is so difficult to understand.

Of course, as we just saw, everything depends on which side of the border one is on. U.S. producers want dollars for their products, since they can't pay their bills in yen, and for the same reason Japanese exporters want yen, not dollars. So when the products are exchanged dollars and yen must also be exchanged. This means U.S. demand (for example) for Japanese products is also the U.S. demand for yen and, of course, vice versa. If, as is usually the case, the United States is demanding more of Japanese exports (imports to us) than they are demanding U.S. exports (Japanese imports), then there is more demand for yen than there is demand for dollars, and the price of yen in terms of dollars should rise accordingly. Looked at another way (in this example), we are supplying more dollars than the Japanese are supplying yen, so the yen price of dollars should fall accordingly.

This is shown in figure 4–6. The Japanese demand for dollars is *derived* from their demand for our exports, but the *supply* of dollars comes from U.S. demand for their exports. These two countervailing forces make up a market for dollars in terms of yen. Of course, to make a market for yen in terms of dollars, everything is reversed.

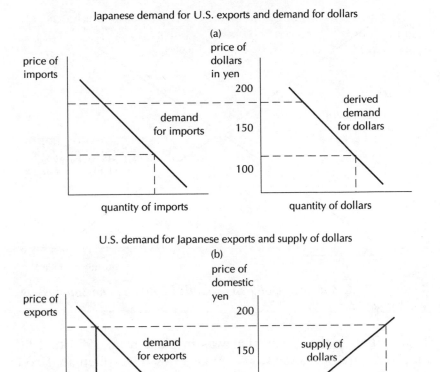

Figure 4–6. *Currency and Goods in U.S.–Japanese Trade*

Free-flexible Exchange Rates:
Possibility Number One

Assuming that exchange rates are flexible and automatically adjust according to supply and demand, they would (as shown in figure 4–7) adjust to equilibrium at the point at which 150 yen equal 1 dollar. At that price exports and imports between the two countries would be equal. Neither would have a deficit or a

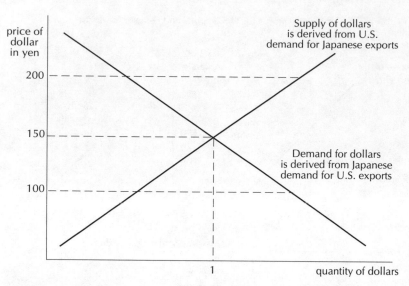

Figure 4–7. *Quantity of Dollars Demanded by Japan and Supplied by the United States*

surplus. This is the system that was in place from 1973 to 1985 and, as figure 4–5 shows, exchange rates have fluctuated considerably over the period—not however, sufficiently to bring trade into balance, for reasons to which we will return shortly.

If we lived in this theoretical economists' world of *free-flexible exchange rates,* adjustment of balance of payments surplus or deficit by gold transfers or central bank intervention would not be necessary. Exchange rates would simply adjust automatically according to the laws of supply and demand. Nations with strong competitive economies would see their currencies appreciate in terms of other currencies and weak economies would see their currencies depreciate.

To see how this might work in a real-world case let's consider, for example, the case of trade between the United States and West Germany, as shown in figure 4–8. The demand for German marks is downsloping because as marks cost less German goods become cheaper for Americans. But, the supply of marks is upward sloping because at higher dollar prices for marks, U.S. goods become cheaper for Germans, thus, the dollar price per mark falls.

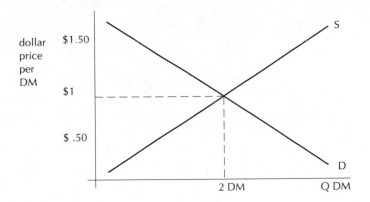

Figure 4–8. *U.S. Dollar vs. West German Deutsche Mark*

The equilibrium price (in figure 4–8) is set by the forces of supply and demand at $1 = 2DM. Supply and demand is, in turn, set by a host of factors including tastes, income levels, relative interest rates, relative inflation levels, and speculation on all of the above.

Now let's assume there is a change in U.S. tastes—desires—for German goods as shown in figure 4–9. Then:

1. At first, if nothing else happens, this creates a balance of payments deficit for the United States in the amount of AB, thus, there is a shortage of marks for us to buy German goods.

2. Now U.S. exports to Germany earn us only OA marks, but we want OB to buy those Mercedeses.

3. So, with a free-flexible system this problem resolves itself, because market forces change the dollar price of marks from $1 = 2DM to $1.50 = 2DM. So it costs us more dollars to buy the marks than we have to have to buy German goods, given they couldn't care less about having dollars because they can't spend them at the beer garden.

4. Now with German goods costing more, we import less of them, and everybody moves toward a new equilibrium around point C. And until something else comes along to change our desire for German imports, new "balance" in the balance of payments accounts is restored.

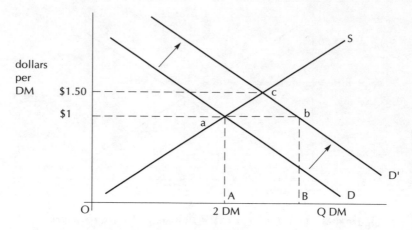

Figure 4–9. *U.S. Dollar vs. West German Deutsche Mark (Change in U.S. Tastes Increases Demand for German Goods)*

Many economists favor this type of system because it provides for the mechanisms of the free market to replace governmental controls. But governments these days generally do not like to see the value of their currency subjected to the uncertainty of the world money market. Thus, as we shall see soon, other systems have been devised.

The Gold Standard: Possibility Number Two

Most people think the present monetary system is based on some sort of *gold standard*. It is a reassuring feeling to know that the cash you have in your pocket or in a bank is, in some way or other, backed up by gold. But nowadays no nation's money supply is actually backed up to any significant degree by gold in any way whatsoever. The value of money depends instead, for the most part, on people's psychological acceptance of simple, inexpensive pieces of paper as a medium of exchange. The *international* monetary system, although somewhat more complicated, works much the same way. It depends, to a large extent, on psychology and "good faith" on the part of trading nations. It must be emphasized again that the world is *not* on the gold standard. Gold is simply one of several "stores of value" used in international commercial transactions.

In its time, the gold standard did operate with some degree of success during various periods of the 1800s and, in various forms, up to the First World War. But, since January 31, 1934, when the United States devalued the dollar, and *officially* went *off the pure gold standard,* the rest of the world also abandoned the gold standard and no one has seriously suggested since that we return to it.

But, since the gold standard is a reasonably possible way to organize an international financial system, let us see how the system would operate *if we were* on the gold standard.

First of all, all standard monetary units would be strictly defined in terms of a fixed quantity of gold. For example, before 1934, the U.S. dollar was defined as 23.22 grains of fine gold and the British pound sterling "contained" 113.0016 grains of fine gold.

Second, for the pure gold standard system to operate, there must be *free conversion rights* of gold into paper money and vice versa. All citizens then have the right to buy and sell (or hoard) gold and to freely import and export it to and from other countries. Since there is free conversion, gold becomes the *standard of money* or, in reality, *the money* of all countries. This system requires all nations to keep on hand large supplies of gold to be able to pay off all comers on demand as well as for use in international transactions. In general, this system (when it was in common use) proved quite cumbersome and very difficult to control whenever there was a loss of confidence in the strength and stability of any nation's economy and, as we have seen, it was officially abandoned in 1934.*

---

*It is interesting to note that under the pure gold standard exchange rates could never fluctuate more than the "mint par" price plus transportation costs. Otherwise, speculators would buy gold and sell it in another country for a profit. Under the gold standard this provided a small "band" (equal to transportation costs) within which exchange rates could fluctuate. But, as long as governments were willing to buy and sell gold at some fixed price, the exchange rate never fluctuated more than the "mint par" price plus or minus the cost of transporting gold between countries.

The United States and the Price of Gold

When the United States officially went off the gold standard with the passing of the Gold Reserve Act of 1934 the world monetary system was altered considerably. *Within* the United States, from then on, the following "rules of the game" were adopted:

1. Legal title to all gold went to the U.S. Treasury.
2. The U.S. dollar was redeemable to U.S. citizens *only* in other credit money and not in gold.
3. Metallic gold could only be used legally by private citizens for industrial, professional, and artistic uses.
4. Private citizens were forbidden to hold gold within the country or to deal in gold trading outside the country.
5. Gold could legally be used by the central bank as reserves or for settling international accounts.
6. And, finally most importantly, the official price of gold was set at thirty-five dollars per fine troy ounce. The U.S. government thereby agreed to *buy* gold at that rate and to *sell* gold at the same rate to any foreign nation holding dollars that wanted to exchange them for gold.

This final section of the act had the effect of "pegging" the world price of gold at thirty-five dollars per ounce. Logically, then, no country would ever *buy* gold at any higher price because it could always be obtained from the United States at thirty-five dollars; but on the other hand, no one could *sell* gold for more than thirty-five dollars per ounce (or would sell for less) for the same reason. Therefore, as long as the United States had a sufficient gold stock to make good on this promise, the price of gold was effectively set at thirty-five dollars per ounce. This offer to buy and sell gold at a fixed price has since played a key role in determining the operation of the actual present international monetary system, which, as we shall soon see, is based primarily on the value of the dollar itself and *not* on gold.

Fixed Exchange Rates

The gold standard or any sort of fixed exchange rate system, such as the Bretton Woods system—to which we shall return—opens up a Pandora's box of problems. To see why, look at figure 4–10. Here we start out again with the dollar–mark rate of exchange fixed at $1 = 2DM. Now we have another uncontrollable desire to start importing more German goods. Then, since exchange rates are not able to adjust automatically as they would under the free-flexible system:

1. The United States has to somehow dig up some marks so that we can increase the supply of them. To do that we have to use some marks that we have been saving, borrow some from the IMF, or sell some gold for marks, or something to come up with the marks to pay for the increased imports.

All that has the effect of shifting the supply curve for marks to the right, and we are back at equilibrium, happy again at point B, where now $1 = 2DM and everything is in balance again.

2. Or, if we don't want to do that, or if we can't scare up enough pounds to do it, we can just discourage German exports

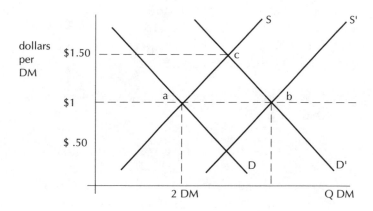

Figure 4–10. *Adjustment under Fixed Exchange Rates*

by slapping a tariff on them, or by imposing some other protectionist measure.

3. Or, we can simply ration the supply of marks, to make it harder for anybody to get them to buy German exports.

4. Or, if all else fails, we can apply deflationary macroeconomic policies to slow down the U.S. economy, reducing everybody's income and consequently their desire to import those expensive German products.

Problems with Free-flexible and Fixed Exchange Rates

It should be clear by now that there are numerous problems associated with both the free-flexible and the fixed exchange rate systems. The free-flexible doesn't as a practical matter work very well because:

1. Exchange rates tend to fluctuate a lot and cause exporters and importers and particularly investors to be nervous about the uncertainty of the returns they might expect. They can hedge against this but that's cumbersome and inconvenient and doesn't always work anyway.

2. Stronger or weaker currencies tend to cause all kinds of problems in the export and import industries.

3. Depreciation is inflationary because it causes import prices to increase. But appreciation makes exports more expensive and less competitive and causes unemployment.

But fixed exchange rate systems cause even more serious problems, in that they:

1. Require large amounts of reserves, which most countries don't have. So they don't offer much of a solution to long-run balance of payment disequilibrium problems such as those the United States has been experiencing for the past decade.

2. And they usually require difficult and politically unpopular macro policy adjustments, and a loss of control of domestic economic policy.

Consequently, since 1985, the industrialized world has been attempting to manage exchange rates with varying degrees of success.

Managed Exchange Rates: Possibility Number Three

As we move into the world of managed exchange rates we begin to approach the present real-world system. Our discussion of the free-flexible system and the gold standard was important to provide a theoretical base for the understanding of the present complex system of international finance. But since we are considering various possibilities, let us look briefly at how the economic authorities could (and sometimes do) actually manage exchange rates.

Exchange Controls

Since, as we have seen, the goal of most countries is to maintain balance of payments equilibrium, we need to understand that one possible way to accomplish this is via *direct* exchange *controls*. That is, it is possible, and in fact quite common in many countries today, to set a legal limit on the amount of currency that citizens can take out of the country, either in person as tourists, or as capital for business transactions. This type of control, while effective in theory, is quite difficult to administer in a practical sense, because unless the currency in question is nonconvertible, there are many ways to get around this type of restriction. And, at any rate, black market operations are usually quick to develop to defeat the purpose of the system. But, in spite of this, it remains a commonly used method for maintaining exchange stability.

Multiple Exchange Rates

Another similar system that has been tried by some countries with persistent balance of payments problems is the establishment of different rates of exchange for different types of international transactions. If, for example, a developing country wanted to encourage the import of capital goods and discourage the import of luxury goods it would be possible to set *different* rates of exchange for these different items. In such cases, usually a special government agency must be established to control the sale and purchase of *all* foreign exchange. Then *low* selling prices (in terms of some reserve currency) are set for items the government wants to discourage being exported. At the same time, *high* selling rates are set for items the government does not want imported. For all other goods, a free market rate generally prevails.

Most economists feel that multiple exchange rates are a rather inefficient method of exchange control because they require quite close policing, and a considerable amount of administrative red tape. And besides, at any rate, they argue, the same goals could be accomplished by tariffs or other types of duties which, while they may not be desirable in terms of facilitating world trade, are at least more efficient and less cumbersome.

Exchange Stabilization Funds

A final possible system of exchange control that was quite common in the 1930s and 1940s is the Exchange Stabilization Fund. During that period, many nations (especially Great Britain and the United States) set aside large sums of gold or foreign exchange to be used to enter the foreign exchange market to stabilize the currency any time its price approached a predetermined upper or lower limit. Any market price can be controlled if there is a sufficient stock of the commodity (in this case foreign exchange) available to meet demand. When demand is high more of the commodity is put on the market to meet it. This obviously has the effect of lowering price. On the other hand, if the price is falling the commodity is purchased and the resulting scarcity tends to raise the price. Thus, as long as the available reserves hold out, the market price is effectively stabilized.

As the world's monetary system became more and more closely pegged to the dollar, the use of exchange stabilization funds became less important, and as a *specific tool* to manage exchange rates, they were largely abandoned by most countries. However, as we shall soon see, the basic idea is still an important part of the world monetary system.

Managed Exchange Rates in Theory and Practice

The free-flexible exchange rate system in place from 1973 to 1985 worked fairly well until around 1982, when the U.S. current account deficit began to grow at alarming rates, as seen in figure 3–2. Concerned that things were getting out of hand, the Group of Five industrialized countries, at the initiative of U.S. Secretary of Treasury James Baker, met at the Plaza Hotel in New York and agreed to begin (again) managing exchange rates. This agreement—known as the Plaza Agreement—was a momentous change in international economic policy.

Managing exchange rates simply requires participating countries to intervene in the foreign exchange markets whenever any country's balance of payments appears to be moving toward disequilibrium. To more clearly understand how this works, simply consider any market—for example, wheat in the commodities market. Anyone who owns enough wheat can control wheat prices by entering the market and supplying wheat any time the price of wheat begins to rise. This has the effect of stabilizing or destabilizing wheat prices, depending on the goal of the seller.

Since the foreign exchange market is simply a market for a commodity (money) and is subject to the laws of supply and demand, it can be controlled (or manipulated) by anyone who holds large amounts of currency. This process is shown in figure 4–11. At price Px, the demand for dollars exceeds the current supply; therefore, there is a tendency for market forces to push the price even higher, toward the equilibrium price Pe. If the United States and/or its trading partners don't want that to happen (because, for example, it would make U.S. exports more expensive), they can intervene in the market and supply (sell) an amount AB of additional dollars. This has the effect of keeping the price of the dollar where it is, at Px, which also in this case means that the dollar is undervalued (it is "weak") in terms of other currencies and that the United States would run a balance of payments surplus in the amount of A dollars, represented by the distance between points A and B in figure 4–11. On the other hand, if the exchange price of dollars were Pm, then the dollar is overvalued and the United States would be running a balance of payments deficit (since the dollar is too strong) in the amount of AB in this example.

Since the objective of managing exchange rates is to move toward balance of payments equilibrium, the monetary authorities—under a managed system—attempt to intervene in the market and cause exchange rates to move the system toward a longer term equilibrium. Under a free-flexible system this should happen automatically. If the world were really that simple then trade between nations could be balanced and everyone would benefit equally from the international trade process. But, in economics, things are seldom as simple in practice as they appear in theory. Neither the free-flexible system of 1973–85 nor the attempts at managing the system since have brought about international trade equilibrium.

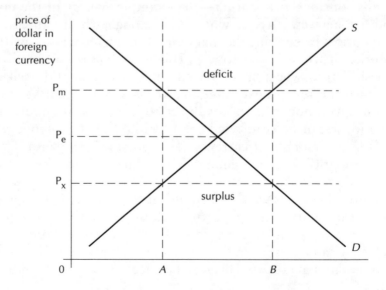

Figure 4–11. *Managed Exchange Rates*

Paradox of the Strong Dollar

Since 1982, the United States has been running gigantic trade deficits. In 1988, the trade deficit approached $150 billion. This is, to say the least, historically unprecedented. Given the theoretical considerations we have just examined, it would seem that under such circumstances, the value of the dollar would *fall* and that, accordingly, U.S. exports would be cheaper, imports would be more expensive, and the trade imbalance would be corrected. But this hasn't happened. The reason it hasn't is an integral part of the present international financial crisis.

Let's look first at the data. Figure 4–12 compares the balance of trade with the value of the dollar (as weighted against a selected group of foreign currencies) and clearly shows that while the dollar has become stronger, the trade deficit has become larger. This, of course, is the opposite of what—theoretically—should have occurred. As we have demonstrated, whenever a nation runs a trade deficit, there has to be a compensating flow in one or more of the other accounts to balance the accounts. That is, the difference has to be made up by earnings from foreign investments, by net flows of new investments, or by borrowing from reserves. By looking at the U.S. balance of payments history shown in tables 4–4a and 4–4b, we can see the paradoxical events that have made the dollar strong even in the face of a large trade deficit. First of all, in the current account, income from U.S. investments abroad generally helped reduce the net effects of the merchandise deficit over the period 1979–82. That income averaged about $30 billion over that period.

Also, in the capital account, large annual (incremental) increases in foreign investment in the United States, coupled with *decreases* in U.S. investment abroad, provided a huge U.S. surplus in the investment account. This annual inflow of new private investment (shown as capital inflow of private assets), which amounted to $125 billion in 1985, more than anything increased foreign demand for the dollar and kept it strong when, in the face of a large trade deficit, it should have been weak.

There are several reasons for this unprecedented shift in the patterns of investment. One is that foreign investors seem to feel that the U.S. economy is a safe haven for investments compared to

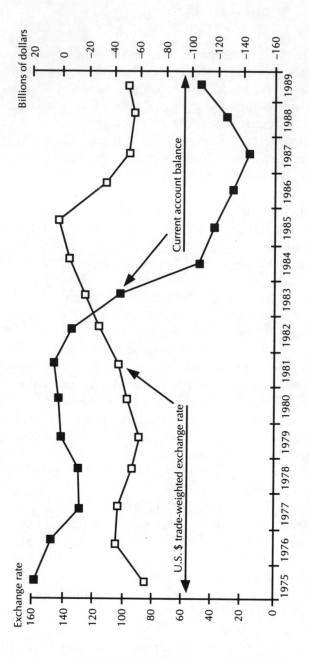

Figure 4–12. *The U.S. Dollar versus the Current Account Balance*

Table 4–4a

U.S. International Transactions, Current Account, 1970–1988

[Millions of dollars; quarterly data seasonally adjusted, except as noted. Credits (+), debits (−)]

Year	Merchandise [1] [2]			Investment income [3]			Net military transactions	Net travel and transportation receipts	Other services net [3]	Balance on goods and services [4]	Remittances, pensions, and other unilateral transfers [1]	Balance on current account [4]
	Exports	Imports	Net	Receipts	Payments	Net						
1970	42,469	−39,866	2,603	11,747	−5,516	6,231	−3,354	−2,038	2,329	5,773	−3,443	2,331
1971	43,319	−45,579	−2,260	12,707	−5,436	7,271	−2,893	−2,345	2,649	2,423	−3,856	−1,433
1972	49,381	−55,797	−6,416	14,764	−6,572	8,192	−3,420	−3,063	2,965	−1,742	−4,052	−5,795
1973	71,410	−70,499	911	21,808	−9,655	12,153	−2,070	−3,158	3,406	11,244	−4,103	7,140
1974	98,306	−103,811	−5,505	27,587	−12,084	15,503	−1,653	−3,184	4,231	9,392	5 −7,431	1,962
1975	107,088	−98,185	8,903	25,351	−12,564	12,787	−746	−2,812	4,853	22,984	−4,868	18,116
1976	114,745	−124,228	−9,483	29,286	−13,311	15,975	559	−2,558	5,027	9,521	−5,314	4,207
1977	120,816	−151,907	−31,091	32,179	−14,217	17,962	1,528	−3,565	5,679	−9,488	−5,023	−14,511
1978	142,054	−176,001	−33,947	42,245	−21,680	20,565	621	−3,573	6,459	−9,875	−5,552	−15,427
1979	184,473	−212,009	−27,536	64,132	−32,960	31,172	−1,778	−2,935	6,214	5,138	−6,128	−991
1980	224,269	−249,749	−25,480	72,506	−42,210	30,386	−2,237	−997	7,793	9,466	−7,593	1,873
1981	237,085	−265,063	−27,978	86,411	−52,329	34,082	−1,183	144	9,278	14,344	−7,460	6,884
1982	211,198	−247,642	−36,444	83,549	−54,883	28,666	−274	−992	9,320	278	−8,956	−8,679
1983	201,820	−268,900	−67,080	77,251	−52,376	24,875	−243	−4,227	9,908	−36,766	−9,480	−46,246
1984	219,900	−332,422	−112,522	85,908	−67,419	18,489	−2,099	−8,604	9,760	−94,975	−12,102	−107,077
1985	215,935	−338,083	−122,148	88,837	−62,901	25,936	−3,431	−10,049	9,600	−100,093	−15,010	−115,103
1986	223,969	−368,516	−144,547	90,110	−66,968	23,142	−4,372	−9,344	11,600	−123,520	−15,308	−138,828
1987	249,570	−409,850	−160,280	103,756	−83,381	20,375	−2,368	−10,281	12,035	−140,519	−13,445	−153,964
1988	319,251	−446,466	127,215	107,775	−105,548	2,227	−4,606	−2,633	20,335	−111,892	−14,656	−126,548

Source: *Economic Report of the President*, Jan. 1989, p. 424.

[1] Excludes military.
[2] Adjusted from Census data for differences in valuation, coverage, and timing.
[3] Fees and royalties from U.S. direct investments abroad or from foreign direct investments in the United States are excluded from investment income and included in other services, net.
[4] In concept, balance on goods and services is equal to net exports and imports in the national income and product accounts (and the sum of balance on current account and allocations of special drawing rights is equal to net foreign investment in the accounts), although the series differ because of different handling of certain items (gold, capital gains and losses, etc.), revisions, etc.

Table 4–4b
U.S. International Transactions, *Capital Account, 1970–1988*

[Millions of dollars; quarterly data seasonally adjusted, except as noted.]

Year	U.S. assets abroad, net [increase/capital outflow (–)]				Foreign assets in the U.S., net [increase/capital inflow (+)]			Statistical discrepancy
	Total	U.S. official reserve assets 6	Other U.S. Government assets	U.S. private assets	Total	Foreign official assets	Other foreign assets	Total (sum of the items with sign reversed)
1970	–9,337	2,481	–1,589	–10,299	6,359	6,908	–550	–219
1971	–12,475	2,349	–1,884	–12,940	22,970	26,879	–3,909	–9,779
1972	–14,497	–4	–1,568	–12,925	21,461	10,475	10,986	–1,879
1973	–22,874	158	–2,644	–20,388	18,388	6,026	12,362	–2,654
1974	–34,745	–1,467	5 366	–33,643	34,241	10,546	23,696	–1,458
1975	–39,703	–849	–3,474	–35,380	15,670	7,027	8,643	5,917
1976	–51,269	–2,558	–4,214	–44,498	36,518	17,693	18,826	10,544
1977	–34,785	–375	–3,693	–30,717	51,319	36,816	14,503	–2,023
1978	–61,130	732	–4,660	–57,202	64,036	33,678	30,358	12,521
1979	–64,331	–1,133	–3,746	–59,453	38,752	–13,665	52,416	25,431
1980	–86,118	–8,155	–5,162	–72,802	58,112	15,497	42,615	24,982
1981	–110,951	–5,175	–5,097	–100,679	83,032	4,960	78,072	19,942
1982	–121,153	–4,965	–6,131	–110,058	93,746	3,593	90,154	36,085
1983	–49,777	–1,196	–5,006	–43,576	84,869	5,845	79,023	11,154
1984	–22,304	–3,131	–5,489	–13,685	102,621	3,140	99,481	26,760
1985	–32,636	–3,858	–2,829	–25,950	129,900	–1,196	131,096	17,839
1986	–97,991	312	–2,000	–96,303	221,253	35,507	185,746	15,566
1987	–75,987	9,149	1,162	–86,297	211,490	44,968	166,522	18,461
1988	–82,110	–3,566	2,999	–81,543	219,299	38,882	180,418	–

Source: *Economic Report of the President,* Jan. 1989, p. 425.

Note: Quarterly data for U.S. official reserve assets and foreign assets in the United States are not seasonally adjusted.

5 Includes extraordinary U.S. Government transactions with India.
6 Consists of gold, special drawing rights, foreign currencies, and the U.S. reserve position in the International Monetary Fund (IMF).

other options. This is partly because of the sheer size of the U.S. economy and partly because of the political and economic uncertainty and turmoil in much of the rest of the world. Another reason is that the rate of inflation in the United States has been relatively low since 1982. This means that the real rate of return (as compared to the nominal rate) on investments in the United States has remained relatively quite high. Also, especially from 1982 to 1984, interest rates in the United States remained high compared to the rest of the world. Even as rates later fell, the real rate of interest (interest rate minus inflation rate) was high by historical standards.

So the primary reason the U.S. dollar has remained strong is that investors have confidence in the U.S. economy. Real interest rates have remained high, since inflation is still relatively low. Now, the question is: What does this unexpected, unprecedented, and paradoxical turn of events mean? There are three important issues here, all of which are analyzed in more detail in other chapters.

Emerging Financial Crisis

To begin with, there is the question of the increasing fragility of the international financial system. One important result of the massive inflows of foreign investment over the past several years is that it has financed much of the U.S. *internal* deficit (the U.S. national debt). If there were a sudden loss of confidence in the U.S. economy because of, say, a Third World debt default, these funds could be withdrawn almost overnight. This would almost certainly precipitate a rapid drop in the value of the dollar and a financial panic, if not a total collapse, of the U.S. economy, and with it a collapse of the international economy.

Second, the world economy now finds itself between the proverbial "rock and a hard place." Third World countries are now facing an external debt burden that exceeds *$1 trillion*. If they are to have even the remotest chance of repaying it, they must be able to earn foreign exchange by exporting. This means the United States *must* continue to run a huge trade deficit; it must continue to buy the exports of the Third World. This, in turn, means that the U.S. trade deficit must continue to be financed by foreign investments from the other industrialized countries, which also means that the U.S. economy will continue to enjoy the benefits of cheap imports, a lower inflation rate, and an internal deficit financed by someone else's savings. In many ways, this is a case of being able to eat your cake and have it too, but at the price of losing the U.S. industrial sector's world dominance and the millions of jobs associated with it to foreign competition.

Finally, this dramatic and ironic shift of roles in the international economy means that the United States has already become a debtor nation for the first time since 1914. There is nothing inherently wrong with being a debtor country. Historically, *developing* countries have borrowed from more advanced countries—as the United States did during the 1800s—to finance investments in capital stock, which then stimulate productivity and growth, ideally at a rate that provides a rate of return higher than the interest on the loans. If that happens, then the loans can be repaid and everyone gains. But for the most developed, richest, and most productive economy in the world to also be a debtor nation is, to put it mildly, somewhat unusual.

A nation, like a household, becomes a net debtor when it spends more than it earns by incurring obligations in its capital account that exceed its net income from exports and the net inflow of foreign investments. By accepting foreign investments, a nation incurs an obligation to pay a stream of income to investors over a long period of time, indefinitely in the case of direct investments. And, because of compounding, portfolio investments (such as U.S. Treasury bonds) tend to grow at an increasing rate, thus worsening the outflow of funds, as the Third World debtor countries can now testify with some clarity and, we might add, anger.

As shown in figure 4–13, sometime in the fall of 1985 the United States became a debtor nation. The outflow of payments (in current account) to foreign investors exceeds the inflow of funds from U.S. foreign investments abroad. This, in itself, would not be an event of historical significance if it were not for some

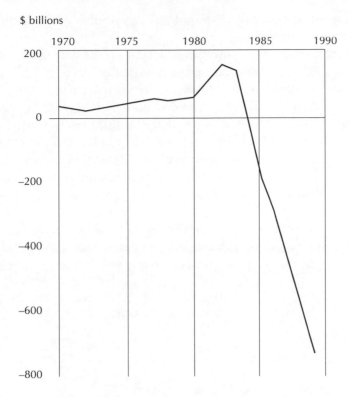

Source: U.S. Department of Commerce, *Survey of Current Business*, Vol. 68, No. 6, June 1988.

Figure 4–13. *U.S. Net External Assets, 1970–1989*

disturbing longer-run trends. Even under the most optimistic conditions, estimates are that the U.S. external debt will exceed $1 trillion by 1992. That is half of the U.S. (internal) national debt and roughly 20 percent of the total U.S. output of goods and services.

One result of such a staggering external debt is that it will engender an estimated outflow (on current account) of some $100 billion annually in interest and dividend payments to other countries. If present trends continue, this would push the total current account deficit into the $200-300 billion range, which would, in turn, cause the external debt to double to $2 trillion by the turn of the century.

The reason for this unsettling turn of events is that while U.S. investment abroad has declined dramatically since 1982, foreign investment in the United States has been increasing rapidly. As shown in figure 4–14, the annual inflow of investments made in the United States began to exceed the annual outflow of investments abroad in the summer of 1982. The reason U.S. investments abroad have declined so rapidly is that investors are concerned about the fragility of the international financial system and a possible default by one of the heavily indebted Third World countries.

Since new investments typically yield a lower rate of return in the early stages (as new factories are built, and so on), it took some time for the outflows on the new investments in the United

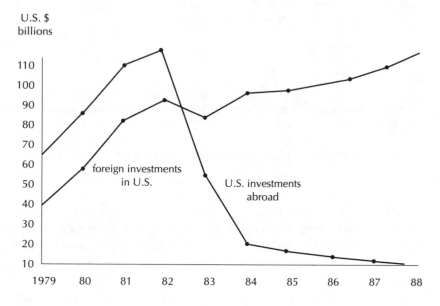

Source: *Economic Report of the President,* 1986.

Figure 4–14. *Annual Flows of Foreign Investment in the U.S. Capital Account, 1979–1988*

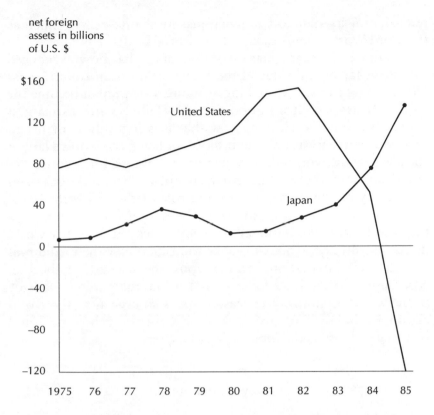

net foreign
assets in billions
of U.S. $

Sources: 1975–1984 data are from the U.S. Department of Commerce and
Japanese Ministry of Finance; 1985 projections come from Kemper Financial
Services.

Figure 4–15. *The United States and Japan as Debtor and Creditor
Countries, 1975–1985*

States to exceed the inflows from the more mature U.S. investments abroad, but, as we have seen, that did begin to occur by
1985. What this means is, first, that as larger and larger shares of
the U.S. internal national debt are owned by foreign interests,
more and more U.S. resources will have to flow abroad to service
the debt. This will mean that the benefits of cheaper imports currently enjoyed by the United States will no longer be possible. The
United States will be forced into austerity programs and a general

reduction of its standard of living just to pay its debts—much as the Third World countries have been forced to do.

Moreover, it means that the United States has now exchanged roles with Japan and some of the Western European countries. By 1985, as you can see by looking at figure 4–15, Japan became the world's largest creditor nation and the United States the largest debtor. It should be clear by now that it is logically inconsistent for one country to sustain the position of being the world's largest spender *and* the world's largest debtor at the same time.

Much will depend on how the international financial community continues to perceive the role of the United States in the world economy and, especially, the role of the U.S. dollar as the world's key international currency. Since the Western world decided at Bretton Woods to make the U.S. dollar the medium of exchange for international transactions, the strength of the U.S. economy—and the U.S. dollar—has become the paramount issue in the world economy. The reason this is so crucial to the world economic balance of power and to continued international financial stability is the topic of later chapters.

Key Concepts

Balance of Payments
Current Account
Capital Account
Exchange Rate
Appreciation
Depreciation
Devaluation
Managed Exchange Rate
Gold Standard
U.S. Debtor Nation

Discussion Questions

1. What are the primary differences between the current and capital account of the balance of payments?

2. If a country is year-after-year running a current account deficit, what conclusions can be generally drawn?

3. What is the basic determinant of a country's exchange rate? (How can it be explained that the demand for a country's currency is a "derived" demand?)

4. What would be the likely explanation for the appreciation of a country's currency? (Depreciation?)

5. What is a managed exchange rate?

6. Assume a country decided its currency was overvalued: the country abandoned its fixed exchange rate for a free-flexible exchange rate. What would happen to the exchange rate?

7. Why has the United States become a major debtor nation?

8. What are the primary macroeconomic consequences of a balance of payments deficit? (Surplus?)

5
Multinational Corporations and Developing Countries

Since the end of the Second World War no aspect of international political economy has generated more controversy than the global expansion of multinational corporations. Some consider these powerful corporations to be a boon to mankind, superseding the nation–state, diffusing countries, and interlocking national economies into an expanding and beneficial interdependence. Others view them as imperialistic predators, exploiting all for the sake of the corporate few while creating a web of political dependence and economic underdevelopment.[1]

—Robert Gilpin

Introduction

To fully understand the significance of the emergence of the modern multinational corporation and its impact on developing countries, one must examine the theory behind the multinational firm, the challenges of economic development for developing nations, the various competing schools of thought on economic development, the case for and against multinational firms in developing countries, and the likely prospects for both multinationals and developing countries in the 1990s.

Economic Rationale for Multinational Corporations

The evolution of the modern multinational corporation in the post–World War II era is clearly one—if not the most important—factor determining the character of the international economic and financial system. The emergence of the MNC has challenged the profession to consider how the international system actually works in the context of how economic theory says it works when confronted with this new reality.

As we have seen in previous chapters, much of the theory of international trade and finance assumes that goods and services are being produced in one country and exported to another under the theoretical rationale of comparative advantage. But, as we are all well aware these days, a large proportion of international trade takes place within the same company—intrafirm trade. This forces us to reconsider the very basic assumptions of trade theory and the character of the firms that are involved.

The multinational corporation has a number of distinguishing characteristics. The common definition is that a multinational corporation is a firm that owns and manages production units in two or more countries. It is a firm that approximates the theoretical model of an oligopoly. Such a firm typically has a coordinated global strategy and is fully integrated in terms of ownership, management, production, and sales. It can take advantage of economies of scale, financial assets, and technological change because of its size and barriers to entry for other firms. As such the modern MNC has been at the center of the historical process of integrating the global economy. The rapid internationalization of production through the increased international specialization and division of labor has placed the MNC as the driving force behind international capital movements and trade.

In terms of size, many of the largest MNCs can challenge many countries with respect to annual product. For example, in 1985, General Motors had gross sales of $96.4 billion, which made it the twenty-second largest country/company in the world. Exxon was twenty-fourth, with gross sales of $86.7 billion. Each of these giants had annual gross sales larger than the GNPs of Indonesia, Saudi Arabia, or South Korea. IBM is larger than Venezuela or Egypt and Texaco larger than Yugoslavia.[2]

As indicated earlier, the larger MNCs tend to be classic oligopolists in the sense that they control a large percentage of their market and have considerable, but not total, control over price. The institutional organizational structure of most MNCs provides for a home-based corporate headquarters, usually—but not always—in the country from which they originated. From this headquarters the financial decisions and strategic corporate planning decisions are made. Other administrative and managerial decisions are decentralized throughout the global institutional structure, as are the operations related to the actual production of goods and services, marketing, and sales. Their major goal is obviously to maximize profits. This requires them to find ways to produce goods and services at the lowest possible cost by taking advantage of lower fixed and variable production costs that exist in countries other than their base country. Such efficiencies have resulted in dramatic increases in the productive capacities of many developing and advanced country economies at the price, however, of a shift in control of the host country's economy to external interests. This has, to say the least, engendered great controversy.

By the 1960s the United States was home base for many of the world's largest multinational corporations. Many experts during this period warned that the day was not far off when these corporate giants would control and dominate the entire global economy. Europeans were particularly concerned about the prospect of their economies being bought up by American corporations, as was evidenced by the point of view presented by Jean Jacque Servan-Schriber in his popular book, *The American Challenge*.[3] Little did he know at the time that Europe would be marching toward full economic integration by 1992 and that the United States would be expressing dismay and concern about Japanese investments in the United States.

In retrospect it is clear that the Europeans did not have to worry. The decade of the 1970s, with its stagflation and spiraling oil prices, positioned the OPEC nations at the center of the global financial system and made life very difficult for most large non–oil-producing MNCs. The slow growth and stagnation of the decade reduced the pace of MNC expansion and redirected the location of what direct private foreign investment did occur. Most of the major MNCs began to look less and less to the developing world and more and more to the advanced nations.

The Multinational Firm in Theory

In addition to the basic assumptions and characteristics normally attributed to an oligopolistic firm, the origins of the multinational firm are to be found in the theoretical formulations of the product cycle developed by economist Raymond Vernon.[4]

Product cycle theory explains the various stages of the development and production of a product, with particular importance attached to the location of each activity in the process.

There are three basic phases: 1) the *innovative phase*, 2) the *maturing* or *process development phase*, and 3) the *standardized* or *mature phase*. Let us examine each of these in some detail.

The innovative (or introductory) phase occurs when new technology is first developed and the product is first produced and no other competitor has the new technology or product. Usually first-phase developments occur in the more advanced industrialized countries. Typically, new products are marketed domestically at first. As foreign demand begins to grow it then makes economic sense to consider producing abroad to circumvent trade barriers and maximize the advantages of proximity to markets and the range of production costs possible outside the home-base country.

This second phase is also characterized by increasing competition as the technology is diffused. In time, the product is produced by a number of other competing firms from other advanced countries. This will push the product and its production into the third phase.

The third phase of standardization (mature phase) is characterized by the shifting of production to the developing countries, especially the NICs. In these countries the multinational can compete principally on the comparative advantage of wage labor costs. Thus, for many multinational corporations, locating production in developing countries essentially allows them to use these countries as export platforms.

Product cycle theory is useful in explaining how and why it is that a multinational corporation can gain from operating globally, what role it plays in the international diffusion of technology, and how international trade becomes an integral part of the multi-national's integrated global strategy.

What it does not explain is how, even in the long run, the multinational can compete with host country corporations even in highly industrialized countries.

This, however, can be explained by what is commonly called *vertical integration theory*, which has its roots in industrial organization theory.

Vertical integration, in the standard sense of the term, means obtaining ownership and control of the production process at all stages. To be simplistic, if a grocery chain sells bread, the firm would own the farm where the wheat is grown, the mill where the wheat is processed, the transportation system the flour is shipped on, the bakery where the bread is baked, the machine that packages the bread, and the trucks that deliver the bread to the store where the bread will be sold.

By establishing a production system that is vertically integrated, a multinational corporation can spread internationally the various stages of production to reduce production costs. The rapid development of technology and its application to production is driven by the multinational firm's ability to devote sizeable resources to research and development. The process of managing and coordinating an international production strategy is made possible by the advances in transportation and communications in the last twenty years. The ultimate goal of reducing costs and maximizing profits is made possible by the placement of various stages of production in different locations around the globe. It is not necessary nor even desirable to produce a product completely in one single country. This allows the multinational firm to take advantage of differential tax rates, host country subsidization of direct private investment, differential tariff structures, foreign exchange fluctuations, and differential competitive environments.

In the 1980s it was possible to observe some of the many dynamic dimensions of this vertical integration in both developing and advanced nations. For example, a few years ago *Business Week* devoted a cover story to the "Hollowing of American Industry."[5] The story described the process by which American firms were no longer producing products themselves but were becoming brokers for other producers. U.S. firms would buy parts of products and ship them to specific locations to be assembled. This now-common process is not explained by either product theory or vertical integration theory.

The decline in domestic manufacturing output and employment, in part a consequence of this "outsourcing" of production, combined with the tremendous increase in the production of services (especially information system and financial services), represented a historic transformation of the U.S. economy. U.S. multinational production became more and more characterized by the increased decentralization of production internationally. It is not uncommon to find a finished product that has been made from parts from over forty nations and assembled in three to four different nations. The *maquiladora,* or twin assembly plants, on the U.S.–Mexico border are perhaps the best example of this kind of production process. On the U.S.–Mexico border are more than five hundred plants that often have a twin manufacturing facility on each side of the border. This allows a firm like Zenith, engaged in the assembly of electronics consumer products, to ship components from the United States across the border to its assembly plant in Mexico. The final product will be fully assembled at the Mexican plant, where labor rates are sixty cents an hour, compared to wage rates in the United States of anywhere from $5.45 to more than $12 an hour. Once the product is assembled in Mexico it will be shipped across the border (paying only taxes on the value added) to the Zenith plant on the U.S. side. From this plant, the product will be distributed to retailers across the country.

While this changing production system is having significant consequences for the U.S. economy, it is not clear yet whether the net result will be good or bad. Clearly, the fears surrounding the "deindustrialization" of the United States are well-founded; yet the recent experience of Japanese automobile companies' setting up production facilities inside the United States has not only brought employment and investment but much-needed competition for the U.S. Big Three. This successful penetration of the U.S. automobile industry from internal production is forcing

Detroit to totally reexamine every single facet of its operation, from relationships to suppliers to the worker on the assembly line.[6]

The point of all of this is that no nation is untouched by the constantly evolving multinational corporation.

But a more important point is, what is the impact of multinational corporations on developing countries? This can only be understood in the context of the basic economic problems facing developing nations and the basic competing schools of thought on economic development in the Third World.

Basic Economic Problems of Developing Countries

Development processes are both cruel and necessary. They are necessary because all societies must come to terms with new aspirations and irresistible social forces. Yet the choices they face are cruel because development's benefits are obtained only at a great price and because, on balance, it is far from certain that achieving development's benefits makes men happier or freer.[7]

Most developing countries confront a series of related economic problems: rapid population growth combined with declining growth of the Gross Domestic Product, unequal distribution of income, the macroeconomic problems of deficit spending, inflation, and unemployment, and the international trade and finance related problems of high import needs, declining exports, balance of payments problems, foreign exchange depreciation, and external debt.

Population and Economic Growth

In 1989, developing countries had a total population of 4 billion people out of a total world population of 5 billion. Between 1980 and 1986, developing countries had an average annual population growth rate of 2 percent, compared with the 0.6 percent average annual population growth rate of industrial countries. The GNP per capita for developing countries in 1980 was $670, compared to $10,760 for industrial countries (see tables 5–2 and 5–3).

Table 5–1
GNP Per Capita in 1986 Dollars

Low-income countries	$ 270
Middle-income countries	1,270
Upper-middle income countries	1,890
Industrial market countries	12,960
Developing countries	610
Oil exporters	930
Manufacturing exporters	540
Highly indebted countries	1,400
Sub-Saharan African countries	370

Source: World Bank, *World Development Report, 1988*
(New York: Oxford University Press, 1988).

Between 1980 and 1987 developing countries had a 1.9 percent average growth of real per capita Gross Domestic Product, compared to growth rates of 3.2 percent for the 1973–80 period and 3.9 percent for the 1965–73 period. In terms of the growth of the real Gross Domestic Product, developing countries averaged only 3.2 percent for the 1980–85 period, compared to the impressive rates of 5.4 percent and 6.5 percent for the 1973–80 and 1965–73 periods, respectively (see tables 5–4 and 5–5), so the decline in real economic growth in the underdeveloped world has been dramatic.

It is obvious that even with strong growth rates of the Gross Domestic Product, the pressure from strong population growth rates will essentially eliminate any of the real economic gains that might have been possible. It is even worse in the current context in which growth rates of GDP and GDP per capita are below historic levels. Therefore it is clear that developing nations must attempt to slow down their population growth rates while struggling to stimulate their economies. It is particularly important for the very poorest nations to do this because they have the lowest GDP per capita ($270/yr) and usually the highest population growth rates (3 percent or higher).

Income Distribution

Almost all developing countries reflect dramatic inequalities in the distribution of income (as can be observed from table 5–6,

Table 5–2

Population Growth, 1965–1986, and Projected to Year 2000

Country group	1986 population (millions)	Average annual growth (percent)				
		1965–73	1973–80	1980–86	1986–90	1990–2000
Developing countries	3,528	2.5	2.1	2.0	2.1	1.9
Low-income countries	2,374	2.6	2.0	1.9	2.0	1.8
Middle-income countries	1,154	2.5	2.4	2.3	2.2	2.0
Oil exporters	475	2.6	2.6	2.6	2.5	2.3
Exporters of manufactures	2,081	2.5	1.8	1.6	1.7	1.5
Highly indebted countries	570	2.6	2.4	2.4	2.3	2.2
Sub-Saharan Africa [a]	399	2.7	2.8	3.1	3.3	3.2
High-income oil exporters	20	4.8	5.5	4.2	4.0	3.4
Industrial countries	742	1.0	0.7	0.6	0.5	0.4
World [a]	4,290	2.2	1.9	1.8	1.8	1.7

Source: World Bank, *World Development Report, 1988* (New York: Oxford University Press, 1988), p. 187.

[a] Excludes nonmarket industrial economies.

looking at the percentage share of household income by percentile groups of households). For example, in Kenya the lowest 20 percent receives 2.6 percent of household income, while the highest 20 percent receives 60.4 percent. In Mexico, the highest 20 percent receives 57.7 percent of household income, while the lowest 20 percent receives 2.9 percent. The inequality of the distribution of income from an economic development perspective means that there will be a low level of domestic savings, investment, and tax revenues. In addition, there will be a low level of domestic demand for goods other than very basic necessities. It also means that the affluent members of the society will be inclined to invest their money in advanced countries and spend on expensive imported luxury goods. So, the inequality in the distribution is not merely an issue that involves questions of fairness but critical issues related to the requirements of a modern growing economy. What seems to be a growing consensus is that developing countries must overcome the stagnation of the 1980s and achieve strong and sustained economic growth that will allow for a change in the distribution of income that will specifically improve the standard of living for the bottom 40 percent of the population.

Table 5-3

Population and GNP per capita, 1980, and Growth Rates, 1965 to 1987

Country group	1980 GNP (billions of dollars)	1980 population (millions)	1980 GNP per capita (dollars)	Average annual growth of GNP per capita (percent)					
				1965–73	1973–80	1980–84	1985	1986[a]	1987[a]
Developing countries	2,096	3,130	670	3.9	3.1	0.7	3.3	3.1	1.8
Low-income countries	573	2,124	270	2.9	2.6	5.1	7.2	4.2	3.1
Middle-income countries	1,523	1,006	1,510	4.5	3.1	-1.4	1.1	2.3	1.1
Oil exporters	523	407	1,290	4.8	3.1	-2.4	1.3	-1.7	-1.3
Exporters of manufactures	949	1,889	500	4.7	3.9	3.4	6.4	5.8	3.5
Highly indebted countries	876	494	1,770	4.5	2.8	-3.7	1.7	1.9	-0.5
Sub-Saharan Africa	198	331	600	3.7	0.7	-4.9	2.9	-0.2	-4.6
High-income oil exporters	227	16	14,540	4.2	5.6	-7.7	-8.2	-10.1	5.7
Industrial countries	7,701	716	10,760	3.6	2.1	1.3	2.4	2.0	2.2

a. Preliminary.

Source: World Bank, *World Development Report* (New York: Oxford University Press, 1988), p. 187.

Table 5–4

Growth of Real Per Capita GDP, 1965–1995

(annual percentage change)

Country group	Actual			Projected, 1987–95	
	1965–73	*1973–80*	*1980–87*	*Base*	*High*
Industrial countries	3.6	2.1	1.9	1.8	2.6
Developing countries	3.9	3.2	1.8	2.2	3.6
Exporters of manufactures	4.8	4.0	4.6	3.4	4.9
Highly indebted countries	4.2	2.9	−1.3	1.0	2.5
Sub-Saharan Africa	3.8	0.5	−2.9	0.0	0.7

Source: World Bank, *World Development Report, 1988* (New York: Oxford University Press, 1988), p. 230.

Note: All growth rates for developing countries are based on a sample of ninety countries.

Macroeconomic Problems

Developing countries experience a number of basic macro-economic problems and challenges. Obviously the goal of attaining sustained and vigorous economic growth is a primary consideration. Without growth rates in the 5–7 percent range it is

Table 5–5

Growth of Real GDP, 1965–1987

(annual percentage change)

Country group	*1965–73*	*1973–80*	*1980–85*	*1986*	*1987*
Industrial countries	4.5	2.8	2.4	2.7	2.9
Developing countries	6.5	5.4	3.2	4.7	3.9
Low-income	5.5	4.6	7.4	6.4	5.3
Excluding China and India	3.4	3.4	3.0	4.8	4.5
China and India	6.1	4.9	8.6	6.8	5.4
Low-income Africa	3.6	2.0	0.7	3.7	3.0
Middle-income	7.0	5.7	1.6	3.9	3.2
Oil exporters	7.0	5.9	0.9	0.3	0.8
Exporters of manufactures	7.4	6.0	5.8	7.2	5.3
Highly indebted countries	6.9	5.4	0.1	3.5	1.7
High-income oil exporters	8.7	8.0	−2.5	−8.1	−2.9

Source: World Bank, *World Development Report, 1988* (New York: Oxford University Press, 1988), p. 23.

Note: Data for developing countries are based on a sample of ninety countries.

Table 5–6
Income Distribution

Country	Year	Lowest 20%	Second Quintile	Third Quintile	Fourth Quintile	Highest 20%	Highest 10%
Bangladesh	81-2	6.6	10.7	15.3	22.1	45.3	29.5
Kenya	76	2.6	6.3	11.5	19.2	60.4	45.8
Philippines	85	5.2	8.9	13.2	20.2	52.5	37.0
Cote d'Ivoire	85-6	2.4	6.2	10.9	19.1	61.4	43.7
El Salvador	76-7	5.5	10.0	14.8	22.4	47.3	29.5
Peru	72	1.9	5.1	11.0	21.0	61.0	42.9
Costa Rica	71	3.3	8.7	13.3	19.8	54.8	39.5
Brazil	72	2.0	5.0	9.4	17.0	66.6	50.6
Mexico	77	2.9	7.0	12.0	20.4	57.7	40.6
Portugal	73-4	5.2	10.0	14.4	21.3	49.1	33.4
Panama	73	2.0	5.2	11.0	20.0	61.8	44.2
Argentina	70	4.4	9.7	14.1	21.5	50.3	35.2
South Korea	76	5.7	11.2	15.4	22.4	45.3	27.5
Venezuela	70	3.0	7.3	12.9	22.8	54.0	35.7
Trinidad/Tob.	75-6	4.2	9.1	13.9	22.8	50.0	31.8
Hong Kong	80	5.4	10.8	15.2	21.6	47.0	31.3
Spain	80-1	6.9	12.5	17.3	23.2	40.0	24.0
Italy	77	6.2	11.3	15.9	22.7	43.9	28.1
Netherlands	81	8.3	14.1	18.2	23.2	36.2	21.5
Sweden	81	7.4	13.1	16.8	21.0	41.7	28.1

Source: World Bank, *World Development Report, 1988* (New York: Oxford University Press, 1988), table 26; John A. Peeler, *Deepening Democracy and Democratic Consolidation in Latin America,* September 1989.

impossible for a developing nation to absorb the numbers of new people entering the labor force each year and find employment for the great numbers of people who are already unemployed or underemployed. While the official unemployment statistics from many developing countries tend to understate the magnitude of the unemployment–underemployment problem, most experts would agree that in many countries over 30–40 percent of the population is either without gainful employment or working few hours on an irregular basis.

Even if a country manages to achieve vigorous economic growth and create employment in both the private and public sectors of the economy, it is difficult to do so without the destabilizing consequences of inflation. It is not uncommon to observe rates of inflation from 150 percent to 2,000 percent in many developing countries. While the character of hyperinflation in developing nations is complicated, it is nevertheless easy to appreciate the problems and difficulties that it generates. The purchasing power of the domestic currency is eroded and the standard of living declines. In addition, the uncertainty that inflation brings to an economy is enough to scare off potential investment and invite local capital to flee the country in search of more stable investment opportunities.

The challenge of stimulating economic growth and employment with price stability is further complicated by the steady increase in annual deficits and public debt—both internal and external. Prolonged stagnation, as was the case for most of the 1980s, puts enormous pressure on a government to engage in deficit spending in a desperate attempt to maintain public consumption and investment levels. However, tax revenues cannot keep up with the expenditure stream and deficits mount. As deficits become a larger and larger problem, there is pressure on the government to spend within its means, but this has decisive political and social consequences for a government. In some instances the social and political unrest from unpopular economic policies and programs can lead to social instability. As a government reins in its budget, it is not uncommon to see subsidies for the poor and middle class eliminated, expenditures for health and education decrease, and public capital expenditures

Table 5–7
Inflation in Selected Heavily Indebted Countries, 1971–1987

(CPI percent December-over-December)

Country	Average, 1971–80	1981	1982	1983	1984	1985	1986	1987
Argentina	121	131	210	434	688	385	82	175
Bolivia	20	25	297	328	2,176	8,170	66	11
Brazil	38	101	102	178	209	249	64	321
Chile	131	10	21	23	23	26	17	23

Sources: 1971–86, IMF, *International Financial Statistics*; 1987, World Bank data; World Bank, *World Development Report, 1988* (New York: Oxford University Press, 1988), p. 70.

drop. While these basic fiscal policy issues are self-evident, the monetary policy issues are also critical. As the government of a developing country wrestles with these macroeconomic problems, its policies with respect to interest rates, the money supply, and the domestic currency become crucial.

International Trade and Finance

Lastly, the developing country confronts a set of interrelated international economic problems. To implement any kind of economic development strategy, it needs to import goods, usually capital goods that are vital for agriculture and industry. As we have seen in earlier chapters, a country needs to sell exports to earn foreign exchange to purchase imports. What becomes crucial is the terms of trade—that is, the price of a country's exports relative to its imports. As can be seen in table 5–8, the terms of trade for developing nations was 1.6 percent from 1973 to 1980 and a negative 0.9 percent from 1980 to 1984. A declining terms of trade, as we have seen, means that the price of a country's exports is declining relative to the price of its imports. As shown in table 5–9, it is clear that developing nations from 1980 to 1986 experienced sizeable trade deficits as reflected in their overall current account balance. Related to that is the reality of external debt for developing nations (shown in table 5–10). By 1987 the debt–GNP ratio for developing nations was 37.6 percent and the debt-service ratio was 21 percent. But for the most highly indebted countries, the debt–GNP ratio was 55.9 percent and the debt-service ratio was 32.7 percent. Balance of payments problems of this nature and magnitude make it all but impossible for a developing nation to generate dynamic real economic growth except by severely restricting imports and redirecting internal production to the export market while continuing to borrow money (loans from private banks) to service past debt. This is a treadmill that many countries have been on for many years, especially Argentina, Brazil, and Mexico (see table 5–11).

For a country that is experiencing balance of payments problems, the solution appears to be one of exporting more and

Table 5–8
Change in Export Prices and Terms of Trade, 1965–1987
(average annual percentage change)

Country group	1965–73	1973–80	1980–84	1985	1986a	1987b
Export prices						
Developing countries	6.4	14.0	–3.2	–4.0	–6.4	12.2
Manufactures	7.2	8.1	–2.7	–1.1	12.0	10.9
Food	5.3	9.1	–2.3	–9.8	4.9	–4.3
Nonfood	4.5	10.3	–4.1	–13.8	0.1	23.8
Metals and minerals	2.5	4.7	–5.2	–5.5	–4.2	13.2
Fuels	8.0	27.1	–4.0	–3.5	–47.2	23.9
High-income oil exporters	7.6	26.9	–4.1	–2.6	–45.3	20.8
Industrial countries						
Total	4.8	10.4	–3.5	–0.6	13.9	8.4
Manufactures	4.6	10.8	–3.4	0.9	19.8	9.4
Terms of trade						
Developing countries	0.7	1.6	–0.9	–2.3	–7.3	0.6
Low-income countries	1.7	–2.5	0.0	–3.6	–2.0	0.5
Middle-income countries	0.6	2.2	–1.0	–2.1	–7.9	0.4
Oil exporters	0.0	10.0	–1.8	–3.1	–38.7	9.3
Exporters of manufactures	1.8	–2.7	0.3	–0.4	3.9	–2.4
Highly indebted countries	1.4	3.5	–0.7	–2.3	–14.3	–0.5
Sub-Saharan Africa	–8.4	4.8	–1.4	–5.9	–23.5	1.1
High-income oil exporters	0.3	13.4	–2.3	–2.2	–49.1	7.6
Industrial countries	–1.0	–3.0	0.1	1.7	9.5	–0.1

Source: World Bank, *World Development Report, 1988* (New York: Oxford University Press, 1988), p. 191.

a Estimated.
b Projected.

importing less. In recent years most developing countries have been forced to devalue their currency to make exports more attractive and imports more expensive. This policy is actually encouraged by multilateral institutions like the International Monetary Fund. Usually the IMF's recommendations are linked to economic stabilization policies required by the IMF as a quid pro quo for loans. Yet, austerity programs and new loans piled on top of old loans do not provide the resources necessary to stimulate dynamic economic growth. In fact, as is clear in Mexico's case, the net resource transfer (the difference between debt service and new

Table 5-9

Current Account Balance, 1973–1987

(billions of dollars)

Country group	Average, 1973–79	Average, 1980–82	1983	1984	1985	1986	1987
Industrial countries	-5.1	-34.9	-23.3	-60.8	-50.4	-19.7	-50.3
Developing countries	-27.5	-82.2	-44.7	-18.5	-23.5	-21.3	2.1
Low-income	-3.4	-9.7	-2.7	-4.2	-22.4	-16.6	-9.6
Excluding China and India	-3.6	-8.5	-4.9	-4.2	-5.7	-5.3	-5.9
China and India	0.1	-1.1	2.2	0.0	-16.8	-11.2	-3.6
Low-income Africa	-2.3	-5.8	-3.5	-2.9	-2.9	-3.2	-4.4
Middle-income	-24.1	-72.5	-42.1	-14.3	-1.1	-4.7	11.7
Oil exporters	-5.8	-15.6	-5.9	3.2	0.1	-18.5	-8.8
Exporters of manufactures	-10.2	-25.9	-5.8	5.2	-4.7	10.3	25.9
Highly indebted countries	-14.2	-43.4	-13.9	1.0	0.6	-11.4	-7.2
High-income oil exporters	22.7	53.6	-0.2	1.7	7.4	2.7	1.0

Source: World Bank, *World Development Report* (New York: Cambridge University Press, 1988), p. 31.

Notes: The total current account balance for industrial, developing, and high-income, oil-exporting countries is less than zero primarily because of counting and measurement discrepancies in the balance of payments reporting, especially on trade in services and on the income of foreign assets.

Table 5-10
Debt Indicators in Developing Countries, 1975–1987
(percent)

Country group and debt indicator	1975	1980	1981	1982	1983	1984	1985	1986	1987[a]
All developing countries									
Debt service ratio	13.7	16.2	17.9	21.0	19.7	19.5	21.8	22.6	21.0
Debt-GNP ratio	15.7	20.7	22.4	26.3	31.4	33.0	35.9	38.5	37.6
Highly indebted countries									
Debt service ratio	24.0	27.1	30.7	38.8	34.7	33.4	33.9	37.7	32.7
Debt-GNP ratio	18.1	23.3	25.6	32.4	45.4	47.5	49.5	54.1	55.9
Low-income Africa									
Debt service ratio	10.2	13.6	14.6	14.2	14.2	15.1	17.9	19.9	34.7
Debt-GNP ratio	25.2	39.8	44.2	48.0	55.1	62.0	68.9	72.1	76.2

Source: World Bank, *World Development Report* (New York: Cambridge University Press, 1988), p. 31.

Notes: Data are based on a sample of ninety developing countries. The debt service ratio is defined as the dollar value of external debt payments (interest and amortization) on medium- and long-term loans expressed as a percentage of the dollar value of exports of goods and services. The debt-GNP ratio is defined as the dollar value of outstanding medium- and long-term debt expressed as a percentage of dollar GNP.

[a] Estimated. Ratios do not assume further buildup of arrears. This accounts for the sharp increase in the debt service ratio for low-income Africa in 1987.

Table 5-11

Capital Importing Developing Countries: Indicators of Economic Performance, 1969–1992

(in percent per annum, unless otherwise indicated)

	Actual 1969–78[1]	1979–83	1984	1985	1986	1987	1988	1989	Actual 1990–92
Real GDP	5.7	3.2	4.9	4.2	4.5	3.8	4.2	4.3	4.8
Real GNP	5.3	2.2	4.7	4.2	4.8	3.7	4.1	4.4	5.0
Investment ratio[2]	24.0	25.5	22.5	22.8	23.2	22.3	22.6	23.0	23.7
Export volume	4.9	3.7	11.0	3.9	8.5	8.6	6.9	6.2	6.4
Terms of trade	1.2	0.3	2.3	-2.9	-11.4	1.9	0.3	-0.1	—
Import volume	5.9	1.7	5.3	2.2	-1.6	5.0	8.7	6.2	6.4
Private lending[3]	23.4[4]	14.6	2.8	2.2	1.0	0.5	-0.1	0.5	1.3
Official lending[3]	18.6[4]	17.8	11.5	9.2	11.0	8.9	6.8	5.9	4.9

(As percentage of exports of goods and services)

	1978	1983	1984	1985	1986	1987	1988	1989	1992
Current account balance	-14.3	-14.2	-4.2	-4.6	-4.4	0.5	-0.5	-0.6	-0.3
Total external debt	129.6	164.1	156.9	172.5	184.3	171.9	159.1	149.0	123.6
Debt service payments	18.7	22.0	22.8	23.7	24.3	20.9	20.9	18.7	15.4
Interest payments	6.8	13.3	13.6	13.8	12.7	10.0	10.9	9.7	7.9
Amortization	11.9	8.7	9.2	9.9	11.6	10.9	10.0	8.5	7.6

Source: World Bank. *World Development Report*, 1987 (New York: Oxford University Press), p. 29.

1 Excluding China.
2 As a percentage of gross domestic product.
3 In billions of dollars.
4 1970–78.

loans) has been negative since 1983 and has grown to a negative $9.6 billion in 1988 (see table 5–12 and figure 5–1). The difference between Mexico's debt service and its new loans must be made up with export earnings. What is true is that the greater the level of export earnings that must be used to service external debt, the less there is for other competing needs related to the overall economic development process and for paying for imported goods. In Mexico's case (we can see in table 5–13 and figure 5–2) in 1988 export earnings were $20 billion, while interest payments alone on the external debt were equal to 40 percent of export earnings. In the same year, total debt service (interest and principal) was $15 billion, or about 75 percent of export earnings. As figure 5–2 illustrates, from 1983 to 1989 Mexico paid a level of debt service that was as low as $11.3 billion and as high as $17.8 billion. Hypothetically, if Mexico had paid only a maximum of 30 percent of its export earnings to service debt, it would have paid from 1983 to 1989 only $44 billion, compared to the $100 billion actually paid. This would have produced an additional $56 billion for Mexico, or an average of $8 billion per year to be used for economic development. This is

Table 5–12
Mexico's External Debt, Debt-Service, and Net Transfer, 1970–1988

(in millions)	Foreign debt	New loans	Principal repaid	Interest repaid	Net transfer[a]
1970[b]	$5,966	$1,375	$1,017	$283	$75
1975[b]	15,609	5,255	1,509	1,104	2,642
1980	57,450	11,600	4,760	4,590	2,249
1981	78,297	17,016	4,508	6,133	6,375
1982	86,111	12,509	4,531	7,784	194
1983	93,057	7,196	4,837	8,181	–5,792
1984	94,908	7,276	5,657	10,262	–8,644
1985	96,875	5,025	5,122	9,393	–9,489
1986	101,054	5,461	4,562	7,737	–6,838
1987	107,882	8,550	4,333	7,091	–2,874
1988[c]	101,900	5,600	6,400	8,829	–9,629

Source: World Bank, *World Debt Tables* (Washington, D.C.: World Bank, 1989).

a Difference between new loans and payments on old loans.
b Excludes short-term debt.
c Estimate.

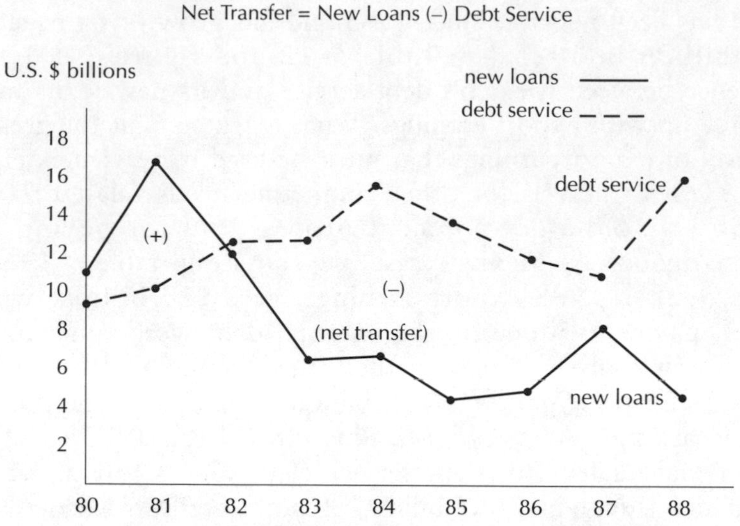
Net Transfer = New Loans (–) Debt Service
U.S. $ billions
new loans
debt service
18
16
14
12
10
8
6
4
2
(+)
(–)
(net transfer)
debt service
new loans
80
81
82
83
84
85
86
87
88

Source: Steve Stamos, "The Brady Plan and Mexico: A Critique and Alternative Debt-Relief Proposal," unpublished paper, 1989.

Figure 5–1. *The Negative Resource Transfer*

the kind of debt relief that many experts are recommending for the highly indebted nations to generate the economic resources they so desperately need to stimulate economic growth.

These then are the four basic economic problem areas that every developing nation must confront. Population growth that is typically more rapid than economic growth has resulted in a decline in real living standards. Unequal distribution of income promotes capital flight and diverts much-needed savings into luxury consumption. Macroeconomic problems tend to cause hyperinflation and huge domestic deficits. Finally, international economic imbalances, declining terms of trade, and ever-growing foreign debts force underdeveloped countries to attempt to maximize exports at the expense of much-needed imports. This has created a crisis in most of the underdeveloped world, which is only partially explained by the various competing schools of thought.

Table 5–13
Mexico's Debt-Service Burden and Resource Transfer, 1983–1989:
Actual versus Debt-Service Limited to 30% of Export Earnings
(Stamos Proposal)

Year	Exports[a]	i % Exp.[b]	i/$	+	a	=	DS[c]	DS/30% Exp.[d]	Net T[e]	vs.	Net T[f]
1983	22.3	37%	8.1		4.8		12.9	6.6	−5.8		+0.6
1984	24.1	40%	10.2		5.6		17.8	7.2	−8.6		0.00
1985	21.6	40%	9.3		5.1		14.4	6.6	−9.4		−1.6
1986	16.0	50%	7.7		4.5		12.2	4.8	−6.8		+0.6
1987	20.6	35%	7.0		4.3		11.3	6.3	−2.8		+2.2
1988	20.9	40%	8.8		6.4		15.2	6.3	−9.6		−0.7
1989	20.0	55%	11.0		5.0		16.0	6.0	na		na

[a] Export earnings (billions dollars U.S.).
[b] i % Exp. (interest payments as a percentage of export earnings).
[c] i + a = DS (interest plus principal equals debt service/billions $).
[d] DS/30% Exp. (Debt service limited to 30% of export earnings).
[e] Net T (Net Transfer = New loans minus debt-service payments/actual).
[f] Net T (Net Transfer = New loans minus debt service [30% exp]).
na = not available.

Competing Schools of Thought on Economic Development

The Traditional Model

The *traditional model* assumes that developing nations must adopt modern capital and technology to have strong economic growth. Underdevelopment is assumed to be a natural condition characterized by backward and archaic institutions and values. This condition of underdevelopment must give way to progress and modernization characterized by the following: (1) industrialization, (2) the mechanization of agriculture, (3) urbanization, (4) secular values, and (5) political stability.

The traditional model explains underdevelopment as a consequence of geography, culture, the lack of capital and technology, and the vicious cycles of unproductive labor and poverty. In this overall context of underdevelopment, this model asserts that a developing nation must create dynamic markets in land, labor, and capital. The emergence of dynamic and smooth-functioning markets along with the expansion of free trade is seen to be the road to progress. Yet it will take the inflow of foreign

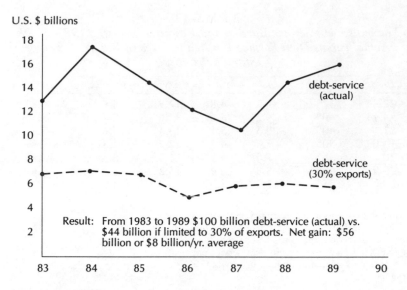

U.S. $ billions

Result: From 1983 to 1989 $100 billion debt-service (actual) vs. $44 billion if limited to 30% of exports. Net gain: $56 billion or $8 billion/yr. average

Source: Steve Stamos, "The Brady Plan and Mexico: A Critique and Alternative Debt-Relief Proposal," unpublished paper, September 1989.

Figure 5–2. *Actual Debt-Service vs. Debt-Service Limited to 30 Percent of Export Earnings*

capital and the transfer of modern technology to be the catalysts and provide the stimulus for sustained growth.

Early proponents of this model used a simple version of the *Harrod-Domar growth model* to explain the problem. The Harrod-Domar growth model suggested that the rate of growth of a nation (G) was equal to the savings rate(s) divided by the capital-output ratio (k), or

$$G = s/k$$

where, for example, country X's savings rate of 12 percent with a capital-output ratio of 3 percent would yield a growth rate (G) of 4 percent. Such a model demonstrates the importance of a high level of domestic savings for a developing nation with a given capital-output ratio. A more elaborate derivation of the Harrod-

Domar growth model would also demonstrate the relationship between savings and investment and the importance of the level of domestic investment as well. For proponents of the traditional model, this growth model demonstrated the need for high levels of domestic savings and investment and given the absence of each in developing nations, it was clear that only capital from outside the country could be the stimulus. Hence, foreign capital in the form of direct private foreign investment becomes the most important factor in the development process. This, of course, puts the multinational firm in a critical role in terms of its ability to provide the capital and the transfer of modern technology.

The Growth with Equity Structuralist Model

In contrast to the traditional model, the growth with equity structuralist model argued that the traditional model's basic analysis of the reasons for the state of underdevelopment, as well as its proposed solutions, were fundamentally flawed.

While it was obviously true that developing nations lacked capital, modern technology, and dynamic markets in land, labor, and capital, critics argued this was not because of any natural condition. Underdevelopment, they said, can only be understood in historical context. It was important, for example, in the case of Latin America, to recognize the profound influence the period of colonization (fifteenth to the nineteenth century) had on shaping the economies of Latin America and the manner in which it was progressively integrated into the modern world economic system. Such a view of history can partially explain the character of land holding, the ownership of primary raw materials, the distribution of wealth, the concentration of political power, and the composition of trade.

Proponents of the growth with equity structuralist model argued in the 1960s and 1970s that internally the root problems of underdevelopment were the land tenure systems that allowed only a small minority to own the majority of the most fertile land. It would, they argued, be necessary to have a major redistribution of land for genuine economic development to be achieved. They also argued that infusions of foreign capital had not really yielded the results that were expected. There was modernization but of a dualistic and uneven character that juxtaposed poverty alongside affluence in sprawling urban areas, while the rural agricultural sector was being modernized with high fossil-fuel–dependent technology to produce goods for export rather than domestic consumption. The traditional model, they argued, created an internal elite that was becoming wealthy and politically powerful. Lastly, they argued that even in the rare cases in which dynamic economic growth was produced, it had not improved the standard of living of the bottom 40 percent of the population.

Supporters of the growth with equity structuralist model argued for land reform, a more diversified economy less reliant on primary commodity exports, government policies that would emphasize agriculture for domestic consumption, import substitution industrialization, and thoughtful use of foreign capital and technology. They also expressed skepticism about the relevance of modern Keynesian economics as practiced in the advanced nations to the unique and specific needs of a developing country economy. In this vein, they were critical of the pressure often brought upon Third World nations from multilateral institutions and even from developed country governments in terms of aid and loan conditions. Also, supporters of this school of thought found the structure of the international financial system to be fundamentally stacked against developing nations. The record of the terms of trade, balance of payments deficits, currency instability, and external debt was proof enough that the way in which the global system functioned was working against the developing nations. Any long-term solution to the problem of underdevelopment must address this structural analysis.

The Dependency Model

By dependence we mean a situation in which the economy of certain countries is conditioned by the development and expansion of another economy to which the former is subjected. The relation of interdependence between two or more economies, and between these and world trade, assumes the form of dependence when some countries (the dominant ones) can expand and can be self-sustaining, while other countries (the dependent ones) can do this only as a reflection of that expansion, which can have either positive or negative effect on their immediate development.[8]

In the 1960s a new way of looking at the problem of under-development based in Marxian analysis challenged both the traditional and structural theories. It assumed that it is necessary to view underdevelopment as a consequence of the historical evolution of capitalism and the integration of developing countries into the expanding sphere of capitalist production globally. This model is based upon a generalized application of a Marxist methodology drawn from philosophy, history, sociology, political science, and economics. The character and structure of a developing country's economic and political system, as well as its class and social stratification system, are explained by its historical experience with colonialism and the subsequent expansion of capitalism.

Supporters of this school of thought argue that most developing nations have passed through stages of integration into the world economy. Each stage can be characterized and distinguished by its economic approach to development. For example, the early stage was characterized by the trading of goods based upon the simple logic of comparative advantage. This kind of specialization and division of labor, according to the dependency models, did not benefit the colonial countries. It resulted in an unequal exchange between advanced and developing nations because of the declining terms of trade. The second stage of "import substitution" was characterized by a strategy of reducing capital goods imports from advanced nations while attempting to build up a domestic manufacturing sector that could eventually compete in international markets as well as produce goods for internal consumption that were previously imported. This required government subsidization of these new industries and protection from foreign competition until they could be mature enough to compete freely. The dependency model argued that this model also failed and further reinforced the dominance of developing countries' economies by the advanced nations. This failure was in part explained by the third stage, which highlighted the emergence and impact of the modern multinational corporation.

Multinationals were criticized for not performing the positive role that the traditional model theorized. The MNC was supposed to fill in the savings gap, the investment gap, the foreign exchange gap, the tax gap, and the technological gap. In practice, the dependency model argued, the MNCs actually lowered domestic savings and local investment. In the long run, they decreased the availability of foreign exchange and paid very little in domestic taxes to enhance government revenues. And, overall, they neither contributed positively nor in large scale to the transfer of technology and management skills.

In addition, the character of the development and economic growth they did generate produced an uneven development that exacerbated the inequalities in income and wealth that already existed. They did not use local raw materials and resources to the extent that they could have, or if they did it was to produce goods that contributed very little to the basic needs of the host country. Many of the products themselves created consumption patterns and adverse impacts from the technology used that resulted in net negative economic, political, and environmental consequences.

The Marxian critique also focused on the impact of MNCs on the market structure of developing nations. Because of economies of scale, barriers to entry (technology, financial resources, advertising, and restrictive business practices) MNCs are able to restrict competition from local firms, charge higher prices, and earn larger profits. Their control of technology and the character of research and development in the context of the product cycle further reinforced MNC control over local markets. Critics also point to the small level of employment actually generated by foreign direct private investment and the lack of backward and forward linkages characteristic of most MNC production. Such firms, they argued, do not create additional economic growth for domestic firms but replace them.

Dependency critics point to the practice of transfer pricing as an example of a behavior designed to benefit the MNC at the expense of the developing nation. Transfer pricing is the practice of overpricing imports and underpricing exports. Since MNCs often buy from their own subsidiaries, they can overprice their own imports and underprice their own exports as a way to accomplish the following: 1) increase the amount of profits that they repatriate to themselves out of the country; 2) pay themselves larger fees and royalties for services; 3) pay lower local taxes, which are based on lower reported profits; 4) escape the constraints of local protectionist measures; and 5) escape the constraints of foreign exchange controls.

In that context, it is easier to understand why few developing countries have been able to generate balanced, sustained economic growth that is equitable and improves the standard of living for the majority.

The dependency model essentially argues that the central issue is the transfer of the economic surplus from the developing nation to the advanced nation. This transfer of the economic surplus is carried out not only by the systemic behavior of the multinational corporation or financial institution but also by institutional practices of the host government and multilateral institutions (IMF, World Bank, and others). What is at the core of this transfer of the surplus is the extraction and control of raw materials, the access to and exploitation of cheap labor, and access to internal markets. The economic surplus is appropriated by foreign capital and its agents and then transferred to the advanced country. The result is that developing nations do not have the economic surplus—the resources necessary—to generate sustained economic growth and development because their resources are being systematically appropriated and transferred to the advanced nations. This process, sometimes called imperialism, reflected a stage of capitalist development as the system was beginning to expand globally.

The worldwide dominance of the MNCs has made an easy target for the dependency critics because much of what they say seems logical if not self-evident. Yet, assuming that the critique is valid, the question then becomes: What should be done? To answer this question it is tempting to consider socialist solutions: more economic planning, regulating the market system, excluding or regulating multinationals, restricting direct private investment, and a host of other considerations.

Yet, in this context, there is a need to be pragmatic. It is clear from the experiences of many socialist countries and countries undergoing socialist transition that becoming self-reliant and reducing the negative features of being integrated into the global capitalist system is not easy, nor is it clear that it is entirely desirable. With respect to multinational direct private foreign investment, the experience of the 1970s and 1980s seems to suggest that it is a fundamental part of the reality of the global system and that it is an institution that must be reckoned with for better and worse. The challenge is to find a way of taking advantage of the benefits, however limited they may be, while minimizing to the extent possible the negative consequences.

The Future

Economic conditions for developing countries in the 1980s and early 1990s have been extremely poor. The 1980s were correctly labeled "The Lost Decade." The tremendous level of developing countries' external debt and annual debt service has created a generalized condition of capital scarcity. Government public investment has slowed, as has direct private investment. So, oddly, the situation is one in which multinational investment capital is badly needed even though the costs and consequences are very well understood by most host country governments.

The 1980s saw the coming into vogue of economic policies and strategies that emphasized privatization, free trade, and the opening of many countries to increased direct private investment. To stimulate economic growth and earn the vital foreign exchange necessary to import goods and service their external debt, many developing nations consciously adopted an export-led development strategy while attempting adjustment and stabilization policies internally that have required prolonged austerity and a dramatic decrease in their standard of living. This export-led strategy was implemented in the context of a conscious attempt to redefine and reduce the role of the government sector in the economy and expand the role of the private sector. The experience with this strategy in the 1980s was quite mixed and it is as yet unclear to what extent it can be continued in the 1990s. This will depend to a large extent upon whether the U.S. economy continues to expand as it did in the 1980s and whether a fundamental long-term solution of the external debt problem is implemented. Neither seems likely.

Key Concepts

Multinational Corporation (MNC)
Intrafirm Trade
Product Cycle Theory
Export Platform
Vertical Integration Theory
Outsourcing
Transfer Pricing
Net Resource Transfer
Debt Service
Traditional Model
Growth with Equity Structuralist Model
Dependency Model
Harrod-Domar Growth Model
Export-Led Growth
Import Substitution
Foreign Investment

Discussion Questions

1. What is a multinational corporation?

2. What are the three phases of product cycle theory?

3. What is vertical integration for a MNC?

4. What are the four basic economic problem areas that all developing nations confront?

5. What is the relationship between population growth and economic growth for a developing nation?

6. What are the negative consequences of a highly unequal distribution of income for a developing nation?

7. What is the basic set of macroeconomic problems that developing nations face?

8. What is the basic balance of payments problem for most developing nations? How does an import-substitution strategy affect the developing nation's balance of payments?

9. What is meant by the expression *net resource transfer*?

10. Why is a declining terms of trade undesirable?

11. According to the traditional model, direct private foreign investment should play a positive role in the economic growth of a developing nation. Why?

12. What does the Harrod-Domar growth model demonstrate?

13. What are the criticisms of the traditional model made by the growth with equity structuralist model? Do these criticisms seem valid to you? (Explain.)

14. What are the criticisms of the behavior of multinational corporations made by the dependency model?

15. What is meant by the expression *export-led growth*?

16. What kind of a role do you think MNCs can play in developing countries?

Part III

Policy and Practice

6
The International Financial System in Historical Perspective

A delicate but decisive transition is under way. It is a transition from stop–go policies and inflationary expansion to a program of monetary and fiscal stability aimed at sustained growth. A good start has been made. But persistence and international cooperation are now required to insure that the needed growth occurs, while further progress is made in removing imbalances. . . .

For their part, the developing countries can best improve their growth performance and their access to credit markets by their choice of macroeconomic and structural policies.

Significant progress has been made over the past few years. Economic policies are now better attuned to economic realities, and inflation—which had been poisoning the financial system for fifteen years—has finally been brought under control in the industrial world.

But much remains to be done. External payments imbalances among the larger industrial countries are a disturbing source of instability and tensions. The erosion of commodity prices has adversely affected the developing countries at the very time when they more than ever need increased export earnings to grow and to service their debts.

In a world that is increasingly interdependent, it is proving more complex than ever to cope with these problems. A satisfactory solution requires not only an understanding of the interaction among national economic policies but also firm adherence to the fundamental principles of monetary stability and strengthened commitment to international cooperation.

Economic policy coordination among industrial countries is no longer a matter of theoretical preference. It is instead a prerequisite for growth with instability. Industrial countries must work together to complete the process of disinflation, to maximize the sources of economic growth, and to assure an open international trading system.[1]

International finance is a complex web of exchange rates, international agreements (and disagreements), balance of payments, letters of credit, hedging, arbitrage, current accounts, capital accounts, and most important for our purposes here, credit arrangements between nations. It's a system highly dependent on political nuances, power politics, and economic policies.

But, in many ways it is merely a system of "gentlemen's agreements" to which all nations abide so that international trade, with all its presumed benefits, can take place. When it functions smoothly—and equitably—everyone benefits. When it doesn't, everyone loses. But over the past few decades the web of international finance has become so tangled that the losers far outnumber the winners. The system is slowly collapsing under its own weight. To understand why, one must—as always—understand the history of the problem. Nothing makes any sense unless it is put in historical context.

The Enigmatic Role of Gold

As we have seen, it is commonly thought that gold has, historically, played a major role in international trade transactions. Gold is scarce, virtually indestructible, and because of that has been used as a standard of monetary exchange since classical antiquity. Wars have been fought over it, nations conquered and exploited for it. Indeed, for centuries, many nations based their international economic policies on the now-curious assumption that the accumulation of gold brought with it wealth and well-being. It was this belief, which dominated economic thinking from 1500 to 1750—which we now refer to as mercantilism—that first inspired Adam Smith to write *The Wealth of Nations*, which laid the groundwork for our modern theories of international trade and caused many of the problems the world now faces.

Paradoxically, the times during which the world was on the international gold standard are still referred to as the "good old days of the gold standard." They were not, in fact, such good times and and they didn't last very long.

The gold standard, which is but one of several ways to arrange international economic affairs, only existed in its pure variation for about forty years, roughly from 1875 to 1914. Gold functions well as a standard of monetary value and exchange only as long as every nation agrees to value its currency equal to a given weight of gold, and as long as gold is freely tradable internationally. International disruptions, most notably, wars, tend to bring out everyone's regard for their own interests and under such conditions international agreements tend to fall by the wayside. This was the fate of the gold standard during World War I, when it was abandoned, much to the chagrin of those disposed to nostalgia.

Beyond the difficulties of ignoring self-interest under duress, gold exchange standard agreements are a very cumbersome and inconvenient way to handle international financial transactions. This is partly because it is expensive, if not ridiculous, to ship gold between countries to settle balance of payments disequilibria, but more importantly because the gold standard extracts a high degree of economic discipline domestically as well as internationally. This is inconvenient for the stronger players in the game of international trade and can be disastrous for the minor leaguers.

A gold standard requires that nations maintain a favorable (or equilibrium) balance of trade and payments or come up with the difference in gold. That means, of course, that countries with trade deficits lose their gold supply to those with trade surpluses, and/or that they institute appropriate economic policies to correct the (perceived) undesirable situation. That is, they must put in place deflationary domestic policies (increase unemployment and slow down economic growth) to decrease the price of their exports, which will allow them to become more competitive internationally. At the same time often-needed imports are reduced because of the lower overall domestic demand.

Such discipline can be politically inconvenient in certain situations and, accordingly, the gold standard was abandoned by most of the major economic powers during the early years of the Great Depression. While there were numerous attempts to revive it during the 1930s, gold didn't resurface as a monetary standard until after World War II, then linked in a tenuous fashion to the U.S. dollar, which replaced gold as the international medium of exchange. This development, as we shall see, was to have far-reaching consequences.

Bretton Woods Conference

The United States emerged from World War II not only as a military victor but as an economic victor as well. It was by far the strongest economic power in the world and, by 1945, had accumulated some $25 billion in gold reserves, almost 75 percent of the world's gold supply.

This is of course meant that the United States was in a very powerful position to reorganize the international financial system to serve its own best interests. Gold, almost everyone agreed, was clearly not up to the task of providing the necessary liquidity to finance world trade. The price of gold had been set at thirty-five dollars an ounce by President Roosevelt in 1933, but the general price level had almost doubled since then, so gold was a very underpriced commodity, scarce even for commercial uses. Therefore everyone realized a new system was needed.

With the war winding down and victory apparent, the monetary authorities of the leading allied nations gathered at Bretton Woods, New Hampshire, in 1944 to work out a new international monetary arrangement. The delegation from Great Britain, headed by economist John Maynard Keynes, argued that an international central bank should be established that would monitor trade imbalances and have the power to force deficit countries to adjust their economic policies any time deficits drifted out of line. But turning the power of control over domestic economic policy to an international institution was more than most countries could accept and the United States, in essence, vetoed any such plan.

Out of that meeting came one of the more dramatic historical examples of what is sometimes referred to as the Golden Rule: "Whoever has the gold makes the rules." The gold standard was replaced with the *dollar standard* and the United States was accordingly exempted from the traditional discipline of international finance.

The United States, since it had most of the world's gold supply anyway, agreed to make the dollar "as good as gold," redeemable on demand by any central bank at the rate of thirty-five dollars an ounce. This meant the dollar became the accepted medium of exchange for international transactions. This seemingly routine event was to have far-reaching implications for the international financial system, certainly far beyond what anyone would have imagined at the time.

Since the dollar was now as good as gold, the rest of the world could, and did, use dollars instead of gold to settle international payments, for international transactions in general, *and* for their own reserves. The system was generally acceptable to most of the Bretton Woods participants (with the notable exception of France). Dollars were more liquid than gold and didn't have to be stored or shipped and, most importantly, dollar deposits can earn interest while gold simply gathers dust in a bank vault.

The new system did not, however, exempt anyone (except the United States, which could create money and spend it at will) from the discipline of international finance. Now dollars, instead of gold, provided that discipline. All countries' currencies were now tied to the dollar instead of gold. The dollar, in turn, was pegged to gold at the rate of thirty-five dollars an ounce. Trade imbalances now had to be settled in U.S. dollars. The Bretton Woods Conference had made the dollar the world's key currency, and in so doing the stage was set for an unprecedented series of developments.

The Bretton Woods Conference also established a quasi-international bank: the International Monetary Fund. The IMF was created to monitor and discipline trade and to provide temporary loans to countries with balance of payments problems. Such loans were conditioned on deficit countries' "getting their houses in order" promptly—slowing down their inflation rate, stimulating their export sector, and/or reducing imports, if they were running trade deficits. Funds for the IMF operation were provided by contributions from member nations, who in turn had a voice (a vote) in its operations proportional to their contribution. The United States, which made the largest contribution, had the controlling vote. Thus, it was no coincidence that the headquarters of the IMF was situated in Washington, D.C.

Evolution of the Dollar Glut

The new system worked well for a number of years. As long as the United States held a large percentage of the world's gold supply other countries were willing to accept dollars in payment for international transactions. Under such conditions the United States could run trade deficits at will and simply pay for the difference with dollars. But in the early years of the agreement this didn't happen because the United States was consistently running trade surpluses, which, in fact, caused a dollar shortage, something hard to imagine now (see figure 6–1). Since then the world moved from a dollar shortage to a dollar glut. How and why this happened is crucial to understanding the current international situation.

First, we must remember that, by definition, balance of payments accounts must always be in balance. Or to put it another way, total dollar expenditures abroad by the United States must equal total dollar receipts for the rest of the world. This means that if the United States is running an export surplus —exporting more than it is importing—then it must also provide the means to finance it, either through loans, gifts, or foreign investments. There is no other way for a country to get the dollars needed to purchase U.S. goods.

In the years just following World War II the United States was running huge export surpluses and was at the same time providing the wherewithal to pay for them.

$ billions

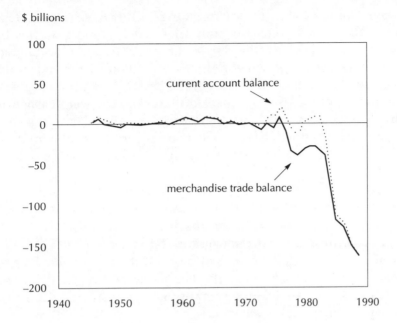

Source: U.S. Department of Commerce, *Survey of Current Business,* Vol. 68, No. 6, June 1988.

Figure 6–1. *U.S. Current Account and Trade Balance, 1946–1988*

The United States ran a huge *balance of trade* surplus—almost $32 billion—during the 1946–1949 postwar period as it furnished much-needed capital goods to the war-damaged countries of Europe. But, since by definition balance of payments accounts *must always balance,* something else had to happen in the other accounts to offset this large credit item. In this case, the credits in the current account were largely balanced by debits in the capital account in the form of loans and grants made to the European countries under the Marshall Plan. If these loans had not been made it would have been impossible for the United States to run such large trade surpluses. During this early period this caused no special problem with the international monetary system since the United States was easily able to make these loans. In fact, if anything, it had a positive effect on the U.S. economy and the rest of the world.

But soon all that began to change. During the 1950–1957 period the United States not only financed its export surplus but *overfinanced* it, so that the rest of the world began to accumulate dollar balances to the tune of almost $9 billion by the end of that seven-year period. At the same time, the United States began to lose some gold as part of these dollar balances were cashed in. This was a clear indicator of trouble ahead but was not considered by most economists to be a serious problem at the time. However, the situation began to change rapidly around 1958.

During the 1958–1965 period the United States still maintained a balance of trade surplus and continued granting loans and foreign aid and increasing its investments abroad. But the total value of these loans and grants far exceeded the U.S. trade surplus and large dollar balances began to be accumulated by the rest of the world. This was the beginning of the "dollar glut," which is still with us and remains a significant factor in the current international financial crisis.

Eurodollar Market

By the early 1960s another significant event occurred that was to have far-reaching implications: the development of the *Eurodollar* market. Eurodollars are dollars deposited in any bank (not necessarily in Europe) outside the United States and kept there as dollar-denominated deposits. European banks, many of which are heavily involved in foreign trade transactions, found it convenient to begin accepting dollar deposits and using them in their day-to-day business. This avoided bothersome exchange transactions and earned them interest as well. And, since the dollar was backed by gold, this development seemed not only logical but safe to everyone concerned.

There was one catch, however, which later turned out to be Catch-22. U.S. banks are required to maintain a percentage of their deposits as reserves. This requirement limits the extent to which they can expand their asset base by loaning out deposits, since they must keep a portion of them as reserves. By controlling this reserve requirement the U.S. Federal Reserve Bank (the U.S. central bank) can maintain some control over the U.S. money supply. An increase in the reserve requirement, for example, causes a contraction of the money supply and is a powerful, but not often used, monetary policy tool. But foreign banks, in general, have no such requirement. As a result, Eurodollar deposits could be expanding infinitely through a process called the multiple expansion of deposits—since there are no reserve requirements there are no limits to banks' ability to create money.

In addition, European banks are allowed to pay interest on very short-term deposits, while U.S. banking laws require that a deposit must be held for at least thirty days before any interest can be paid. Therefore, since the 1960s was a period of rapid expansion of U.S. multinational corporate activities all around the world, many MNCs, which routinely move large sums of surplus funds between countries to finance their off-shore production activities, found Eurodollar deposits to be a very attractive option compared to holding their surpluses in U.S. banks. Accordingly, large sums moved into the Eurodollar market.

All this had the effect of creating an entirely new money supply, based on and denominated in dollars, that did not exist before. This had two effects. One was that the U.S. bank authorities lost control of a very large portion of the U.S. money supply, which severely reduced their ability to control inflation with monetary policy, one of the primary macroeconomic policy tools. The other was that it further solidified the role of the U.S. dollar as the cornerstone of the international monetary system. These days Eurodollar deposits amount to more than $2 *trillion* (nobody knows for sure), roughly equal to the basic U.S. money supply itself. So one-half of the U.S. dollars in existence are outside any kind of control whatsoever by the U.S. banking authorities, which, among other things, makes it easier to understand why the entire world maintains a lively interest in the health of the U.S. economy and, especially the U.S. rate of inflation.

Demise of Gold

The other relevant (and unexpected) development that occurred in the 1960s was that the United States continued to run balance of trade deficits and its gold supply began to dwindle. Although, in theory, anyone should have been willing to accept dollars in payment for international trade transactions (given that the dollar was supposed to be "as good as gold," convertible on demand), some countries, notably France, were beginning to doubt the long-term viability of a system that substituted pieces of green paper for gold.

U.S. gold reserves fell from a high of $25 billion in 1950 to $10 billion in 1970. During the same period foreign dollar claims against the U.S. gold supply increased from about $5 billion to $70 billion. Clearly, by then, it no longer made any sense at all to say that the dollar was convertible to gold on demand since the potential dollar claims against the U.S. gold supply were seven times larger than could be honored.

Faced with a building crisis of confidence, President Nixon cut the link between the dollar and gold (on August 15, 1971). The United States would no longer honor its pledge to redeem dollars for gold. This meant that the rest of the world was left holding $70 billion that were worth only what the U.S. government said they were worth. Surprisingly, most foreign governments accepted this as an inevitable reality and continued to use dollars as reserves and as the international medium of exchange. There was no alternative. This, then, was the final step in establishing that the international financial system was a dollar system. Gold eventually became just another commodity that could be bought and sold on the commodity markets at whatever price it would bring.

By the end of 1971, the United States was experiencing a major balance of payments problem. The U.S. current account deficit had grown to a deficit of $1.4 billion and the trade deficit had reached an unprecedented $2.2 billion. The Nixon administration responded to this situation on December 18, 1971, by initiating the historic Smithsonian agreement.

This agreement formalized the results of President Nixon's New Economic Policy (NEP). The NEP, in addition to halting the convertibility of the dollar into gold, provided for a 10 percent tax on the value of all imports and the floating of the dollar. In effect, the United States would neither buy nor sell currency on the foreign exchange markets. Exchange rates would be left to determine their own level or be influenced by the intervention of other governments. Floating the dollar and cutting its link to gold violated the established operational guidelines of the IMF. So, in essence, the Smithsonian agreement represented the collapse of the Bretton Woods system.

Petrodollar Recycling

By 1973 the dollar was firmly entrenched as the world's key international currency and the stage was set for the beginning of the most serious crisis ever faced by the international monetary system. Interestingly, what happened was as much a political problem as it was an economic one.

Outraged by the U.S. support of Israel during the Yom Kippur War, the Organization of Petroleum Exporting Countries (OPEC), which had gained a dominant position in the world oil market by the early 1970s, placed an embargo on oil sales to the United States. Later, when that was relaxed, OPEC dramatically raised the price of oil (from $1.30 a barrel in 1970 to $10.72 by 1975). Since most oil transactions are carried out in dollars and because, at the time, the United States was dependent on OPEC for almost 50 percent of its oil imports, this sent an inflationary shock through the U.S. economy and the rest of the world.

Having no short-run alternative, the United States and the rest of the world paid the price. One result of the OPEC price increase was one of the most massive transfers of wealth in history. Hundreds of billions of dollars were transferred from oil-consuming nations to the Middle Eastern oil-producing countries. The OPEC nations were then faced with the ironic and paradoxical problem of what to do with this windfall. Clearly their own economies couldn't absorb such an injection of funds without risking runaway inflation. They had no alternative but to look for other places to invest them.

In spite of the problems caused by the oil shock the U.S. economy was still the strongest in the world. So, the only logical thing for the dollar-rich OPEC nations to do was to cycle the oil revenues back into U.S. and European banks. By 1976 the OPEC countries had placed nearly $100 billion in deposits in U.S. and European banks. Now it was the banks that were faced with a paradoxical dilemma. They had billions of new dollar deposits and, with a recession (caused in part by the higher oil prices) going on in the United States, nowhere to put them to work. Since banks must pay interest on deposits it follows that they can only survive if they are able to loan out those deposits at higher rates than they have to pay depositors. Within the ramifications of this elementary fact we find the roots of the present economic crisis.

Most Third World countries were desperate for outside development capital, especially since most of them are also dependent on oil imports and were, along with the industrialized nations, forced to pay the higher oil prices. Therefore, they were prime candidates for loans from U.S. and European commercial banks. So, in what seemed to many to be a logical process at the time (capital moving to where it is needed) the underdeveloped countries were only too willing to absorb the banks' excess funds. Everybody was happy. Bankers lined up at the doors of finance ministers' offices with loan money in hand. And the cycle was complete. Almost.

The process, shown in Figure 6-2, now called "petrodollar recycling" involved the Middle Eastern countries' shipping the oil to the United States and Europe, which, in turn, had sent along the dollars to pay for it to the Middle East. The OPEC countries then deposited those same dollars back in U.S. and European banks, who in turn, loaned them to the capital-poor Third World countries. Unfortunately, as everyone now knows (in hindsight), this is where the cycle stopped, and where the seeds of the present debt crisis were planted.

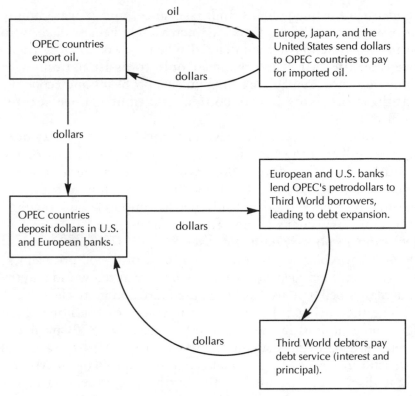

Figure 6–2. *OPEC Petrodollar Recycling*

Oil Shock of 1973–1974

The system of floating exchange rates was severely challenged by the shock of the 1973–1974 OPEC oil embargo. The dramatic rise in oil prices severely disrupted the international monetary system; nevertheless, the recycling of petrodollars took place without the catastrophic disruption and disequilibrium that many experts had predicted.

By the middle of the 1970s chronic balance of payments problems plagued most developing nations, particularly those that needed to import oil. These balance of payments deficits placed greater and greater pressure upon the International Monetary

Fund for adjustment loans and assistance, and it was rapidly
becoming clear that the IMF was increasingly being called on to
perform a function never intended when it was created. At its
inception the IMF was organized only to assist nations with
temporary short-run balance of payments problems and economic
stabilization. Now it was confronting much more serious
problems.

By the middle 1970s, these chronic balance of payment
deficits reflected the long-festering structural problems of the
Third World. Most developing nations were facing a constant
deterioration of their terms of trade and an outflow of capital to
pay for their oil and other badly needed imports. This required
even more new loans to pay for oil imports and to adjust to
declining export revenues caused by the U.S. recession of
1974–1975, which was another by-product of the oil price shock.
So the general interdependence of the industrialized world and the
underdeveloped nations was becoming more and more clear.

The increasing collective consciousness of the nonaligned
developing nations in the late 1960s and early 1970s produced
extensive debate and dialogue centered on the need for a global
restructuring of the international economic and financial systems.
These discussions resulted in the Sixth Special Session of the
United Nations in April of 1974. At this session of the U.N.
General Assembly two resolutions were drafted and adopted. The
first called for the establishment of a New International Economic
Order (NIEO). The second resolution outlined a Programme of
Action to bring about the creation of the New International
Economic Order.

With these actions, the Group of Seventy-seven (the
developing nations) evidenced a new global posture vis-à-vis the
developing world. They substituted "defiance for the deference of
the past."

On December 12, 1974, at the regularly scheduled Twenty-
ninth Session of the U.N. General Assembly, the call for an NIEO
was reaffirmed in the adoption of the "Charter of Economic
Rights and Duties of States." Later, in 1975, the United Nations
called for the "full and complete economic emancipation" of the
developing world.

The "Declaration of the U.N. General Assembly on the Establishment of a New International Economic Order" stated in part:

We, the Members of the United Nations,

Having convened a special session of the General Assembly to study for the first time the problems of raw materials and development. . . .

Solemnly proclaim our united determination to work urgently for THE ESTABLISHMENT OF A NEW INTERNATIONAL ECONOMIC ORDER based on equity, sovereign equality, interdependence, common interest and cooperation among all States, irrespective of their economic and social systems, which shall correct inequalities and redress existing injustices, make it possible to eliminate the widening gap between the developed and the developing countries, and ensure steadily accelerating economic and social development and peace and justice for present and future generations, and, to that end, declare:

1. The greatest and most significant achievement during the last decades has been the independence from colonial and alien domination of a large number of peoples and nations, which has enabled them to become members of the community of free peoples. Technological progress has also been made in all spheres of economic activities in the last three decades, thus providing a solid potential for improving the well-being of all peoples. However, the remaining vestiges of alien and colonial domination, foreign occupation, racial discrimination, apartheid, and neocolonialism in all its forms continue to be among the greatest obstacles to the full emancipation and progress of the developing countries and all the peoples involved. The benefits of technological progress are not shared equitably by all members of the international community. The developing countries, which constitute 70 percent of the world's population, account for only 30 percent of the world's income. It has proved impossible to achieve an even and balanced development of the international community under the existing international economic order. The gap between the developed and the developing countries continues to widen in a system which was established at a time when most of the developing countries did not even exist as independent States and which perpetuates inequality.

2. The present international economic order is in direct conflict with current developments in international political and economic relations. Since 1970, the world economy has experienced a series of grave crises which have had severe repercussions, especially on the developing countries because of their generally greater vulnerability to external economic impulses. The developing world has become a powerful factor that makes its influence felt in all fields of international activity. These irreversible changes in the relationship of forces in the world necessitate the active, full, and equal participation of the developing countries in the formulation and application of all decisions that concern the international community.

3. All these changes have thrust into prominence the reality of interdependence of all the members of the world community. Current events have brought into sharp focus the realization that the interests of the developed countries and those of the developing countries can no longer be isolated from each other, that there is a close interrelationship between the prosperity of the developing countries and the growth and development of the developing countries, and that the prosperity of the international community as a whole depends upon the prosperity of its constituent parts. International cooperation for development is the shared goal and common duty of all countries. Thus the political, economic, and social well-being of present and future generations depends more than ever on cooperation between all the members of the international community on the basis of sovereign equality and the removal of the disequilibrium that exists between them.

These words, now long forgotten, were much more prophetic than anyone realized at the time.

International Monetary Fund

To qualify for a trade adjustment loan from the International Monetary Fund, a country is usually required to agree to a set of economic policies judged by the IMF to be appropriate for stabilizing the economy and eliminating what it determines to be the causes of the country's balance of payments problems. Quite often, the IMF's economic stabilization package requires the country to adopt an austerity program that includes measures to reduce imports and increase exports, currency devaluation, reduction in government spending, tax increases to reduce the rate of inflation, and policies designed to attract more foreign investment.

These economic policy measures are generally meant to result in a period of declining economic growth and austerity. Usually the understanding between the IMF and the borrowing country was that some short-term sacrifice was necessary to restore long-term economic growth and stability. But while a country's governmental officials may have understood this, such policies were not popular with the majority of citizens who had to pay the price—a reduced standard of living.

The economic chaos of the Carter years exacerbated the situation seriously as it set the stage for higher interest rates and a precipitous increase in debt-servicing costs. A second round of OPEC price increases sent the U.S. economy into a three-year period of stagflation—from 1979 through 1981. The oil price increase brought higher interest rates, soaring inflation, coupled with declining economic growth, and increasing rates of unemployment. Moreover, the oil import bills of all industrialized nations increased, as did those of the oil-importing developing nations. And OPEC, once again, was faced with the financial challenge of prudently allocating oil revenues for internal development and investing the surplus in European and U.S. banks and government securities.

At the same time, as a consequence of the higher oil prices (and many other factors such as declining trade, spiraling inflation, compounding past loans, and rising interest rates), the oil-dependent developing nations increased their demand for loans from the IMF and now, more importantly, from private commercial banks. The IMF's limited loan capability was not sufficient to meet the avalanche of credit demand. So, the private commercial banks eagerly stepped in to fill the gap. Flush with petrodollar deposits and facing limited demand for credit in their own countries (because of the prolonged recession), the banks were only too happy to oblige, to put it mildly. Because of tight U.S. monetary policy, interest rates were at record highs, so bankers faced the pleasant prospect of making and often encouraging what they thought would be extremely profitable loans to developing nations with what appeared to be little risk.

Emergence of the Strong Dollar Syndrome

The new policy prescriptions of the Reagan administration were to have far-reaching consequences for the international financial system in general and the debt crisis in particular. Reagan had campaigned on a platform of supply-side economics. His goals were to reduce taxes and government spending on domestic programs. According to supply-side theories, this policy mix would generate a burst of economic growth and output sufficient to reduce inflation, decrease unemployment, and balance the budget all at the same time. In addition, Reaganomics emphasized the continuation of free-floating exchange rates and strongly supported free trade, even though the U.S. trade deficit was growing worse.

The supply-side economic program was accompanied by a very tight monetary policy on the part of the Federal Reserve Bank between 1981 and 1983. This policy induced the worst recession since the 1930s and finally broke the back of inflation but only at a very high social and economic price: two years of severe unemployment, declining economic growth, a record high federal budget deficit, *and* an increasing balance of trade deficit.

By 1982 the U.S. economy had begun to recover. But by then the seeds of crisis had been sown. The high interest rates of this period strengthened the U.S. dollar once again, as foreign investment flowed in seeking the higher returns, but this was to have far-reaching implications. Most importantly, the strong dollar directly made the U.S. trade deficit even worse as it made U.S. exports more expensive and imports cheaper (see table 6–1).

For the developing nations, the continued high level of interest rates made their annual trek to the bank and the IMF even more expensive. Their balance of payments problems were exacerbated by a further slowdown in world trade and economic growth. And their exports and foreign exchange earnings fell precipitously.

Table 6–1
U.S. Trade Deficit, 1977–1988

Year	Trade Deficit (billions)
1977	$ –31.0
1978	–33.9
1979	–27.5
1980	–25.5
1981	–29.9
1982	–36.4
1983	–67.2
1984	–112.5
1985	–122.1
1986	–144.5
1987	–160.0
1988	–132.5

Source: *Economic Report of the President* (Washington, D.C.: Government Printing Office, 1989).

In 1978 there was a capital *outflow* to the Third World countries from the industrialized nations of $37.5 billion. But the situation began to deteriorate rapidly in the early 1980s and by 1984 there was a net drain—that is, an inflow in the capital account—of $34.6 billion. This was mostly caused by a sharp reduction in new bank loans to the underdeveloped countries, while interest and principal amortization payment obligations continued. In 1982, at the depth of the U.S. recession, when both interest rates and oil prices were still high, the current account deficit—balance of trade plus investment income flows—reached a crushing $90 billion. By then it was becoming obvious that the Third World debt situation was reaching crisis proportions. However, it took a near collapse of the Mexican economy to bring the problem to world attention.

Mexico Crisis of 1982

On Friday the 13th of August in 1982 Mexican Finance Minister Jesus Silva-Herzog arrived in Washington with what amounted to a bombshell in his briefcase. Mexico was bankrupt. It owed $81 billion in foreign debts—$68 billion of that to commercial banks—and could not pay *even the interest* on its obligations. Mexico would need an immediate loan of $3 billion just to cover interest payments coming due in August and September. Later it would need more, he informed the startled monetary authorities at the U.S. Treasury and the Federal Reserve Bank. Otherwise, Mexico would be forced to default.

A default by Mexico would have meant losses of about $12 billion for the six largest U.S. banks. That alone would have reduced the value of their capital (shareholder's equity) by almost 50 percent, and it would severely damage all of the fourteen hundred U.S. banks that had loans out to Mexico. Citicorp, the largest U.S. bank, would lose more than $3 billion—two-thirds of its capital. A crisis of this magnitude would put strains on the international financial system far beyond what the U.S. government could allow. It was not Mexico that was in trouble, it was the United States. The saying, "If you owe a bank a thousand dollars and can't pay, you're in trouble. But if you owe a bank a million dollars and can't pay, the bank is in trouble," had turned out to be all too true.

The U.S. monetary authorities, under the leadership of Federal Chairman Paul Volcker, quickly put together a rescue loan package that, temporarily at least, averted total collapse. The package was made up of a $1 billion advance payment by the Department of Energy for oil destined for the U.S. strategic petroleum reserve, $1 billion from the Department of Agriculture, $700 million from the Federal Reserve Bank, and $300 million from the U.S. Treasury in the form of a "currency swap" arrangement. Later Mexico got an additional $1.85 billion line of credit from the Bank of International Settlements and, with unprecedented rapidity, almost $4 billion from the International Monetary Fund, on the condition that the commercial banks cough up an additional $5 billion, which they did reluctantly.

By December the rescue package was completed. Mexico had borrowed enough to meet its immediate obligation and, in the process, ended up some $14 billion further in debt. And the phrase, "Third World debt crisis" had become part of the national lexicon.

Mexico's debt crisis simply focused worldwide attention on an international financial problem that had been brewing for many years. But few were willing to acknowledge its magnitude until it reached the crisis stage. Now the global debt crisis was added to the seemingly unending list of global economic problems. But the major Western countries' governments were so preoccupied with their own stagnating economies that they did not confront the wide-ranging, long-run implications of the crisis. It suddenly became clear that not only was Mexico in trouble but so were Argentina, Brazil, Chile, Venezuela, Peru, Nigeria, the Philippines, Turkey, Poland, Romania, and many others—most of the underdeveloped world.

The Reagan administration's response was to facilitate the extension of additional loans by the IMF and private commercial banks to enable the debtor countries to continue meeting their obligations with borrowed money. If this meant they would face domestic economic austerity, the United States argued, that would be necessary until global economic growth and the recovery of the industrialized nations could improve the export capacity of developing nations.

The expected recovery did come in 1983. By 1984 world trade had expanded at an annual rate of 8.5 percent and world output grew at an annual rate of 4.2 percent. For developing nations, 1984 brought growth rates of 4.1 percent and an increase in exports of 8 percent, compared to only 4 percent two years earlier.

Even with the recovery continuing through 1984 and into 1985 it became obvious that the international economic problems weren't going to go away. Part of the problem, clearly, was the continued strong dollar and the free-flexible exchange rate system.

Plaza Agreement of 1985

At the initiative of Treasury Secretary James Baker, the United States invited the five largest industrial nations (United States, Great Britain, France, West Germany, and Japan) to New York to discuss the exchange rate problem. At this meeting, held at the Plaza Hotel in September of 1985, this "Group of Five" agreed to return to an informal system of managed exchange rates. Yet, in spite of the "Plaza Agreement," the major problems—the U.S. trade deficit and the huge Third World debt—remained and were two of the primary issues on the agenda of the Tokyo Economic Summit in May of 1986. The others were the pace of industrial world growth, the direction of the U.S. dollar, the possibility of policy coordination, high interest rates, and the U.S. federal budget deficit.

While overall world industrial growth was increasing, most participants continued to express concern over the slowing of economic growth in the United States. The Reagan administration took the position that Japan and West Germany should stimulate their economies to speed up their economic growth rates to increase their demand for imports, especially U.S. exports. Japan and West Germany didn't agree, because they felt such stimulation would be excessively inflationary.

The major issue at the Tokyo Summit was that of policy coordination. Since each nation's economy had started to converge (declining interest rates, real growth continuing, and lower inflation), it was possible to begin thinking seriously about coordinating economic policies. But since unemployment rates and trade deficits varied considerably in each country, the prospects for workable economic policy coordination appeared to be remote, and there was no formal agreement.

The summit participants did, however, acknowledge that another year had gone by without a Third World debt crisis. (Except, of course, for the unique case of Mexico.) Declining interest rates and oil prices had brought an easing of the debt problems for most developing nations. The summit group also endorsed a plan developed by Secretary Baker to aid debtor countries by generating an additional $29 billion in loans from the IMF and the World Bank ($9 billion) and private commercial banks ($20 billion), to be spread among seventeen countries.

At the conclusion of the Tokyo Summit, there appeared to be a renewed spirit of cooperation and a determination to work toward a more cooperative and coordinated set of economic policies that would simultaneously promote and protect the interests of each individual nation while considering the consequences and ramifications on the group as a whole. But, except for some coordinated interest rate reductions, little was accomplished at that meeting. There was general agreement that the U.S. dollar was "too strong" and that something should be done about it. Therefore, in a historically significant departure from the free-flexible exchange rate system that had prevailed since the Nixon administration—that is, since 1971—the Group of Five industrialized nations agreed to intervene in the exchange markets to bring down the value of the dollar. They were successful. This was tacit recognition that the huge U.S. trade deficit was one of the major international economic roadblocks to solving the imbalance of trade.

Reducing the value of the dollar, the G-5 leaders felt, would make U.S. exports cheaper and the price of imports higher, thus eventually reducing the U.S. balance of trade deficit. The dollar fell by 40 percent against the yen over a six-month period beginning in September of 1985. By the spring of 1986 it was at the lowest level it had been since 1947—140 yen to the dollar. But the trade deficit didn't budge. This defied a long-standing economic theory and sent the international economists back to the drawing boards.

What is supposed to happen in such a devaluation is that a so-called J-curve effect takes place. At first, because imports suddenly become more expensive in dollar terms the trade balance gets worse. But soon, as there is time to adjust, imports decline and exports increase and trade is brought back into balance.

But for a number of complicated reasons this didn't happen. Partly it was because the dollar wasn't strong for the reason it normally would have been—because of a strong international trade position. Instead, it was strong because a huge sum of foreign investment money was flowing into the United States seeking "safe haven" investments *and* because of the high rates of return available because of high interest rates in the United States compared to the rest of the world. Devaluing the dollar didn't change that significantly.

Beyond that, while the dollar did fall against *some* U.S. trading partners, such as Japan and West Germany, it did *not* fall against others, notably Canada, Mexico, and especially against the increasingly important Newly Industrialized Countries, such as Taiwan, South Korea, and the Pacific Rim countries that tie their currencies to the value of the dollar. In addition, U.S. demand for imports appears to be insatiable because most Americans seem to have become convinced that foreign-made products are superior in quality to U.S. products.

As a consequence, in spite of the fall of the dollar, the U.S. trade deficit didn't improve at all. It exceeded $156 billion in 1986 and was $174 billion in 1987. And it was a major agenda item on the Venice Economic Summit in June of 1987.

Venice Summit

In a climate of having to bail Mexico out of another debt-servicing crisis in 1986, only to be faced with a moratorium by Brazil—the largest Third World debtor—on most of its foreign debt, continued high U.S. budget and trade deficits, and a U.S. president weakened by the Iran-Contra scandal, the leaders of the seven largest industrial nations met once again in Venice to try to resolve the continuing economic chaos. Their communiqué declared:

> We, the heads of state or government of the seven major industrialized countries and the representatives of the European Community, have met in Venice from 8 to 10 June 1987, to review the progress that our countries have made, individually and collectively, in carrying out the policies to which we committed ourselves at earlier summits. We remain determined to pursue these policies for growth, stability, employment, and prosperity for our countries and for the world economy.
>
> We can look back on a number of positive developments since we met a year ago. Growth is continuing into its fifth consecutive year, albeit at lower rates. Average inflation rates have come down. Interest rates have generally declined. Changes have occurred in relationships among leading currencies which over time will contribute to a more sustainable pattern of current account positions and have brought exchange rates within ranges broadly consistent with economic fundamentals.

In volume terms the adjustment of trade flows is under way, although in nominal terms imbalances so far remain too large. . .

We now need to overcome the problems that nevertheless remain in some of our countries: external imbalances that are still large; persistently high unemployment; large public sector deficits; and high levels of real interest rates. There are also continuing trade restrictions and increased protectionist pressures, persistent weakness of many primary commodity markets, and reduced prospects for developing countries to grow, find the markets they need, and service their foreign debt.

The correction of external imbalances will be a long and difficult process. Exchange rate changes alone will not solve the problem of correcting these imbalances while sustaining growth. Surplus countries will design their policies to strengthen domestic demand and reduce external surpluses while maintaining price stability. Deficit countries, while following policies designed to encourage steady low-inflation growth, will reduce their fiscal and external imbalances . . .

We also agree on the need for effective structural policies especially for creating jobs. To this end we shall:

- Promote competition in order to speed up industrial adjustment;

- Reduce major imbalances between agricultural supply and demand;

- Facilitate job creating investment;

- Improve the functioning of labor markets;

- Promote the further opening of internal markets;

- Encourage the elimination of capital markets' imperfections and restrictions and the improvement of the functioning of international financial markets . . .

We note rising protectionist pressures with grave concern. . . . Recognizing the interrelationship among growth, trade, and development, it is essential to improve the multilateral system based on the principles and rules of the General Agreement on Tariffs and Trade and bring about a wider coverage of world trade under agreed, effective, and enforceable multilateral discipline. Protectionist actions would be counterproductive, would increase the risk of further exchange rate instability and would exacerbate the problems of development and indebtedness . . .

We attach particular importance to fostering stable economic progress in developing countries, with all their diverse situations and needs. The problems of many heavily indebted developing countries are a cause of economic and political concern and can be a threat to political stability in countries with democratic regimes. We salute the courageous efforts of many of these countries to achieve economic growth and stability.

We underline the continuing importance of official development assistance . . .

- We support the central role of the IMF through its advice and financing and encourage closer cooperation between the IMF and the World Bank, especially in their structural adjustment lending . . .

- We support a general capital increase of the World Bank . . .

- In the light of the different contributions of our countries to official development assistance, we welcome the recent initiative of the Japanese Government in bringing forward a new scheme which will increase the provision of resources from Japan to developing countries.

For the major middle-income debtors, we continue to support the present growth-oriented case-by-case strategy . . .

There is equally a need for timely and effective mobilization of lending by commercial banks. In this context, we support efforts by commercial banks and debtor countries to develop a "menu" of alternative negotiating procedures and financial techniques for providing continuing support to debtor countries . . .

We recognize the problems of developing countries whose economies are solely or predominantly dependent on exports of primary commodities the prices of which are persistently depressed. It is important that the functioning of commodity markets should be improved . . .

We note that UNCTAD VII provides an opportunity for a discussion with developing countries with a view to arriving at a common perception of the major problems and policy issues in the world economy.

On the surface the joint communiqué of the Group of Seven leaders at the Venice Summit seemed impressive. The public acknowledgment of the need for better coordination of economic policies, the recognition that the problem of Third World debt must be resolved, and the need to address trade imbalances all seemed to point to some sort of action-oriented solution. But, in fact, almost nothing at all happened at or after the Venice Summit. What *did not* happen is more significant than what did.

Most importantly, what did not happen is that no one was ready to acknowledge that the United States no longer enjoys hegemony over the world economy; that it has, instead, become a prisoner of international economic forces that now seem far beyond its control. But the dollar remains the lynchpin currency, used in more than 50 percent of all international transactions. Since everyone knows the situation cannot continue, without at some point precipitating a crisis, it is clear that something will need to be changed.

What can be done is that a new system can be put in place that is more consistent with the present realities of the modern-day world. Instead, the Venice Summit simply endorsed a continuation of the Band-Aid trial and error muddle-along efforts that clearly are not working.

The short-run solutions proposed were: first, reduce the U.S. budget deficit, which is supposed to somehow magically solve all the world's problems. But there is no evidence to indicate that is going to happen any time in the foreseeable future, and *if it did* there is no reason to think reducing the deficit alone would solve the problem of structural trade imbalance. And, in any case, President Reagan's response to those proposals was that the United States is already doing all it can to reduce its deficit.

Second, Japan, West Germany, and the other European countries were encouraged to stimulate their economies on the assumption that faster growth would absorb more U.S. exports. But growth rates in those countries are nearly stagnant and are showing no signs of improvement. Moreover, there are no signs that anyone wants to do anything about it. But, *even if* they did, there is no evidence that faster growth would resolve the longer-run festering problems. Several studies show that even a 1 percent growth rate increase in Japan and West Germany would only improve the U.S. trade deficit by 25 percent over a five-year period.[3]

Third, it was generally recognized that the United States needs to become more competitive in world markets, but the United States—still the most productive economy in the world—*has* become more competitive, that is, productive, in terms of output per man hour, especially in the manufacturing sector where productivity increased at a rate of 2.6 percent in the first half of 1987, but United States exports have hardly increased at all, and *even if* they did that would not resolve the longer-run problem, unless imports—which have remained constant—were cut back drastically.

Fourth, there was agreement that the value of the dollar should be reduced, or at least maintained at the lower levels achieved by central bank interventions after the Plaza Agreement in 1985. But by the end of 1987 the lower value of the dollar had not improved the U.S. trade deficit *at all* and, *if it did*, the risk of a systemic collapse would be greatly increased. A lower dollar exchange rate would increase the price of U.S. imports even more and put inflationary pressures on the economy that would force the monetary authorities to increase interest rates, tighten the money supply, or both. That, in turn, would push the economy into a recession, which would reverberate throughout the world.

A weaker dollar also means lower rates of return for foreign investors as their dollar-denominated investments translate into smaller rates of return in terms of their home-country currencies. That means that the risk of a foreign investment pullout is greatly increased and if that happened a dollar collapse or a dollar panic would be inevitable. So simply depreciating the value of the dollar isn't a viable short-run *or* long-run solution. It is, at best, a delicate balancing act between possible chaos on the one hand, the recession on the other.

Fifth, there was general agreement that protectionist legislation, especially in the United States, should be avoided at all costs, and the G-7 nations recommitted themselves, rhetorically at least, to the continuing GATT negotiations to reduce tariffs and import quotas. But, even if *all* trade restrictions were removed it is estimated that the U.S. trade deficit wouldn't improve by more than 3 percent. And, beyond that, the Omnibus Trade Bill that became law in 1988 was the most protectionist trade legislation passed by the U.S. Congress since 1932. So talking about reduction of trade barriers in these times has a hollow ring. Free trade is an attractive theory, but an unlikely reality.

Finally, the Third World debt crisis was hardly discussed, although there was some acknowledgment that the impoverished nations of Africa need some special attention. Yet, as we have seen, the Third World debt problem has been getting worse at an increasing rate.

Interestingly, the one significant thing that did happen at the Venice Summit was largely unnoticed in the press. The Group of Seven agreed to adopt an international economic plan developed by their finance ministers during 1986. This is a significant and unprecedented development.

U.S. Treasury Secretary James Baker announced that from now on the Group of Seven nations would begin tracking their economies using a newly developed series of economic indicators, and that when any member of the group begins to drift off course—meaning presumably, the status quo—the ministers would meet to determine what to do about it.

What exactly these indicators are will be kept secret but most likely they will include trade balance data, interest rates, budget projections, inflation and growth rates, and currency exchange rates.

One reason this hasn't been done before is that each nation has its own method of keeping track of these data so that comparisons between countries are often meaningless. For example, because of the way it is defined, a cut in the Japanese or West German discount rate means much less than it does in the United States. Unemployment rates are calculated differently, and so on. Under the new agreement everybody will use the same system and the results will be much more meaningful. However, the agreement is nonbinding because no country is ever going to consent to a binding agreement that could subvert its control of its own economy. The only "automatic" thing about it is that the finance ministers did agree to meet any time things seem to be getting out of hand.

The Venice Summit merely reaffirmed a set of anachronistic Band-Aid solutions that have been tried but haven't worked economically and are not politically feasible. Subsequent summits held in Toronto in 1988 and Paris in 1989 mostly ignored the building storm. Neither the outgoing Reagan administration nor the new Bush administration was willing to acknowledge that the world economy is in a period of transition that needs to be managed and coordinated in an orderly manner. It has become clear that the United States can no longer manage its own interests. A new system of coordination is badly needed and, to put it in place, a new conference on the order of Bretton Woods.

Key Concepts

Gold Standard
Bretton Woods Conference
Dollar Glut
Eurodollar Market
Petrodollar Recycling
New International Economic Order
Strong Dollar Syndrome
Plaza Agreement

Discussion Questions

1. Assume the world economy was on the gold standard now. What would have happened? Who would have all of the world's gold supply?

2. The Bretton Woods Conference set up a new system sometimes called the "dollar standard." How did it work? Who benefited from it?

3. Currently, are we in a "dollar glut" or a "dollar shortage"?

4. What, specifically, is a Eurodollar?

5. What is the relationship between petrodollar recycling and the Third World debt crisis?

7

The Triple Debt Crisis

I n the 1980s debt has come to dominate the news from every angle. It is no longer buried in the financial pages. The explosive growth of debt everywhere has become *the* economic issue of the decade. And it's not going to go away. Indeed, a *triple debt crisis* has evolved; the U.S. national federal debt exceeded *$2.8 trillion* in 1989, more than *double* what it was only five years earlier. In the fall of 1985 the United States became a *debtor nation* for the first time since 1914. U.S. external debt reached $600 billion in 1989 and is expected to exceed $1 trillion by 1992. On top of that, in 1989 Third World debt to the industrialized countries stood at nearly $1.3 trillion. Most Third World debt is owed to U.S. banks, who have publicly acknowledged that the chances of it being repaid are slim to nonexistent. Such a buildup of debt is historically unprecedented, and it has sown the seeds of a major crisis, if not a total collapse of the international financial system.

Debt has always played a significant and important role in economics. It is often said that the real measure of one's wealth is "not how much you have, but how much you can borrow." But, in the American psyche, the word debt has a negative connotation. People are supposed to "save their money and live within their means." Nonetheless, people go into debt for a number of perfectly legitimate reasons: to buy a home or a car or to finance a college education. As long as one's income increases as fast or faster than a new debt does, there is no particular problem as long as the interest on the debt can be serviced. Indeed, managing debt properly is an important part of prudent financial planning. Debt is an integral part of the American way of life. Of course, if a household's debt begins to exceed its capacity to pay its interest and principal obligations then it is in trouble, and bankruptcy often follows.

Businesses, too, go into debt for perfectly legitimate reasons. Businesses borrow to invest in expanding capacity, to finance inventories, to build new plants, and for a host of other reasons. Virtually all businesses depend on debt to operate. So it's not at all clear that debt is a "bad thing" in the context of prudent business management.

The point of a business going into debt, of course, is that there is a presumption that the rate of return generated by the investments made possible by borrowing will exceed the rate of interest on its loans. That way, the earnings from the investment project will be more than sufficient to repay the money used to finance it. That's one of the reasons interest exists. Money—financial capital, as it is called—is presumed to be "productive" in the same sense that investing it creates a rate of return higher than the "price" of money which is, of course, the interest rate. Otherwise banks wouldn't exist. When a business's debt exceeds its capacity to service it then it, too, is in trouble and bankruptcy will eventually ensue.

As with households and businesses, so with the nations of the world. There are a variety of reasons for countries to go into debt: to finance needed defense expenditures, to invest in public works, and so on. But now the situation becomes a bit more complicated. Nations can go into debt in two different ways. They can borrow internally, that is, from their own citizens, or they can borrow externally, from other nations. Either way can make perfect economic sense, or either can get out of control. This is what happened in the United States and most of the Western world in the 1980s.

The U.S. National Debt and Deficits

The federal government's huge debt ranks high on everybody's list of economic concerns. One poll, conducted by NBC News and *The Wall Street Journal* in 1988, showed that 32 percent of

Americans thought the national debt was the country's single biggest problem. And it may be, but for different reasons than most people think. There are two ways of looking at the national debt question, and that gives rise to a lot of mythology as people attempt to sort it out using different assumptions. There's what might be called the "barnyard economics" way and the economics of public finance way.

Those who look at the federal debt from the "barnyard" perspective argue that it's simply not prudent for the government to spend more than it takes in. After all, if households and individuals can't do it, why should the government be able to? The reason this view doesn't fit very well with the facts is that households and governments don't face the same reality. The reason households have to balance their budgets—"save their money and live within their means"—is that although individuals may be able to spend more than they earn for short periods of time, they can't go on very long. Also, of course, households must attempt to save for retirement, so prudent personal financial management does certainly make sense in that context. Since this is a process deeply ingrained in the American way of life it is not surprising that many would extrapolate it to the government.

But, in general, governments don't face the same fiscal restraints that households do. Governments can raise their incomes any time they need to by increasing taxes. To be sure this may have other, less desirable, side effects but it is possible—and very common. Households obviously don't have this option. Also, since governments, in theory at least, exist in perpetuity they don't have the constraint of needing to save for retirement. If the government retires none of this will matter anyway. So it doesn't make sense to assume that governments have to manage their financial affairs the same way that households do. The commonly drawn comparison is simply a fallacy.

A somewhat more sophisticated view of the national debt issue, which you can find described in virtually every elementary economics textbook, argues that the national debt is not really a problem at all.

The chief reason is that there is a lot of confusion over the question of who owes what to whom. The national debt consists

of the total of all U. S. Treasury bills, notes, and bonds outstanding at any given point in time. When the government runs a
deficit, that is, spends more than it takes in from taxes and other
sources, that amount is added to the national debt as additional
securities are issued and sold. In 1989 the total amount of such
securities outstanding (the national debt) was roughly $2.8
trillion. The relevant and commonly misunderstood question here
is: Who owns these interest-bearing assets? That is, to whom does
the government owe all this money? The interesting answer is
that, in one way or another, most of it is owed to the U.S. citizens.
If you own a U.S. savings bond or any kind of U.S. government
security, then you own part of the national debt. So who owes
whom? For the most part, the government owes the debt to its
own citizens, who not only own it but receive interest payments
on it.

Moreover, a large part of the national debt is owned by the
government itself, or by quasi-governmental agencies. The U.S.
central bank—the Federal Reserve System—owned over $250
billion worth of U.S. Treasury obligations in 1989. The Social
Security Trusts held almost $500 billion. Together these two
quasi-governmental institutions held 27 percent of the total debt.
So the net debt outside of the government itself was only about
$1.9 trillion, as opposed to the more publicized $2.8 trillion.
Much of the rest of the debt is owned by banks (27 percent),
insurance companies (7 percent), state and local governments (11
percent), and other institutions. Only 9 percent is owned by
individuals directly (figure 7–1).

The other reason that most economists have tended to
downplay the importance of the federal debt is that historically
both the economy and the government's income have grown much
faster than the debt. They point out that, as a percentage of
national income, the debt has been getting smaller and smaller. So,
in that context, it has become a decreasing burden on the
government. And that, as shown in figure 7–2, was indeed the
case, at least until 1980.

In 1946 the national debt, mostly accumulated during the war,
stood at 127 percent of the U.S. GNP. By 1986 that percentage

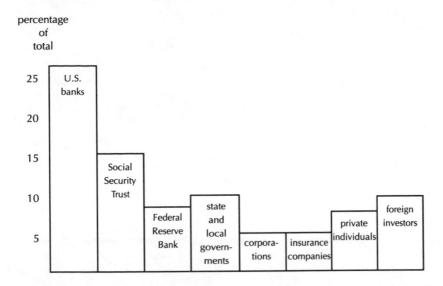

Source: *Economic Report of the President* (Washington, D.C.: Government Printing Office, 1989).

Note: In 1989 total U.S. public debt was $2.8 trillion.

Figure 7–1. *Ownership of U.S. National Debt, 1989*

had dropped to 54 and, if the Federal Reserve and Social Security holdings are netted out, the debt was only 36 percent of the country's GNP that year. Clearly that's a lot, but even by household comparisons it's not overwhelming. If anything, rather than hindering economic growth and general prosperity, as some would argue, the debt has probably stimulated it. So, put in that context the national debt—many economists feel—is not a serious problem.

That has been the conventional wisdom in economics for some time now. But things are changing rapidly and it is becoming more and more apparent that the U.S. economy may have bitten off a lot more than it can chew. Now three new developments are causing even liberal economists and politicians to reevaluate their position on the national debt.

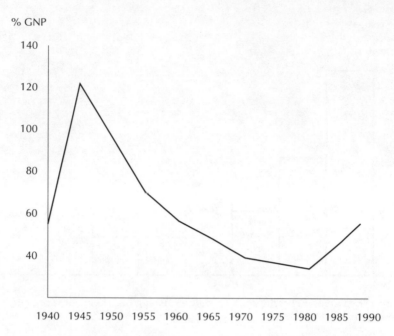

% GNP

Source: Congressional Budget Office, *The Economic and Budget Outlook: Fiscal Years 1989–1993*, February 1988.

Figure 7–2. *Federal Debt as a Percentage of GNP, 1940–1990*

Interest Payments

In 1976 net interest payments—the difference between what the government pays out in interest and what it takes in—came to $26.8 billion, or 6.8 percent of federal expenditures. A decade later, in 1986, the federal government made net interest payments of $135.8 billion, which was 13.2 percent of federal expenditures. Interest payments on the debt are now the third largest category in the budget, after national defense and social security. The problem here is that this is causing a transfer of wealth from the middle class, who pay most of the taxes, to the wealthy, who own most of the government debt. This is becoming an increasingly serious problem, especially when you consider that in the United States the top 20 percent of income receivers already receive 45 percent of all income, while the bottom 20 percent only get 5 percent.

Compounding

Second, and perhaps even more significant, is the seemingly overlooked phenomenon of compounding. Everybody knows that if you leave your money in the bank and let the interest accumulate, your savings will grow at a compound rate. At a 7 percent annual interest rate they will double every 10 years. By the same token, if you borrow money to pay interest on what you already owe, a similar compounding process occurs. And that, of course, is what's happening to the U.S. national debt.

What is important here is the relationship between the growth of the national income and the growth of the debt. As with a household, if income grows as fast as debt then there is no particular problem: the debt can be serviced with no decline in living standards. But, while that's what happened in the United States until about 1980, it's not happening now and there is no reason to expect that it ever will again. The situation is changing rapidly. Since 1980 the U.S. national debt has almost tripled, while the economy grew only by 56 percent—much less than that if the data are adjusted for inflation.

If one makes only very conservative assumptions and extrapolates a bit into the future the numbers defy the imagination. One economist, Alfred Malabre of *The Wall Street Journal,* has estimated that at current rates of growth the U.S. national debt could reach $34 trillion by the year 2010.[1]

Federal Deficits Out-of-Hand

Third, there is little evidence that the federal debt situation can be improved unless drastic and politically unpopular tax increases are implemented.

The Reagan administration came into office on a campaign pledge to cut government spending, balance the federal budget, and reduce the national debt. Normally that would mean cutting spending and increasing taxes. But, instead, the administration chose to adopt a new version of an old theory called supply-side economics, the rationale of which was that if the burden of high marginal taxes is taken off the backs of individuals and businesses they will work harder, save, and invest more. This renewed burst of economic activity, the argument goes, will so stimulate the economy that (contrary to common sense) soon the tax *decrease* will cause an *increase* in governmental tax revenues.

One result of this peculiar variation on the idea of "eating your cake and having it too" was that the wealthy paid fewer taxes but decided to spend their extra money rather than save it or invest it productively. By 1987 the national savings rate was running at less than 4 percent of disposable income and investment had hardly increased. The other result of the tax decreases (in 1981 and again in 1986) was that federal deficits grew to record highs. Whenever the government runs a deficit that amount is added to the national debt. The deficits grew from $40.2 billion in 1979 to $220 billion in 1986 and, as we have seen, the national debt more than doubled during that period.

Moreover, because a large percentage of the federal budget goes either to defense spending or to "entitlement programs" such as social security, federal pensions, and interest payments on the national debt itself, the administration was not successful in reducing government spending. In fact, the federal budget grew from $303 billion to under $1 trillion in 1986—it more than doubled. Congressional efforts to cut spending were unsuccessful. The Gramm-Rudman law, which was to require a balanced budget, was declared unconstitutional by the Supreme Court and largely ignored in spirit both by Congress and the administration, even after it was revised to meet constitutional requirements. The legacy of the Reagan administration and its ill-fated fantasies of supply-side economics is that the national debt was increased by more than the total accumulated debt of all previous administrations combined.

While it was once fashionable to argue that the national debt was not a serious problem, the realities of massive transfers of wealth from the poor to the rich and a runaway compounding of the debt to unimaginable heights means that the national debt problem is something the United States can no longer afford to ignore. The proverbial chickens have come to roost.

The Overall U.S. Debt Picture

The obvious gravity of the situation aside, in a very real sense the U.S. federal debt is a minor problem when it is put in the context of the growth of debt in the U.S. economy as a whole in the 1980s. Consider the following:

- Total personal, business, and governmental debt outstanding in the U.S. economy in 1987 exceeds $7 trillion—up 1 trillion from 1986.

- The ratio of total debt to the Gross National Product stood at 1:7 in 1987, the highest since the 1930s. In 1981 the debt/GNP ratio was only 1:4.

- In 1987 corporate debt as a percentage of net worth grew to 120 percent, compared to 96 as recently as 1983.

- Utility and industrial corporations are so heavily leveraged that by 1987 there were only 27 left in the entire country that merited the top-drawer AAA rating. Ten years earlier there were 56.

- Even though the economy in general was doing relatively well in 1986, some 138 banks—staggering under nonperforming agricultural and oil-based debts—failed. That's compared to only 42 in 1982, and more than in 1933 at the height of the Great Depression.

- In 1987 there were 1,500 banks on the FDIC's "problem bank" list, up from 1,150 a year earlier.

- Household debt as a percentage of disposable income was, in 1987, just over 31 percent, compared to 25 percent in 1983.

- Personal bankruptcy filings climbed to a record 567,000 during the fiscal year ending June 30, 1986, a 35 percent increase over the previous year.

- In agriculture in 1986 some 36 percent of 261,000 FHA borrowers were behind on their payments. Of those, 80 percent had been delinquent for more than three years.
- The percentage of home mortgages being foreclosed doubled between 1982 and 1986 to a postwar high: one out of one hundred outstanding.

Total consumer debt (including home mortgages) exceeded $2 trillion by 1987 and has been growing at over 9 percent annually since 1980. That's about $24,000 for each of the 85 million households in the country. Consumer installment purchases alone in 1987 ran at almost 17 percent of personal income, compared to 12 percent in 1982.

Business debt, which now exceeds $3 trillion, has been growing even faster, at a rate of almost 10 percent annually since 1984, compared to an average of 2.7 percent over the 1975–1983 period. Corporate debt now exceeds total corporate net worth by 12 percent.

What's more, the nature of corporate debt has been changing dramatically. Corporations have traditionally raised capital by issuing stock to the public, but in the past ten years they have increasingly turned to banks and to issuing bonds instead. Bank loans as a percentage of total corporate external fund sources have increased from 22 percent in 1975 to almost 38 percent now, and bonds as a source of borrowing have grown from 34 percent to 45 percent over the same period. So direct debt has largely replaced equity (ownership) financing as a means for corporations to raise funds externally, and the cost of repaying debts is now taking almost 50 percent of total corporate cash flow.

Such a buildup of the debt pyramid is almost unprecedented in U.S. economic history. Yet, amid the euphoria of a rising stock market, it was largely ignored. In the five years of steady, albeit sluggish, economic growth of the U.S. economy between 1982 and 1987, the stock market (as measured by the Dow-Jones average) grew by almost 250 percent, while the economy grew at only a 20 percent inflation-adjusted rate. The only parallel is the 1920s—the "roaring twenties"—when the market, built on a pyramid of credit, grew by 500 percent between 1921 and 1929, until it finally collapsed, taking the U.S. economy and the economies of the other western nations with it into the Great Depression of the 1930s.[2]

In October of 1987 the stock market collapsed. The Dow-Jones average dropped 508 points *in one day* and it became clear that the days of unfettered and unwarranted growth of the market were over. Many analysts predicted a severe recession would follow, but to nearly everyone's surprise the economy continued to grow, albeit slowly.

Whether the debt bubble will ever burst no one knows. But the implications of the debt explosion in the U.S. domestic economy pale by comparison to the developing international debt crisis. Largely as a result of its growing internal debt, the United States has now become a *debtor nation* externally. For the strongest economic power in the world this borders on absurdity. But it is a fact, and the long-run implications are much more serious than even the alarming domestic debt build-up.

It makes economic sense for a nation to borrow from abroad *if* the funds are used productively to develop its economy, and, especially, its export capacity, so that the loans can be repaid. Indeed, the United States borrowed heavily from Europe during the 1800s to finance the development of its industrial plant and the westward expansion. Developing countries are, for the same reasons, usually debtor nations and most economists agree that as a development strategy this is prudent financial management if the loans are invested productively in manufacturing and needed infrastructure. Operating on those assumptions the United States was a debtor nation until 1914. After that it began to show an export surplus, repay the loans, and eventually become the world's largest creditor nation. U.S. export surpluses financed among other things, the reconstruction of Europe after World War II, the expansion of U.S. investment worldwide, and the loan of billions of dollars to the capital-poor Third World developing countries.

But in the fall of 1985 that all changed dramatically. The United States became a debtor nation for the first time in seventy-one years. What this means is conceptually difficult to understand, but, because it is crucial to understanding the nature and dimensions of the international financial crisis, merits closer examination.

What It Means To Be a Debtor Nation

There is a common misconception that, if a nation consistently runs a balance of trade deficit, it is a debtor nation. In some cases that may be true, in others not. The confusion comes over the distinction between balance of trade transactions and overall balance of payments accounting.

By definition, the balance of payments accounts of a country must balance (as in double-entry bookkeeping). So it is possible for a country to run balance of trade deficits without becoming a debtor nation so long as there are offsetting transactions in the balance of payments accounts to make up for the excess of imports over exports. These can be sales of gold or accumulated foreign exchange, debits on Special Drawing Rights from the International Monetary Fund, net positive flows of income from foreign investments, or simply borrowing from other countries. Any of these financial transactions (and some others) will permit a country to import more than it exports. What counts, however, in the long run is flows of capital investments as compared to the return flows of interest or profits from them.

The United States did not become a debtor nation because it went to Japan or Western Europe and "borrowed" money in the literal sense. Rather, what happened was that around 1983 the flow of capital into the United States from abroad—mostly from Japan and Western Europe—began to exceed the outflow of the U.S. capital investments to the rest of the world. Historically, the United States had counted on the *net income* from investments abroad to compensate for trade deficits and to help finance the various military activities it maintains around the world.

U.S. net foreign investment income averaged $14.8 billion annually during the 1970s and peaked at over $34 billion in 1981. But after 1981 it began to decline rapidly as the rate of foreign investments in the United States began to grow at a faster rate than U.S. investments abroad. By 1987 U.S. net investment income had declined to $14.4 billion, and when netted with the huge balance of trade deficit (see figure 7–3), the U.S. current account was a negative $160 billion at the end of 1987.

High interest rates resulting from the (successful) Volcker-Reagan effort to break the back of inflation, the general perception that the United States was a "safe haven" for investment, and the U.S. need for external savings to finance its own domestic national debt, coupled with huge Japanese and West German trade surpluses, all added up to large increases in the flow of

Source: *Economic Report of the President* (Washington, D.C.: Government Printing Office, 1989).

Figure 7–3. *U.S. Merchandise Trade Balance, 1970–1988*

investment funds into the United States. The result was that the accumulated total of U.S. assets held by foreigners began (in 1985) to exceed the total value of foreign assets held by the United States. That's how the United States became a debtor nation.

The United States went from being the world's largest creditor nation to being the world's largest debtor nation in just five years (see figure 7–4). This, in itself, is not a crisis situation, but it has

Source: U.S. Department of Commerce, *Survey of Current Business*, Vol. 68, No. 6, June 1988.

Figure 7–4. *U.S. Net External Assets, 1970–1989*

some significant long-run implications. Certainly, at the least, it signals the erosion of U.S. dominance of the international economy, a dramatic change in the world role of the U.S. dollar's key-currency status and the privileges that go with it; and a shift in the balance of economic power toward Japan and Western Europe, especially Japan, which became the world's largest creditor nation in 1986 (see table 7–1). This unprecedented situation has a number of serious implications for the U.S. economy and for the rest of the world.

The federal debt, which we used to think was not a big problem because "we owed it to ourselves" is now increasingly being bought by foreigners. In 1976 foreign interests held only $70 billion of U.S. government securities, but by 1986 they owned $240 billion worth—a 350 percent increase in just ten years. Interest payments on that, which, it is important to emphasize, flow *out of the country*, now amount to some $20 billion annually. In 1986 Japanese investors purchased about 35 percent of new long-term Treasury issues. If that trend continues, by 1996 foreign interests will own about $1 trillion of U.S. governmental obligations and interest payments on that will be $100 billion (see table 7–2).

But foreign investment involves more than just government securities. It involves direct purchases of U.S. corporations and

Table 7–1

Japan's Growing Role as a Creditor Nation

(billions)

	Net Overseas Investment	
	Japan	United States
1980	$ 11.5	$ 106.3
1981	10.9	141.1
1982	24.7	137.0
1983	37.3	89.6
1984	74.3	3.6
1985	129.8	–111.9
1986	180.4	–263.6

Source: U.S. Department of Commerce, *Survey of Current Business*, Vol. 68, No. 6, June 1988.

Table 7–2

Japanese Foreign Assets in the United States, 1980–1987

(millions)

	Net Purchases[a]		Direct Investment
	Stocks	Bonds	
1980	$ 344	$ 4,285	$ 4,699
1981	240	5,808	8,932
1982	151	6,066	7,703
1983	658	12,507	8,145
1984	51	26,773	10,156
1985	995	53,517	12,217
1986	7,048	98,024	22,320
1987	10,019	48,497	7,461

Source: U.S. Department of Commerce, *Survey of Current Businss*, Vol. 68, No. 6, June 1988.

Note: 1987 figures are for periods ended June 30. Stocks and bonds are based on calendar years; direct investment is based on fiscal years ended March 31.

[a] Excludes transactions of non-Japanese securities through Japanese market.

real estate. Exact data on the extent of such investments are not available, but rough estimates are that foreign interests held $1.3 trillion in U.S. assets in 1987 and that over $200 billion of that was direct investment.* The list of well-known U.S. corporations now controlled by foreign interests is long—and getting longer. As economics columnist Ernest Conine has pointed out:

"If you were to require every foreign-owned enterprise to fly the national flag of its owners for a day, the result would surprise most Americans. Carnation Co. is Swiss. Doubleday, RCA Records, Celanese, and General Tire are all German. Zale Corp., the giant jewelry retailer, is Canadian. Purina Mills, Smith and Wesson, and J. Walter Thompson advertising are British.

"Because the Japanese were late starters, their investments are not much more than one-tenth as large as those of the Europeans. But the Japanese are coming on strong. Direct Japanese investment in the U.S. has more than tripled, to more than $25 billion,

*The rest is portfolio investment—corporate stocks and bonds and governmental securities.

in just five years. Already Japanese banks have the largest foreign presence in the United States; they are especially strong in California.

"The Japanese also are plunging into the commercial real-estate market. Their holdings include the ARCO Plaza and Chase Plaza in Los Angeles, Essex House, the Exxon Building, and Capital Cities-ABC headquarters in New York, plus major structures in Boston, Washington, San Francisco, Honolulu, and other cities.

"About 435 U.S. manufacturers in such disparate fields as auto assembly, chemicals, electronics, auto parts, textile equipment, and steel products are owned wholly or partly by the Japanese.

"In some sectors of the U.S. economy, foreign ownership has reached major proportions. Four of the top ten chemical companies and more than half the cement industry are foreign-owned."[3]

It is often argued that such investments create jobs for Americans and stimulate the U.S. economy. That is obviously true, but unless the profits from direct investments are reinvested in the United States (forever) they eventually flow abroad and exacerbate the already serious current account deficit. And, in the future, the situation is likely to get worse. Consider this possible scenario. In 1987 the balance of trade deficit was $171 billion and the current account deficit (which includes trade *and* net investment flows) was $160 billion. If foreign investment increases at its present rate, the total current account deficit could easily exceed $1 trillion by the mid-1990s. Unless this is offset by capital inflows that exceed the (compounding) profit and interest outflows, the U.S. economy could well be brought to its knees as increasing percentages of its productive capacity are diverted abroad to service its foreign debt.

The net result is that because of the key role of the dollar as the international currency and the general strength of the U.S. economy, the United States has been able to run record-high levels of debt and enjoy the benefits of cheap imports all through the 1980s. All of this is possible because it is being financed by foreign interests. But this situation can't continue forever unless the United States is willing to sell its economy to the rest of the world.

Under the most favorable circumstances the economies of the United States, Japan, and Western Europe will become melded into one giant supernational economy. But a much less favorable scenario is that the U.S. economy will slip into a period of recession, or inflation, and foreign investors will lose faith in it and stop providing the capital—in essence, the loans—now required to service the U.S. federal deficit and the trade deficit and make the current fragile international financial system function. If that happens the dollar could well collapse; imports would become prohibitively expensive, and this would put extreme inflationary pressures on the U.S. economy. To counter that and provide incentive for foreign investors to continue financing U.S. domestic deficits, interest rates would have to be pushed sky-high, which in turn would certainly push the economy into a recession. With U.S. markets shrinking, the rest of the world would also be pushed into a recession that could easily spiral into a full-fledged depression. The dollar would become "Monopoly money" and it would be the end of the "era of privilege" for America.

The ironic situation that the United States is rapidly moving into is similar but not exactly analogous to the even more serious and rapidly deteriorating debt crisis of the Third World. It's different in the sense that most of the U.S. external debt is privately held, whereas most of the Third World debt is governmental; also, of course, the U.S. economy is much larger and stronger than any of the Third World countries—or all of them combined. So in percentage terms the numbers are much less dramatic. But it is similar in the sense that sooner or later the United States will have to pay the price of debt and profligate spending habits by transferring resources out of the country and accepting a lower standard of living in return. That is exactly what is happening in the Third World now, but for a different set of equally ironic reasons.

Third World Debt Crisis

As we saw in the previous chapter, the Third World debt crisis evolved in large part out of an unexpected and certainly unplanned quirk of fate. The Arab oil embargo of 1973 and the subsequent strengthening of the OPEC oil cartel resulted in a dramatic increase of oil prices and one of the largest transfers of wealth in history. Billions of dollars went to the Middle East from the oil–import-dependent industrialized countries. They, in turn, redeposited the money back in western banks, which, in turn, loaned it to the capital-poor developing countries. At the time the process seemed to make sense to most analysts. Petrodollar recycling, as it was called, transferred funds to the place where they were most needed: the Third World.

It is worth reemphasizing that the rationale behind any country borrowing from abroad—especially an underdeveloped country—is that if the funds are used productively, that is, invested in export-expanding sectors of the economy, overall welfare will be increased at the same time that the capacity to repay the loans is developed. On those assumptions, and the now-dubious assumption that governments don't go bankrupt, the international money-center banks zealously facilitated the buildup of the Third World debt. As shown in figure 7–5, Third World foreign debt grew from $100 billion in 1973 to nearly $1.3 *trillion* in 1989.

But as early as 1982 it was becoming increasingly clear that a crisis of unprecedented proportions was brewing. High interest rates in the United States raised the cost of servicing the debt; the U.S. recession of the early 1980s reduced U.S. imports of Third World products, and world commodity prices fell. All this added up to the near-default by Mexico in 1982. The collapse of oil prices in 1986 pushed the oil-exporting Third World countries to the brink of collapse and it was clear that the final link in the petrodollar cycle had been broken: the banks were not going to be repaid.

The idea behind foreign borrowing and foreign investment is, in the case of developing countries, that a net flow of funds *from* the industrialized *to* the developing countries will be engendered by the lending process. If this doesn't happen it's clearly ludicrous for any developing country to be borrowing for development purposes. But, strange as it may sound, that's exactly what happened. The reasons are complicated and, ironically, built into the lending process.

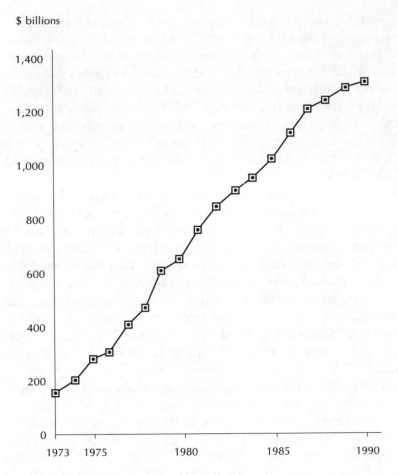

Source: World Bank, *World Bank Debt Tables: External Debt of Developing Countries* (Washington, D.C.: World Bank, 1988–89).

Figure 7–5. *Third World Debt, 1973–1990*

The fundamental problem is that the simple mechanics of the lending process demonstrate that any situation that involves a regular annual amount of borrowing and a conventional repayment schedule will soon lead to a situation in which the debt servicing (the interest and the amortization) will exceed the annual amount of new loans. This process will soon lead to a reverse capital flow (a flow of capital from the capital-poor nations to the

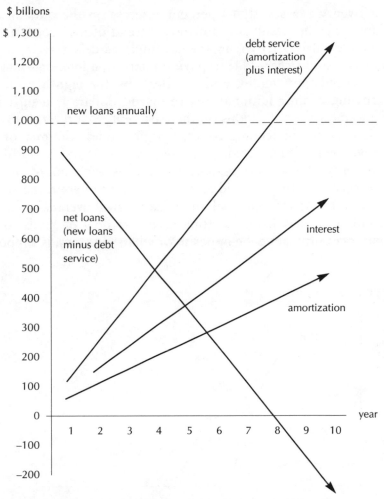

Source: *Monthly Review* (April 1985).

Note: Net capital flow if $1,000 is borrowed each year at 10 percent interest for twenty years.

Figure 7–6. *The Debt Trap*

capital-rich), which, of course, is the opposite of what one would presume was the desired effect.

This process is shown in figure 7–6, which is a hypothetical example. Assume that each year a country obtains a new foreign loan of one thousand dollars to be repaid in equal installments over twenty years with 10 percent interest on the outstanding balance. The net result is a downward trend of net proceeds (the amount left over after paying the accumulated debt service, which gets larger and larger—due to paying interest on interest—making net proceeds get smaller and smaller). By the eighth year, the borrowing of an additional one thousand dollars is insufficient even to meet the obligations on the past debt, so a reverse flow of funds back to the lending country begins unless the rate of the new borrowing is increased.

So, any time a country borrows a constant amount of new funds each year to be repaid at a given rate of interest, the return flow of interest and principal amortization will eventually exceed the inflow of new loans, creating a *reverse* flow of funds to the creditor country, quite the opposite of what, in theory, is supposed

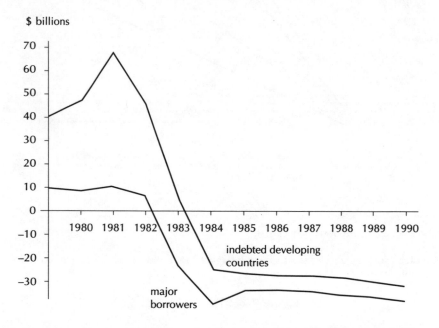

Source: Harold Lever and Christopher Huhne, *Debt and Danger: The World Financial Crisis* (New York: Atlantic Monthly Press, 1986) and authors' estimates.

Figure 7–7. *The Resource Transfer, 1979–1990*

to happen. How long this takes depends on how high the rate of interest is, but in the case of Latin America, for one example, it was about twenty years.

The net inflow of loan funds to the developing countries was increasing until 1981, when it started to decrease (figure 7–7). By 1983 the reverse flow had begun and the creditor countries were receiving more than they were lending. The "development" loan process was causing a net drain of capital from the debtor countries.

The key factor in determining the viability of such a loan-based development strategy is the percentage of total export revenues that a country must commit to debt servicing. If export earnings are increasing faster than the flow of debt service then—by this measure at least—the program is viable. In this context a look at the data is revealing.

Debt service as a percentage of export revenues was 16 percent in 1980, but grew to almost 23 percent by 1984 (table 7–3). This is in a period in which Third World exports have been increasing—in an effort to service the debt—while imports have been pared to the lowest possible level. This has had two effects, both of which are becoming increasingly serious and, at the least, illustrate the senselessness of the entire process.

Table 7–3
Debt and Financial Flows in Developing Countries, 1980–1987
(U.S. billions)

	1981	1982	1983	1984	1985	1986	1987
Debt disbursed and outstanding	$498.0	$556.9	$639.4	$713.8	$783.6	$870.7	$930.5
Disbursements	124.3	116.6	99.1	92.3	88.7	85.7	90.0
(from private creditors)	91.4	84.2	66.5	58.6	57.3	47.5	49.0
Debt service	89.1	98.7	92.1	99.7	109.5	116.4	119.0
Principal repayments	47.5	49.7	44.7	46.8	54.8	60.8	64.0
Interest	41.7	48.9	47.2	52.8	54.7	55.6	55.0
Net transfers	35.2	17.8	7.1	−7.3	−20.8	−30.7	−29.0

Source: World Bank, *World Debt Tables, I* (Washington, D.C.: World Bank, 1988).

Note: The 109 countries reporting under the Debtor Reporting System (DRS). Data for Poland are included only from 1984 onward.

Exports and Imports: A Two-way Street

One way for a country to service increasing debt obligations is for it to increase exports. In an era of falling commodity prices and, especially, declining oil prices this has not generally been a feasible strategy. Third World exports to the industrialized nations did increase during the 1980s, bringing about some improvement in developing countries current account situation. This is shown in table 7–4. But most of the improvement, if that's what it can be called, came not from increases in exports but from *decreases* in imports.

The net effect of this is that badly needed replacement parts, equipment, and new technology have not been available. So, economic growth in most Third World countries has come to a halt, if not become negative. This, coupled with high rates of population growth, has meant that already low standards of living in most of the debtor countries have declined precipitously. The standard of living in Mexico, to take just one example, has fallen to where it was in 1967, causing much human suffering, not to mention political unrest.

The other side of that coin is even more ironic. Third World imports are the exports of the industrialized world (table 7–5). In the United States the loss of exports to Latin America alone accounted (in 1987) for about 25 percent of the U.S. trade deficit.

Table 7–4
Third World Debtor Countries' Trade Balance, 1975–1986

(U.S. millions)

Year	Exports	Imports	Trade Balance
1975	$171,757	$224,343	–$52,586
1980	447,196	550,108	–102,912
1981	470,415	602,047	–131,632
1982	440,839	569,760	–128,921
1983	434,393	521,815	–87,422
1984	471,571	533,843	–62,272
1985	463,018	540,613	–77,595
1986	450,235	529,215	–78,980

Source: World Bank, *World Debt Tables, I* (Washington, D.C.: World Bank, 1988).

Table 7–5

Highly Indebted Countries, GDP Exports:Imports, 1980–1987

(% real increase or decrease)

Year	GDP	Exports	Imports
1980	5.7	3.8	10.9
1981	0.4	−1.1	6.1
1982	−0.6	−5.0	−14.3
1983	−2.9	1.7	−20.2
1984	2.3	12.3	−2.4
1985	2.9	−0.5	0.1
1986	2.9	−2.7	−0.7
1987	2.4	1.5	−0.9

Source: World Bank, *World Debt Tables, I* (Washington, D.C.: World Bank, 1988).

That translated into the loss of about 1 million export-related jobs, or about 13 percent of the U.S. unemployment rate. So, simply to perpetuate the myth that the international banking system is functioning, *both* the industrialized world *and* the Third World are paying a very high price. It is a senseless cycle, a treadmill from which nobody can get off.

Banks and U.S. Government Policy

In the early years of the crisis, from 1980 until 1986, the policy of the U.S. money-center banks was to continue lending more and more money to the debtor countries to allow them to service at least the interest on what they already owed. This, as all of the involved parties know, merely serves to compound and perpetuate a clearly unworkable situation.

The official U.S. government policy, which takes the form of the Baker Plan, is that both private bank and governmental loans should be continued on the condition that the debtor countries "restructure" their economies. This, in essence, means privatizing inefficient state-controlled industries and letting market forces operate more freely under the auspices of an IMF-approved austerity plan. IMF austerity plans typically involve cutting back inflation by keeping a tight rein on the money supply, reducing government expenditures, and instituting wage controls, all of which add up to a reduction in the standard of living.

Some of the larger debtor countries, such as Mexico and Argentina, have agreed to cooperate with the IMF and the commercial banks and new loan packages were arranged for them in 1986 and 1987, adding billions to their overall debt but temporarily forestalling a crisis. Others, notably Brazil and Peru, have balked at instituting austerity measures and have declared moratoriums or similar measures on even interest payments on their debts.

Brazil's recalcitrance prompted a major reassessment of the entire Third World debt problem by the commercial banks. As shown in table 7–6, many of the U.S. money-center banks were (in 1986) exposed in amounts far exceeding their capitalization.* Banks can carry such loans on their books as "performing" so long as interest payments are not more than ninety days in arrears. After that loans must be transferred to a "cash basis," and assets—or what are called assets—reduced accordingly. Faced with such a prospect and the possibility of a domino-like series of defaults in Latin America, Citicorp, the largest U.S. bank and the holder of almost $16 billion in Third World loans, unilaterally called Brazil's bluff and increased its reserves against loan losses by some $3 billion. In the process it took an accounting loss of $2.5 billion in the second quarter of 1987—the largest in U.S. banking history. The other large banks had no choice but to follow suit and by the summer of 1987 loan-loss reserves of the ten largest banks had been increased by $11 billion.

This unexpected action was the first time that the major banks had publicly acknowledged that the Third World debt situation was an "illusionary" game being played with mirrors, and it represents an important turning point in the history of the debt crisis.

The "get-tough" stance by the banks signaled the debtor countries that timely payments were going to have to be made or they would face the prospect of being cut out of badly needed

---

*That is, the amount they are owed far exceeds the total value of their shareholders' equity—the book value of their stock outstanding.

Table 7–6
Bank Loan Exposure to Developing Nations, 1986

(U.S. millions)

Bank	Assets	Total Third World Loans	Loans as a Percentage of Capital
Bank of New York	$ 20,709	$ 505	$ 40
BankAmerica	104,189	6,681	108
Bankers Trust	53,743	2,128	66
Chase Manhattan	94,766	6,700	125
Chemical	60,564	4,367	115
Citicorp	196,124	14,700	137
Continental Illinois	32,809	1,560	63
First Chicago	39,148	1,674	57
First Interstate	55,422	2,267	69
First Pennsylvania	5,888	537	104
Irving	24,233	1,416	111
J.P. Morgan	76,039	3,939	65
Manufacturers Hanover	74,397	7,505	157
Marine Midland	24,790	1,474	90
Mellon	33,406	898	45
Republic Bank of New York	16,814	570	34
Security Pacific	62,606	1,251	34
Wells Fargo	44,577	1,534	50

Source: Bear Stearns, *The Wall Street Journal*, July 14, 1987.

Note: Money-center banks whose loans to developing nations exceeded 33 percent of their capital—that is, equity plus reserves for losses on loans—at the end of 1986.

trade credits. The banks, by increasing their reserves against losses, were saying that they were ready to "take the hit" if necessary. The markets, knowing that Third World debt was already selling at about 55 percent of stated value, generally perceived this move as prudent banking and, indeed, the bank's stock value increased in spite of huge losses.

But the banks' get-tough attitude could easily become the straw that breaks the camel's back. The key point here is that the annual flow of new loans must equal or exceed the return flow of debt service. Otherwise, the debtor country simply slides backward, as has been happening since 1982. If the flow of new loans *stops altogether*, or is curtailed, the old loans, with debt servicing obligations, *are still there*. Under such circumstances any underdeveloped debtor economy will quickly collapse under the weight of payment obligations with no corresponding cash inflow.

Before the banks increased their loan-loss reserves, new loans to the fifteen debtor countries had fallen by $2.8 billion and governmental and international agency loans dropped to $6.6 billion in 1986, compared to an average of $13.8 billion in 1983 and 1984. Since there is no way any commercial bank can make a profit by making dubious, risky new loans while at the same time increasing its loan-loss reserves, it is highly unlikely the flow of new funds to the underdeveloped debtor countries will continue at anywhere near the levels of the early 1980s.

Brady Plan

One new development in this unfolding scenario came in 1989. At the initiative of the Bush administration's new Secretary of Treasury Nicholas Brady, the United States changed its stance toward the Third World debt problem. As we have seen, the Reagan administration's policy, known as the Baker Plan, had presumed that increasing bank loans to the debtor nations would eventually resolve the problem. But, in fact, it simply made the situation worse. Finally recognizing this, the Bush administration announced in the spring of 1989 that it would support a debt-relief plan that involved a desperate combination of new bank loans, exchanges of old loans for new long-term bonds, debt-equity swaps, and support from the United States, Japan, the IMF, and the World Bank.

Mexico, which was a "model debtor" in the sense that it had implemented a series of debt-related reforms, was chosen as the first test case. After six months of negotiations the numerous involved parties agreed in August of 1989 to an accord that generally fit the provisions of the Brady Plan. The debt-relief package covered $54 billion of the Mexican government's $70 billion long- and medium-term bank debt.

Under the agreement the banks have the option of exchanging their old loans at a 35 percent discount for new thirty-year variable rate bonds, or they can exchange the loans at par value for thirty-year bonds at a fixed rate of 6.25 percent, which amounts to an interest rate reduction. In addition, if they so choose, the banks can continue making new loans to Mexico, which, in essence, means paying themselves interest as they have been doing in the past. Other facets include loans from Japan, the United States, the IMF, and the World Bank that will in essence be guarantees of the new long-term debt replacement bonds.

The accord was roundly criticized by many economists on the grounds that it was inadequate, in the same sense that even if all of the banks participate it will only result in a net reduction of $1.5 billion annually of Mexico's $9 billion interest obligations—or 15 percent. This means Mexico will continue to be a net transferrer of resources to the industrialized world—hardly a prescription for a revitalized growing Mexican economy.

Yet the first test of the Brady Plan was a significant development in the history of the Third World debt crisis. For the first time the industrialized world acknowledged that no real progress can ever be made unless the banks are willing to cooperate in genuine debt relief.

At this writing it remains to be seen if the Brady Plan will provide a framework for debt relief programs for the other debtor nations, many of which are in a much weaker position than Mexico and can hardly be considered "model debtors." So the specter of a large Third World debtor nation defaulting unilaterally on its debt still haunts the international financial community. In fact, if the other debtor countries begin to perceive that new funds are not likely to be forthcoming, and as political pressures mount to get off the debt treadmill, the likelihood of a unilateral default is becoming ever greater. If one *major* debtor country should repudiate its foreign debt, it is possible the others will follow. While the banks' recent loan-loss reserve increases would help soften the blow, the international financial system could not withstand such a shock without a major bailout from the governments of the industrialized countries.

If a default did occur, the effects on the U.S. economy would be devastating. No one has put it more eloquently than former Secretary of Treasury and White House Chief of Staff Donald Regan, who in testimony before a congressional committee said:

The American citizen has the right to ask why he or his government need to be concerned with debt problems abroad. With high unemployment at home, why should we be assisting other countries, rather than, say, reducing taxes or increasing spending domestically? Why should he care what happens to the international financial system?

One way to look at this question is to ask what the implications are for workers in Providence, Pascoag, or Woonsocket if foreign borrowers do not receive sufficient assistance to adjust in an orderly way. What if they are late in making interest payments to banks or can't pay principal, and loans become nonperforming or are written off as a loss?

If interest payments are more than ninety days late, the banks stop accruing them on their books; they suffer reduced profits and bear the costs of continued funding of the loan. Provisions may have to be made for loss, and as loans are actually written off, the capital of the bank is reduced.

This in turn reduces the banks' capital asset ratio, which forces banks to curtail lending to individual borrowers and lowers the overall total they can lend. The reduction in the amounts banks can lend will impact on the economy. So will the banks' reduced ability to make investments, which in everyday language includes the purchase of municipal bonds, which help to finance the operations of the communities where individual Americans work and live. Reduced ability to lend could also raise interest rates.

I want to make very clear, Mr. Chairman, that we are not talking here just about the big money-center banks and the multinational corporations. Well over 1,500 U.S. banks, or more than 10 percent of the total number of U.S. banks, have loaned money to Latin America alone. They range in size from over $100 billion in assets to about $100 million. Those banks are located in virtually every state, in virtually every Congressional district, and in virtually every community of any size in the country. Those loans, among other things, financed exports, exports that resulted in jobs, housing, and investment being maintained or created throughout the United States.

If the foreign borrowers are not able to service those loans, not only will U.S. banks not be able to continue lending abroad, they will have to severely curtail their lending in the United States. Let me illustrate this point as graphically as I can. A sound, well-run U.S. bank of $10 billion in assets—not all that large today—might have capital of $600 million. It is required by the regulators to maintain the ratio of at least $6 in capital to every $100 in assets. What happens if 10 percent, or $60 million of its capital, is eroded through foreign loan losses? It must contract its lending by $1 billion. Now realistically, the regulators will not force it to contract immediately, but they will force it to restrict its growth until its capital can be rebuilt.

The new result in either event is $1 billion in loans that can't be made in that community—20,000 home mortgages at $50,000 each that can't be financed, or 10,000 lines of credit to local businesses at $100,000 each that can't be extended.

And of course, this reduction in lending will have negative effects on financing of exports, imports, domestic investment, and production in individual cities and states around the United States, be it in shipping, tourist facilities, farming, or manufacturing. The impact will not only be on the banks—it will negatively affect the individual as well as the economic system as a whole. Higher unemployment and a reduction in economic activity, with all they entail for city, state, and federal budgets, would be a further result. None of this is in the interest of the U.S. citizen.[4]

So the United States has woven itself a complex, spider-like web in which it has now become entangled. The preeminence of the dollar as the international key currency and the privileges that went with it are now history. As shown in figure 7–8, the unplanned, and certainly unexpected, events of the past two decades are inextricably intertwined. The buildup of public and private debt in the United States makes it a prisoner of the international economy, dependent on the goodwill of the new creditor nations, most notably Japan.

Moreover, the apparent inability of U.S. industry to compete internationally and the continuing balance of trade deficits that do not respond to even massive dollar devaluations seem to indicate that a solution is not on the horizon. The interrelated Third World debt crisis, which exacerbates the trade crisis, and shows the vulnerability of the U.S. banking system to external shocks, has every indication of getting worse long before it gets better.

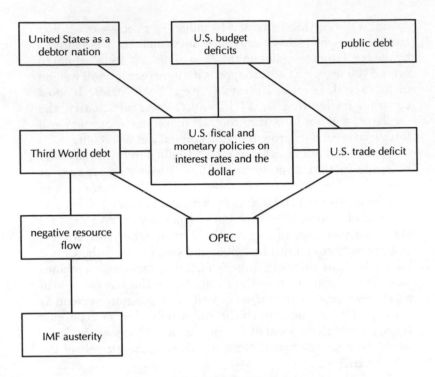

Figure 7–8. *The Triple Debt Crisis*

A triple debt crisis has evolved. U.S. international debt, U.S. external debt, and the Third World debt cannot be allowed to escalate much further, or else we can expect a dramatic shift in the balance of economic power. New, realistic policies are called for. The international financial system must be restructured to reflect the realities of the modern world. If it is not, we can expect a drastic reduction in standards of living.

This is not to say that there is a shortage of ideas about how to solve the problem, just that none will work unless they encompass the longer-run structural contradictions of the United States—once the dominant economic power in the world, able to make its own rules and now being reduced to the status of a debt-ridden country. There *are* solutions, but they will require sacrifices. Above all it is becoming obvious that the world economy cannot continue to function as it has in the past. Change will come. Whether it is planned and orderly, or unplanned and chaotic, is the question yet to be resolved.

Key Concepts

U. S. National Debt
Debt Compounding
Debt/GNP Ratio
Debtor Nation
Trade Deficit
Third World Debt Crisis
Net Resource Transfer
The Debt Trap
The Brady Plan

Discussion Questions

1. What, if anything, is wrong with being in debt?

2. The United States is in debt to the tune of almost $3 trillion. To whom does it owe all this money?

3. What, specifically, does it mean for a country to be a debtor nation?

4. How does a country get to be a creditor nation?

5. Let's assume that one of the large Third World countries decided it was going to unilaterally default—simply refuse to pay—on its foreign debt. What difference would that make to anybody? Who would be affected?

8
Reconstructing the International Financial System

For international trade to function there has to be some system upon which every participant agrees to make international exchange payments possible. As long as everyone agrees that *something* is universally acceptable *and* convertible into local currency, trade will take place to everyone's benefit. That "something" must perform all the traditional functions of money in any economy. It must be a medium of exchange for transactions, a store of value for reserves, and a unit of account, so people, businesses, and nations can keep track of what's going on and plan accordingly.

Taking the long view of history, we know that gold performed that function for many hundreds of years. But, as we have seen, by the end of World War II it was becoming obvious that gold was too cumbersome and limited in supply to perform its traditional role effectively. This was especially complicated by the fact that at that time the United States held most of the world's minted gold supply.

Another option, which was supported by many of the participants in the Bretton Woods conference, would have been to set up a world monetary authority with the power to issue a universally acceptable currency that could be used to settle international accounts. But such a system would have had all the restrictions and limitations of the gold system, and the United States, in particular, opposed it.

Another equally workable system is for the world to simply agree that one country's currency will be acceptable to all at an agreed-upon rate of exchange. Since the United States was the dominant economic power at the time, it was decided that the U.S. dollar would become the world's key international currency. This, as we saw in chapter 2, set the stage for an era of U.S. dominance of the world economy, *and* the stage for the present economic crisis and the eventual demise of the U.S. hegemony.

At first the system seemed to work well. The United States agreed to "peg" the value of the dollar to a set amount of gold—thirty-five dollars an ounce—and to redeem dollars held by foreign countries at that rate on demand. That meant, for all practical purposes, that the dollar was as "good as gold," universally acceptable for international transactions and suitable for foreign bank reserves. It also meant that the United States accepted responsibility for the smooth functioning of the international financial system, which, in essence, meant that the United States was agreeing to maintain the value of the dollar at a constant rate because no monetary system can function if its users don't know from day to day what the value of the key currency will be.

Also at the Bretton Woods Conference, the International Monetary Fund was established to monitor exchange rates within a narrow band (plus or minus one percent) *against the U.S. dollar.* Therefore, a system of international economic discipline was instituted that had all the trappings of the gold standard. If a country was running a balance of payments deficit, thereby causing a drop in the demand for its currency and a consequent drop in its value, it had no option but to institute appropriate *domestic* economic policies to correct the situation. This meant slowing down its rate of inflation at the cost of slower growth and higher unemployment or devaluing its currency, which under the rules of the game required permission of the U.S.-controlled International Monetary Fund.

Every country in the Western world was, therefore, subjected to the discipline of the international financial system *except* the *United States*, which had *carte blanche* to do whatever it wanted—like the eight-hundred-pound gorilla. So long as there was a strong demand for dollars (to pay for much-needed U.S. exports) and the United States had the gold to back them up, the system functioned smoothly for, in fact, about fifteen years. But, by the 1960s, as the war-torn economies of Western Europe and Japan began to recover (in large part because of reconstruction loans from the United States) and become major exporters in their own right, the situation began to change. The U.S. balance of payments surplus dwindled, while Japan and Western Europe, now operating with newer, more productive plants and equipment, began to run large surpluses, selling more to the United States than they were buying *and* accumulating large dollar balances in the process.

Collapse of the Bretton Woods System

By 1971 it had become obvious the United States no longer had the wherewithal, that is, the gold, to back the dollar. Dollar holdings abroad exceeded $70 billion, while the U.S. gold supply dwindled to around $10 billion, and it was clear the world's banker no longer had the reserves to make good on its claim that the dollar was "as good as gold" and in 1971 President Nixon cut the link between gold and the dollar. In December of that year the financial ministers of the Western world met in Washington and reluctantly agreed (the Smithsonian Agreement) that the world was now on a dollar system *with none of the traditional link to gold* and no disciplinary restraints on exchange-rate fluctuations.

The international financial system was now left to the vicissitudes of the forces of the free market. The new system was a free-flexible-floating exchange rate system but *the U.S. dollar was still the world's key international currency*. Put differently, the world economy became dependent on the U.S. economy for stability. The discipline of the gold standard and the Bretton Woods agreements had become history. The problem now was for the United States to discipline itself.

As long as the U.S. economy remained strong and stable there was no particular problem associated with this dramatic change in the rules of how international trade was to be conducted. If dollars are relatively constant in value and in demand they can function as a medium of international exchange as well as anything else. But while dollars continued to be in demand, their value did not remain constant. Several events, which, as we saw in the previous chapter, were largely unanticipated and certainly unexpected, occurred to change that.

Inflation Shocks

On the heels of the Smithsonian Agreement, the OPEC oil embargo and the subsequent fourfold increase in the price of oil by 1973 sent an inflationary shock throughout the U.S. economy. Under such conditions one would normally expect the exchange rate of the dollar to fall as U.S. exports become more expensive, but the OPEC countries demanded that payments for oil be made in U.S. dollars, thereby *increasing* the demand for the dollar worldwide, and at the same time, the recycling of petrodollars to the Third World increased demand for U.S. exports. The dollar became stronger even in the face of higher rates of inflation in the United States. By the time inflation rates peaked in the United States at over 10 percent in 1982, the dollar was still becoming stronger until it peaked in the fall of 1985. (See figure 8–1.)

As a result of this, and many other factors that we shall explore in the following chapter, the U.S. trade balance began to decline precipitously. The U.S. merchandise trade balance went from a deficit of $36 billion in 1982 to a $171 billion deficit in 1987. If, as we have said, a country is going to serve as the world's banker, it has to maintain some stability in its international accounts. If the United States runs a trade surplus, then as foreigners scramble for dollars to buy U.S. products, dollars are taken out of the world economy and international liquidity is reduced, among other things. But if the owner of the world's anchor lynchpin currency runs a consistent trade deficit then something else has to occur in the overall flow of international transactions to cover, that is, *pay for* the deficit, otherwise the value of the currency will fall. Interestingly, these

Source: *Economic Report of the President* (Washington, D.C.: Government Printing Office, 1989).

Index: 1980–1982 = 100.

Figure 8–1. *Index of the Dollar's Value against Fifteen Industrial Country Currencies*

offsetting transactions did occur as other countries continued to pour the dollars earned (from exports to the United States) back into the United States as foreign investment, which is another way of saying the United States borrowed the money to finance its trade deficit. This, as we saw in chapter 3, has caused the United States to move, in just a few years, from being the world's largest creditor nation to being the world's largest debtor, and has precipitated a crisis in the international financial system of unprecedented and seemingly unsolvable proportions.

And ironically, while the United States is the largest debtor nation, it still remains one of the largest creditors in the sense that it holds debts of the Third World—now generally acknowledged to be unrepayable. For the pillar of the world economy to be debtor and a creditor at the same time is clearly untenable over anybody's definition of the long run. Attempts to rectify the situation by devaluating the dollar by some 50 percent between 1985 and 1988 have failed as the U.S. trade deficit has continued at record-high levels. The dollar—the world's key currency—is being propped up by ad hoc intervention in the exchange markets. Clearly, the United States has lost control of its own economy—as debt is replaced by new debt at a compound rate—and most certainly it has lost control of the international economy.

Other factors, external to and clearly outside of U.S. control, have made it clear to most analysts that the world has changed in ways that no one would have expected at the time of the first Bretton Woods Conference. Most importantly, Japan has become the world's largest creditor nation, West Germany and much of Western Europe are not far behind, and gaining on them are the Newly Industrialized Countries of the Pacific Rim: Taiwan, South Korea, and others. This shift in the balance of economic power, which has occurred in only one decade, is unprecedented. All the rules, traditions, and structure of the dollar-based system are coming into question. All this has led an increasing number of observers to call for a new Bretton Woods Conference: a complete restructuring of the international financial system more in line with the reality of the modern world.

A New Bretton Woods?

There is general agreement that any new restructuring of the international financial system must address the problem of more equitable flows of trade and capital. This means, in essence, that the Third World debt problem must be addressed and resolved. Any system that does not resolve this problem will simply prolong and exacerbate the current crisis. There is less agreement, however, on how to go about it, although there is no shortage of suggestions.

The Case Against

There are also those who argue that there is no need for a new system because the current system already has in place mechanisms to correct the imbalance problem. The IMF, some argue, could initiate the necessary discussions and implement appropriate policies. But the IMF already holds annual conferences, and little seems to be accomplished. Indeed, many argue, the conservative policies of the IMF, which attempt to correct exchange rate distortions through "conditional" loans, have been one of the primary causes of the problem.

Others argue that the current problems could easily be resolved if the United States would only put in place appropriate monetary and fiscal policies to end inflation and lower interest rates, but that has already happened over the past several years and the overall situation has simply worsened.

A related argument is that a restructuring of the international financial system is almost certain to be opposed by any U.S. administration, and that, therefore, even thinking about it is a waste of everybody's time. But, like it or not, the crisis has reached such proportions and the trends are so troubling that soon there will be no choice. The question is whether the process will be planned and orderly or forced and chaotic.

As Morris Miller, former executive director of the World Bank, has put it in an insightful analysis of the problem:

> It matters whether the movement toward a new Bretton Woods is made by design or forced by events. The preferred method is to be guided by forethought and design, but even the second-best route to the destination may suffice—if we don't fall off the figurative cliff in the meantime. Once the current debt crisis is seen as an integral part of a deep-seated transformation of the global economic and financial system, the door is open to considering policy approaches that have the breadth and depth commensurate to the problem.[1]

There is a growing recognition that a turning point requiring a series of hard choices is imminent. There is, however, less recognition that the profound changes wrought over the past four decades are of a structural nature both in terms of 1) how trade and finance are handled and the size and direction of these flows, and 2) the ability of the United States to take on the type of leadership responsibilities that were assumed at Bretton Woods and the necessity of sharing such leadership with Japan and other nations.

Under such conditions it is not surprising that, in light of the present instability of the international financial system, there are increasing calls for a new system based on something more stable than the U.S. dollar, which is now out of control, literally and figuratively. Even such staid observers of the international scene as former Secretary of State Henry Kissinger have taken up the cause:

> The biggest politico-economic challenge to statesmen is to integrate national policies into a global perspective, to resolve the discordance between the international economy and the political system based on the nation state . . . The spirit that produced Bretton Woods reflected the realization that in the long run the national welfare can only be safeguarded within the framework of the general welfare. . . . In (today's) circumstances the international economic system operates—if at all—as crisis management. The risk is, of course, that some day crisis management may be inadequate. The world will then face a disaster its lack of foresight has made inevitable. . . . My major point is that the world needs new arrangements.[2]

Put in this context, the rationale for international monetary reform seems overwhelming because first, no system of policy coordination exists to replace the declining U.S. leadership role, second, there is no "early warning" system to signal impending crisis and no adequate response mechanism to cope with crises when they do occur, and third, there is no control mechanism over the mobility of capital. Foreign exchange transactions now conducted instantaneously by computer-links now amount to more than *$200 billion a day.*[3]

So the agenda for a new Bretton Woods is a long one, and the issues are pressing to the point of urgency. As the stock market crash on October 19, 1987—"Black Monday"—dramatically demonstrated, the financial system cannot function efficiently in such a volatile climate.

Agenda for a New Bretton Woods

Those who favor a new Bretton Woods Conference argue that it should not be held in a climate of panic, that it should not be held without considerable prior preparation, and that it should not attempt to map out a plan for what might be done in the future. Rather, they suggest, it must address the fundamental structural imbalances that are disrupting the present outmoded system.

In *Toward World Prosperity,* a penetrating book on the topic, Irving Friedman has suggested that there are six basic issues that must be included in a new Bretton Woods Conference if it is to be successful.

First, a new financial system must be developed that will provide the framework for world prosperity, sustained growth and structural change. Such a system, he argues, must above all protect the developing countries from the continuing and worsening levels of high unemployment, low growth rates, and inadequate rates of saving.

Second, a system of exchange rates must be established that is realistic, equitable, and stable. Many of the present problems have come from the continual roller-coaster-like movements of the dollar from strong to weak, weak to strong, a process that has disrupted the smooth functioning of the system and that has helped no one and generated unnecessary instability and uncertainty.

Third, the whole process of international capital movements must be reexamined. Capital is supposed to move from the more industrialized world to the underdeveloped countries. Instead, as we have discussed earlier, the opposite has occurred. If the system is ever to regain stability this must be corrected. Is it feasible, Friedman asks, for a code of international behavior in this area to be established? If so, who would administer it?

Fourth, something has to be done to stop worldwide inflation, which has reached epidemic proportions in the underdeveloped countries and is a persistent problem in the industrialized world as well. No one knows how to stop inflation without at the same time slowing economic growth and increasing unemployment, a bitter pill that few nations are willing to swallow. Is it feasible, he asks, that exchange rate adjustments could be tied to inflation rates in a more formal manner, perhaps administered by the International Monetary Fund?

Fifth, Friedman asks, "Do the existing governmental rules and practices serve world business, which has become interdependent and integrated to a degree that represents a quantum change from the past? . . .

"Interdependence and global integration have created a world in which nations and their businesses have lost their freedom of action, however, reluctantly and angrily. The linkages of world markets . . . mean new definitions of what is national, what is meant by national interest, and what is meant by unfair national competitive practices."

Finally, he asks, "Is the international financial system suited to a world that has become very different because of the miracles of modern technology?"[4]

The Major Question: Policy Coordination

Any restructuring of the international financial system must be considered in the context of overall *policy coordination* between the major industrial powers and between them and the less-developed countries—which include *80 percent* of the world's population, some 4 billion people.

The present system gives only lip service to policy coordination, while each of the industrial powers continues "beggar-thy-neighbor" policies of studied self-interest that do not have long-run viability.

In a sense there *has* been an international economic policy in place since 1980, a policy of no policy. The theoretical rationale of the Reagan administration has been that capitalism functions best when it is left alone—to the free market. When it became clear in 1985 that *laissez-faire* economics didn't always work to everyone's advantage, especially that of the United States, haphazard intervention in the exchange markets became the "policy" that pushed the dollar down by some 50 percent against the currencies of the major U.S. trading partners. That move produced virtually no results as the U.S. trade deficit hovered at levels over $150 billion two years after the intervention. And "policy coordination," which is simply another way of saying international economic planning, became the buzzword in Washington and in the financial press.

For international policy coordination to have any long-run effect three key questions have to be addressed. First, trade imbalances must be resolved or, at least, financed in an orderly manner. Second, exchange rates must be stabilized and anchored to *something* that provides stability as well as coordinated flexibility. Third, capital flows must be redirected so that they produce growth rather than engender long-run stagnation. In addition, and directly related to the problem of capital flows, the Third World debt crisis must be resolved. Until that happens, talk of a new Bretton Woods Conference and policy coordination will ring as hollow as the rhetoric of laissez-faire.

Coordination and Trade

The issues that must be addressed at a new Bretton Woods Conference fall into three major interrelated categories: trade imbalance, a workable system of exchange rate adjustment, and capital flows, that is, in the present reality, the still unresolved Third World debt question. The latter two are subsets of the overall trade question.

As long as the United States continues to run record-high trade deficits and, essentially, exchange those deficits for recycled paper IOUs, the international financial system will continue to be dangerously fragile *and* the United States will pay the price, as will the Third World debtor countries. The problem could perhaps be resolved by some combination of increasing U.S. manufacturing productivity, that is, restoring the U.S. "competitive position" and/or devising some way to induce reluctant Japan and West Germany (and others) to stimulate their economies to the extent that they could absorb more U.S. exports, or by somehow convincing U.S. consumers to reduce the level of consumption of imported products.

But while there are indications that U.S. productivity is improving, there is little evidence—as we have seen—that the trade imbalance, which is also *gradually* improving, will reverse itself to the extent that it would make any *real* difference in the foreseeable future. A new Bretton Woods Conference can't dictate to American consumers, it can't tell U.S. industry to be more productive, and certainly it can't tell Japanese, European, South Korean, and Taiwanese manufacturers to stop trying to sell their products abroad. Therefore the burden falls on some sort of agreement that will stabilize exchange rates at levels consistent with trade equilibrium, and on some sort of agreement to normalize capital flows, at least to the extent that funds begin flowing *from* the industrialized world to the developing world, instead of the reverse, as is happening now. There are many proposals to modify the exchange rate system and to rectify the Third World debt problem. Some are viable; some, in the current political climate, are not. Whether any kind of change in the exchange rate system would be sufficient to resolve the overall problem of imbalance and inequality in the international arena remains to be seen.

Exchange Rate Problem

As we have already seen, the Reagan administration allowed the value of the dollar to decline in an effort to make U.S. exports more competitive and imports more expensive (see figure 8–1). This strategy has been somewhat less than successful. Even though the dollar declined as much as 40 percent against the yen and deutsche mark, the U.S. merchandise trade deficit for 1987 was a record $171.2 billion. The dollar decline did generate a significant 20 percent increase in manufacturing exports; yet, the U.S. appetite for the even more expensive imports continued unabated.

Several prominent economists, including former chairman of the Council of Economic Advisors Martin Feldstein, have proposed that the dollar should be allowed to fall further.[5] This position suggested that the bottom had not yet been reached. But the Reagan administration was cautious about letting the dollar sink too low, too fast, given the need to finance the federal deficit and maintain interest rates at levels high enough to keep attracting foreign money. So one of two things has happened. Either there is something wrong with the economic theory guiding exchange rate policy or there are structural factors at work in the economy thwarting exchange rate policy. In any case, it is clear that, as Professor Paul Krugman, an international economist at the Massachusetts Institute of Technology, has pointed out, "The U.S. trade balance has shown less turnaround than anyone's model predicted." In theory the decline of the dollar since 1985 should have resulted in a reversal of export and import prices. But instead much less of the yen and deutsche mark appreciation has been passed through to the American consumer in the form of higher import prices than was expected. This explains the high level of imports and the continued high trade deficit. The trade-weighted-dollar has declined 28.8 percent since 1985 while import prices have increased only 18.8 percent.

Many economists have attempted to explain the lack of success of the U.S. exchange rate policy in terms of the J-curve. The J-curve theory, as we saw earlier, argues that at first there will be a rise in the trade deficit after the dollar declines because consumers only slowly adjust to the higher priced imports. After consumers adjust to the new prices of imports, a reduction in imports will occur as exports are expanding and the trade deficit will begin to decline. But this has not been the case. Although there have been some improvements in the U.S. trade deficit, the failure of the J-curve theory continues to be an enigma, and there is no simple explanation.

By the mid-1980s, foreign producers had successfully held down their export prices despite the enormous changes in currency values prompted by the U.S. devaluation of the dollar. So, the relative prices of imports and domestic products did not change significantly. This limited the predicted benefits of a cheaper dollar. What appears to have happened is that foreign companies, especially Japanese firms, are more adept at "pricing to the market"—that is to say, adjusting to competitive conditions, than anyone expected. U.S. firms seem to be less successful in adjusting pricing policies to market conditions changed by currency value shifts.

How do foreign companies manage to hold down export prices in the face of a declining dollar? Or, put differently, why are U.S. firms unable to price to the market? Harvard economist Jeffrey Sachs has argued and demonstrated that the focus on the dollar itself is allowing for a misdirected policy. His argument is that the dollar strategy, which largely is based upon monetary policy—that is, the manipulation of interest rates—is wrong. It is, he argues, ill-conceived because it does not address the reality of the U.S. budget deficits and the relationship of these deficits to the trade deficit. Sachs maintains that the low interest rates required to encourage the decline of the dollar also encourage consumer spending and demand for imports. In addition, the existence of budget deficits (in the vicinity of $160 billion a year) stimulates consumer demand for imports because discretionary income is larger than it would be if taxes were increased or spending decreased in an attempt to reduce the budget deficits. So, both lower interest rates and budget deficits drive the seemingly insatiable demand for imports on the part of American consumers in spite of the falling dollar.

There are, in addition, other factors behind the lack of success of the dollar devaluation strategy, which help explain why the prices of imported goods have not followed the appreciation of the yen and deutsche mark. Economist Robert Kuttner has identified five major explanations.

To begin with, he argues, most raw materials are priced in dollars. Therefore, a 70 percent decline in the dollar also means a 70 percent decline in the cost of oil, iron ore, chemical feedstocks, and other commodities. This, he suggests, substantially offsets the effect of the higher exchange rate on the price of finished products.

Second, all currencies have not appreciated against the dollar. Both American and Japanese producers have increasingly moved production to cheap-currency, low-wage countries like Korea, Taiwan, Singapore, China, and Mexico.

Third, capital costs are far lower in Japan and Germany than in the United States. This means that a Japanese firm can cut profit margins to hold the line on prices, and still make acceptable returns.

Fourth, many foreign producers did not pass along the full savings to United States customers when the dollar was expensive, so they had a substantial cushion to absorb anticipated price increases as the dollar got cheaper.

Finally, he points out, a large share of imports today are marketed in the United States. by American retailers or wholesalers, who often share the foreign producer's interest in holding down the price.[6]

These factors make it clear that the decline of the dollar will not *automatically* reduce the trade deficit. They mean, among other things, that the present one-dimensional policy approach will only result in a decline in the standard of living of U.S. citizens as the cost of imports increases and inflation follows. The gradual resurgence in U.S. exports, while a positive factor, is tempered by the fact that continued export growth is held captive by the continued growth of other advanced industrial nations' export capacity and by the decrease in the demand for U.S. exports by developing nations because of their inability to maintain growth rates and export earnings sufficient to service their debt and at the same time buy more U.S. exports. In addition, a U.S. recession, when it comes, would exacerbate all these issues.

To further complicate this situation, the global economy is suffering from excess capacity, especially for export-oriented goods like steel and automobiles. There is also the problem that many U.S. firms that successfully adapted to the new competitive environment of the 1980s now find themselves so "lean" they are unable to increase output without higher costs or having to expand their capacity. So it is unlikely they will be inclined to rapidly expand capacity in the short run to take advantage of what may be only a temporary increase in demand in the face of a potential global recession in the early 1990s. Also, there is the problem that many firms fully dismantled their marketing net-works when the dollar was strong and are unable to respond swiftly to the new, more competitive conditions. Lastly, there is the maze of regulations peculiar to every nation in this interdependent global economy. Such regulations make doing business more difficult and time-consuming, thus slowing down any rapid response to changing currency swings. Faced with this set of realities and uncertainties, it is virtually impossible for firms to make decisions about whether to expand capacity at all or where to add it in the face of increasing global production.

To conclude, it seems clear that the weaker dollar in itself will not cure the trade deficit. Deborah Allen Olivier, president of Clarement Economics Institute, has argued that "the dollar's plunge against a few key currencies is not and cannot be a broad program of relief from foreign competition. Rather, it is a highly specific and narrow subsidy that will provide only limited help to a few producers." She asserts that the trade balance will be restored only when U.S. industries regain international competitiveness through increased productivity and greater efficiency.[7] Also, economist Michael Hudson has pointed out that the benefits of a cheap dollar are limited. He has maintained that "the really important variables in the comparative trade advantages of countries are their labor costs, interest rates, and tax obligations." Hudson argues that as automation becomes more and more widespread, production will depend more on capital and financing and less on the cost of labor. The problem, he says, with policy makers is that they ignore these realities and choose to concen-trate instead on relative currency values, which are of secondary importance, and, we would add, only a temporary, short-run solution.[8]

The crucial question now becomes: given the seemingly inherent limitations of the declining dollar strategy (currency devaluation) of the United States and the other G-7 countries, is there a workable strategy for the coordination of exchange rates among the G-7 countries that would resolve the problem of trade imbalance?

Exchange Rate Coordination

The one significant thing to come out of the Tokyo Summit of 1986 was a tacit agreement among the G-7 countries to construct an indicator system to help guide the international coordination of macroeconomic policies. This agreement was informal and voluntary, but it was a step toward a mechanism to set target zones for exchange rates.

While the Louvre Accord negotiated in February of 1987 called for the further development of and a commitment to such an indicator system, it become readily apparent that what was really needed was a more formal mechanism by which to establish agreed-upon parameters (target zones) between which exchange rates could fluctuate.

Since the Plaza Agreement in 1985, the G-7 nations have engaged in a form of international exchange rate coordination that has been largely based upon interventionist actions on the part of central banks, rather than on a systematic assessment of domestic macroeconomic policy coordination. For the United States, international monetary policy has essentially involved direct intervention in exchange markets by the Federal Reserve and the manipulation of interest rates to control the decline of the U.S. dollar.

Thus, as we have seen, the dollar debate has been reduced to a discussion of how low the dollar should be allowed to fall, how fast, and how far. But, at the same time, the dollar has been held hostage by the trade deficit and the budget deficit.

The lesson of all this is that it is vital to understand that any reconstruction of the international monetary system will of necessity require a formal method and system for setting and maintaining stability in foreign exchange markets. This means going beyond discretionary interventionism and monetary policy. This policy, for example, forced foreign central banks to buy $115 billion (net) between November 1986 and November 1987. These were, in essence, unwanted dollars that in reality represented loans to the U.S. Treasury to finance the U.S. deficit. This, as Paul Farba, a columnist for *Le Monde,* has argued, is a hidden danger of such currency cooperation because it indirectly fuels U.S. consumers' purchasing power to buy imports and does not contribute to a systematic or structural solution to the continued instability of exchange rates.[9]

As part of a newly conceived international monetary system, it will be necessary to go beyond informal indicators and loose policy coordination. Several such systems have been proposed.

Proposals for Exchange Rate Coordination

Ronald I. McKinnon, an economist from Stanford, has for years been proposing versions of a basic model for currency cooperation. He argues that a trade deficit is not a monetary phenomenon. Instead, he says, it simply indicates that an economy is saving too little or investing too much. In the case of the United States, he (as have many others) identifies the problem as being too large a federal deficit.

For McKinnon the central question is one of being able to establish exchange rates without having to drive the dollar up and down with monetary policy. Therefore, he proposes that the Western world adopt a system of *purchasing power parity* (PPP) as a theoretical guide for central banks and financial markets. Such a "benchmark" would allow for the calculation of nominal exchange rates that would align national price levels of internationally tradable goods as measured by Producer Price Indexes. These exchange rates—within narrow bands—would serve as the official exchange rate target range for governments.

Under such a scheme, international trade and mutual monetary adjustment would ensure convergence to the same rate of commodity price inflation. Eventually, McKinnon argues, tradable goods prices would then be aligned and relative growth in national money claims would reflect differentials in productivity growth.

How would such a system be coordinated? McKinnon suggests that the country with a weak currency would slow its domestic money growth, if necessary raising short-term interest rates relative to those abroad, while monetary policy in the strong currency market became more expansionary. Thus, the aggregate money stock remains unchanged.

While the mechanics of a system such as McKinnon has proposed are certainly more complicated than spelled out here, it is clear that such a system could be implemented without great difficulty *if* a general agreement could be reached.[10]

Another similar proposal has been developed by John Williamson, an economist with the Institute for International

Economics. His proposal calls for the establishment of international macroeconomic policy coordination in a manner that transcends anything the G-7 countries have done to date.

The primary goal of international policy coordination is, of course, to maintain as high a level of economic growth as possible while avoiding excessive inflation and disruptive destabilizing financial disequilibrium—especially excessive trade and budget deficits.

The Williamson proposal calls for the determination of target zones for exchange rates for each of the major G-7 countries. Such target zones would be mutually consistent with the internal domestic policies of each country. The basic policy objectives of increasing growth, lowering inflation, increasing employment, and balancing payments would of necessity have to reflect normal timing lags.

To successfully implement such a program, it would be necessary to set targets for exchange rates and the rate of growth of nominal domestic demand. The exchange rate, which is the central determinant of the division of demand between domestic and foreign sources, and of supply between domestic and foreign markets is, he argues, the central determinant of the current account. Thus, to have a target for the current account means having a target for the exchange rate. Such a target must also focus on the real effective exchange rate because it is this rate that is most relevant to competitiveness and the balance of payments. According to Williamson, such a target would be the fundamental equilibrium exchange rate (FEER), defined as the rate "which is expected to generate a current account surplus or deficit equal to the underlying capital flow over the cycle."

To implement such a scheme, it is necessary to convert a target for the real exchange rate into one for the inflation-adjusted exchange rate, which is a technical exercise. Following this, the need for intervention is eliminated and monetary policy can adequately adjust misalignment if the exchange rate moves out of the agreed-upon zone by a margin of 10 percent. For the purposes of making policy, this would require managing interest rates and overall fiscal policy in each country to achieve the targets for a set of growth rates of nominal domestic demand and (mutually consistent) real effective exchange rates.

To accomplish these objectives, Williamson proposes that all participants would have to agree to modify their monetary and fiscal policies according to the following principles:

1. The average level of world (real) short-term interest rates should be revised up (down) if aggregate growth of nominal income is threatening to exceed (fall short of) the sum of the target growth of nominal demand for the participating countries.

2. Differences in short-term interest rates among countries should be revised when necessary to supplement intervention in the exchange markets to prevent the deviation of currencies from their target ranges.

3. National fiscal policies should be revised with a view to achieving national target rates of growth of domestic demand.[11]

The proponents of such an approach to the coordination of exchange rates have used simulations of such policies for the G-7 countries to demonstrate that if such an indicator system had been adopted between 1980 and 1987 the instability experienced would have been essentially eliminated.

It is important to note that all efforts designed to expand and implement mechanisms for exchange rate coordination and overall international economic cooperation *assume* that the participants will be willing to sacrifice some measure of national sovereignty.

A World European Monetary System?

Experts such as France's Minister of Finance, Edouard Balladur, have proposed that a world version of the European Monetary System (EMS) might provide a guide to the future.[12] Such a model would, as the EMS does, provide for automatic trigger mechanisms and appropriate sanctions. An EMS model would require a monetary reference unit that would be determined by a weighted average of international currencies that would serve as the standard for such a new system. Under such a system, each nation would be required to adhere to margins of fluctuations set around the target rate defined for each currency. Thus, each central bank would have to be prepared to intervene in exchange markets to ensure that its currency did not exceed its limits.

The obligation to intervene to maintain the value of its currency would force each country's central bank to either spend its reserves or to borrow from its trading partners when necessary. These required changes in reserves would be an indirect sanction. If it were necessary to fundamentally redefine the current currency standard (parity realignment), this could occur only with the mutual consent of all.

The all-important difference between such a system and the old Bretton Woods arrangement is that the beleaguered U.S. dollar—now the world's key currency—would be replaced by a world currency. Thus, the redefinition of the role of the U.S. dollar is one of the most important considerations related to the reconstruction of the international monetary system. Hence, it should be among the top priorities at a new Bretton Woods Conference.

The eventual resolution of the crisis of imbalance will require that, in addition to the basic areas of trade and exchange rates, the problem of Third World external debt must be confronted. The central challenge here is to devise an approach that offers genuine debt relief to the overindebted nations, while allowing for the growth and stability of the world economy simultaneously. This is a tall order, but not impossible.

Third World Debt Relief

By 1987 the external liabilities of developing countries had reached over $1.3 trillion dollars. As we have seen in previous chapters, by the early 1980s the problem (especially for the major debtors) had become a debt-service burden that resulted in the net transfer of capital *from* the debtor countries *to* the creditor countries. This reverse capital flow has made it virtually impossible for nations to find the resources necessary to promote balanced domestic economic growth. The need to service debt has forced the debtor nations into transforming their economies into open-export oriented economies with increased emphasis on market solutions for their economic problems. This adjustment and restructuring, which under current arrangements seems necessary, has not been without serious consequences. Third World standards of living have steadily declined even though, on the surface, balance of trade conditions appear to have improved.

While the Bush administration's commitment to the Brady Plan appears to be unwaivering, many experts view it as having been unsuccessful and insufficient. Critics maintain that the Third World debt problem is one of structural overindebtedness—that is, a long-run solvency problem rather than a short-run problem. Virtually all the private commercial banks seem to agree, since they have in recent years drastically reduced the level of new loans to debtor nations. (See table 8–1.) It is also clear that they have begun to recognize that they need to prepare for the time when they will have to accept large losses because the loans will never be paid back. In anticipation, many banks have increased their loan-loss reserves, money set aside to cover potential losses on their Third World loans. Higher loan-loss reserves will enable the banks to reduce their total debt exposure to levels that are more realistic in terms of potential repayment. (See table 8–2.) Such

Table 8–1
Debt Relief and New Loans, 1980–1987
(billions of U.S. dollars)

Debt Relief	January 1980– September 1987	1983	1984	1985	1986	1987 (through September)
Debt restructuring bank	321.4	43.8	87.0	22.9	72.4	84.1
Official creditors	68.4	8.9	4.1	16.4	13.6	18.8
Total	389.8	52.7	91.1	39.3	86.0	102.9
New long-term money disbursed	42.2	13.0	10.4	5.3	2.7	9.5
Concerted short-term credit facilities	36.2	29.4	34.9	32.0	31.5	31.1

Source: World Bank, *World Debt Tables, I* (Washington, D.C.: World Bank, 1988), p. 22.

Table 8–2

Big Lenders to Developing Countries

(billions)

	Loans to LDCs	Added to Loss Reserves	1987 Earnings (Loss)	1986 Earnings (Loss)
Citibank	$15.59	$3.0	$1.06	($1.00)
BankAmerica	10.00	1.1	(0.52)	(0.75)
Manufacturers	8.4	1.7	0.41	(1.05)
Chase	8.7	1.6	0.59	(0.85)
J.P. Morgan	6.0[a]	[b]	0.87[a]	0.92[a]
Chemical	5.9	1.1	0.40	(0.71)
Bankers Trust	4.0	0.7	0.43	(0.18)
First Chicago	2.8	0.8	0.28	(0.44)
Security Pacific	1.9	0.5	0.39	0.15
Wells Fargo	1.9	[b]	0.27	0.33[a]
First Interstate	1.6	0.75	0.34	(0.20)

Source: Morgan Guaranty & Trust Company, 1987.

[a] Estimated.
[b] Nothing added so far in 1987.

losses will inevitably reduce bank equity and capital base. This eventually will be reflected in the bank stock prices and profits.

Viewing the developing-country debt problem as a solvency problem means seriously considering ways in which it is possible to develop a solution that produces concessionary debt relief. Debt relief requires that debt-servicing requirements be significantly reduced so that debtor countries can again begin to generate a positive capital inflow from the advanced creditor nations. Such flows are vital if the debtor nations are to have any chance of developing balanced sustainable economic growth and improvements in their standards of living, which are now sliding backward.

There are numerous debt-relief proposals. Most, however, involve at least one or some combination of the following five categories:

1. Canceling part of the debt or declaring a moratorium on payments for a stipulated period of time.

2. Subsidizing interest rates or in some manner reducing real interest rates.

3. Capping interest rates on variable rate loans or issuing variable maturity loans that become operative when the interest rate exceeds some predetermined limit set in relationship to measurable indicators such as the debt-service/export ratio.

4. Capping the percentage of export earnings to be devoted to servicing foreign debt, or

5. Enabling developing nations to convert part of their short- and medium-term debts into longer-term obligations.

One of the more imaginative plans has been detailed by Morris Miller in *Coping Is Not Enough*.[13] He argues for a comprehensive debt policy that would guarantee debt relief by the rescheduling of principal payments, coupled with reductions in real interest rates, so that the overall debt-servicing burden is significantly reduced.

Miller, however, emphasizes that while significantly reducing the debt-servicing burden is vital, it alone is not enough. It is, as well, necessary for net capital to flow to the debtor nations. The unlikelihood that this will occur through an expansion of private commercial bank loans, he feels, requires that the World Bank increase its capital resources available for debtor nations and additionally liberalize the conditions of the World Bank's structural adjustment loans. Miller also wants to see the International Monetary Fund support debtor nation domestic economic policies that are growth oriented as opposed to austerity driven. John Loxley, in *Debt and Disorder: External Financing for Development*, has detailed how such an approach might work:

> [In summary, such a] . . . policy package would be tailored to the specific structural characteristics of the economy in question. It would rely more on selective policy instruments designed to influence behaviour in particular sectors or industries than on blunt instruments designed to have an economy-wide impact. It would favour gradual shifts in policy over shock treatment. It would be more sensitive to distributional implications and especially to the importance of preserving and/or extending the

provision of basic needs, goods, and services. Above all it would seek to establish broad political support for adjustment efforts, thereby maintaining, or even strengthening, democratic institutions. Such a package would undoubtedly imply less reliance on unfettered market forces and greater use of selective direct controls (including exchange controls, import controls, some price control, and a general incomes policy) than would orthodox packages. It would avoid a blanket commitment to an outward-oriented economy. It would put national economic integration and the meeting of basic needs to the forefront of economic strategy.[14]

Loxley's alternative stabilization approach assumes the debtor countries will undergo significant internal adjustment and economic restructuring but in a way that allows for diversity. This diversity, he argues, should reflect the unique character of each country and its situation.

Several noted proponents of debt-relief proposals focus more specifically on the debt-service problem and less on (somewhat unrealistic) overall comprehensive policies that involve the World Bank, the IMF, and debtor country responsibilities. For example, Stanley Fischer, an international economist from MIT, has made the case for debt relief on distributional (welfare) arguments. He proposes that the debt burden (interest and amortization) tied to commercial bank loans be reduced to 65 percent of the initial contracted value. This would result in a decline of approximately $10 billion a year in interest payments. In his proposal, commercial banks would gradually record these losses without serious financial consequences. However, he feels that such debt relief should be contingent upon each debtor country's agreeing to a comprehensive growth-oriented economic policy program approved by the IMF.[15]

A perhaps more realistic proposal by Jeffrey Sachs, a Harvard international economist, would have an international agency (the World Bank, for example) purchase commercial bank debt at the secondary market rate. The purchase, he suggests, could be made with marketable bonds issued by the agency. This would reduce the debt burden to 60 percent of the current amount. Sachs argues that banks could afford this because their losses have already been reflected in their stock market valuations and loan-loss reserves. As with the Fischer proposal, Sachs also assumes that the debtor nation would agree to pursue adjustment programs approved by the IMF and/or the World Bank.[16]

In the past few years a number of other concessionary debt-relief proposals have been presented. Each involves the creditor commercial banks' absorbing some losses while facilitating an increase in capital flows to the debtor nations and/or increasing availability of foreign exchange. Senator Bill Bradley (D–N.J.) has proposed a plan whereby commercial banks would forgive annually 3 percent of the interest and 3 percent of the principal for a period of three years, after which debtors would resume standard obligations on the remaining debt. His plan also gives each debtor nation control over economic policy during this period.

The commercial banking institutions of the creditor nations, not surprisingly, have refused to consider such a proposal. It is also unclear whether the U.S. Congress could constitutionally legislate such a program, and it is almost certain that the banks would not voluntarily participate in such a program. In addition, it has been estimated by William R. Cline that the Bradley Plan, even if it were enacted, would really do very little to help debtor nations and might even be harmful in the long run. Cline's empirical research on Mexico tends to support these conclusions.[17] So, most analysts feel the Bradley Plan does not go far enough to provide any long-term resolution of the problem.

Others, like Peter Kenen, a Princeton economist, Senator Paul Sarbanes (D–Md.), Congressman John J. LaFalce (D–N.Y.), and Richard Weinert have each proposed versions of a plan whereby some international entity would buy Third World debt from the banks at a discount. And, in fact, such a proposal has recently come from a member of the International Monetary Fund's executive board, Arjun Sengupta. He has proposed that the IMF establish an International Debt Facility. This new entity would then buy portions of a debtor country's debt at an agreed-upon discount. In return IMF bonds would be given to the banks. Then the debtor country's obligation would be to the IMF for that portion of the debt held by the IMF but, in addition, the debtor nation would have to agree to an IMF-specified economic policy program for domestic adjustment and stabilization.[18]

Many such proposals involve creative but complicated technical financial mechanisms as part of the overall debt-relief strategy. Two of the more recent such mechanisms have been the debt-equity swap and the zero-coupon bond option.[19]

The conclusion is inescapable that as long as debt relief schemes, however imaginative, are voluntary and involve banks' accepting losses, they will be generally insignificant, as the Brady Plan has been. They will expand the growing menu of options available but will not themselves bring about long-term, concessionary debt relief.

Clearly, there is no shortage of ideas when it comes to solving the problem of developing countries' external indebtedness (see figure 8–2). The technical mechanisms and imaginative comprehensive proposals we've discussed demonstrate that debt relief is possible, but until there is general agreement that the crisis must be resolved or, more likely, a financial crisis of major proportions, the problem will linger and continue to stifle real economic progress.

A New Bretton Woods: Conclusion

In this chapter we have argued that there is great need for a realignment of international priorities and that to accomplish that a new Bretton Woods Conference is needed. The agenda for such a conference has been outlined and detailed. It is clear that the leaders of the world need to come together to discuss the issues of trade, exchange rates, capital flows, and Third World debt as interrelated problems needing solutions requiring unprecedented international cooperation.

Conservative market-oriented prescriptions have not worked, and liberal structural-adjustment schemes are not realistic as long as the self-interests of the banking community do not coincide with the needs of the deteriorating Third World economies and the desires of the industrialized world.

In his statement at the 1987 Annual Meetings of the IMF and World Bank, James A. Baker, United States Secretary of the Treasury, listed instruments suitable for inclusion in an expanded range ("menu") of financing options for commercial banks participating in rescheduling agreements. The list included the following instruments:

• Trade and project loans, which enable banks to channel more funds directly to the private sector. Such loans, viewed by banks as providing more easily identifiable returns, encourage imports of investment goods.

• On-lending, which enables banks to channel funds to specific end-users (mostly in the private sector) under their general balance of payments loan agreements with their governments, thus supporting their commercial relationships.

• New money bonds, which are viewed by many banks as more attractive than participation in a syndicated loan as the vehicle for new money, as bonds have some characteristics of a senior claim on the issuing country.

• Notes or bonds convertible into local equity, which can facilitate debt-equity swaps, thus helping reduce external debt-service burdens and stimulate domestic activity.

• Exit bonds, which are also known as "alternative participation instruments," were used for the first time in the 1987 Argentine rescheduling. . . . Exit bonds enable banks with small exposure to avoid future new money obligations by accepting negotiable low-interest bonds.

• External debt conversions, which are now established in many countries as a means of reducing debt and debt-servicing burdens. They permit the conversion of external claims into domestic currency denominated bonds and equity, or, in some cases, into currency itself.

• Interest capitalization, which reduces interest service directly. Secretary Baker indicated that mutually agreed interest capitalization may be appropriate in selected cases, particularly for small debtors.

• Balance of payments loans, which are the standard form for new money loans have taken hitherto. Such loans to debtor country governments will continue to be an essential component of future new money packages.

Source: World Bank, *World Debt Tables* (Washington, D.C.: World Bank, 1988).

Figure 8–2. *Debt Relief Financing Options*

To suggest that the leaders of the Western world come together and seriously try to resolve the problem of international imbalance seems almost Pollyannaish. Capitalism is, by definition, a competitive system, not a cooperative one. Beyond that the contradictions of present world economic arrangements may be too great. This was summarized eloquently by Harry Magdoff and Paul Sweezy who, in the fall of 1987, said:

> The idea that far-reaching international cooperation is feasible under these conditions is about as remote from reality as one can get. Each step in an attempt to eliminate imbalance tends to produce a net set of problems. Thus, if the U.S. were to reduce imports sufficiently to eliminate its trade deficit, the economies of countries exporting to the U.S. would suffer. This would especially hurt Third World countries who would then have even greater difficulty servicing their debts. To achieve stability in the foreign exchange markets a lid would have to be put on speculation and some means found to stabilize exchange rates. But how can stability be achieved if an exchange rate that favors one country harms another? To reap balance out of imbalance some countries would have to accept a voluntary reduction in income, leading to growth in unemployment, reduction in welfare, and a possible financial collapse. The list of contradictions could go on and on: the main point to keep in mind is that capitalism and its market system are by their very nature anarchic. To advocate eliminating anarchy—whether in domestic or international affairs—while maintaining the system serves only to foster the worst kind of illusions.[20]

Key Concepts

Policy Coordination
Exchange Rate Coordination
Purchasing Power Parity (PPP)
Fundamental Equilibrium Exchange Rate (FEER)
European Monetary System (EMS)
Liquidity vs. Solvency
New Bretton Woods

Discussion Questions

1. Suppose you were in charge of the international financial system. What kind of exchange rate system would you adopt?

2. If the United States had not severed all links between gold and the U.S. dollar in 1971, what would have happened?

3. Take one side or the other and make the argument *for* or *against* a new Bretton Woods Conference.

4. Suppose the G-7 nations agreed to a system of exchange rate coordination. What would that mean for each of their *national* economic policies.

5. Of the myriad proposals for Third World debt relief, which do you favor? Why?

9
The American Challenge: What Can Be Done?

In 1981 the United States emerged from the confusion and malaise of the Carter era into a new era of optimism. The imperial presidency of Ronald Reagan and those around him helped restore a sense that things were under control again. The things that Reagan stood for—dismantling the federal government, unleashing the power of business to function in a free market setting, and reducing the tax burden on the wealthy—all fit well with the age of the yuppie, the new era of greed, the roaring eighties.

To the average person looking for a panacea, Reaganomics, as it came to be called, provided more than a glimmer of hope. It also gave new meaning to the phrase "common sense." Supply-side economics, as we have seen, was supposed to relieve us of the burden of taxation, while at the same time *increase* federal government revenues. The famed Laffer Curve which, legend has it, was first detailed on a napkin in a Washington restaurant (presumably) over cocktails, purported to prove that there is an optimum tax rate that will maximize tax revenues. Above it taxes are a disincentive to work effort and productivity. So, at any level above the optimum, taxes should be lowered. The resulting stimulus to motivation will so energize people—since they now get to keep more of the money they earn—that overall economic activity will boom. From that *more* taxes will be collected, even at the lower rates.

This new version of "eating your cake and having it too" provided the rationale for the Reagan administration to push through tax cuts in 1981 and again in 1986. The highest marginal tax rate was reduced from 70 percent when Reagan took office to 33 percent by 1988, and thus the stage was set for one of the most important experiments in economic history.

Reaganomics, of course, meant more than just reducing taxes for the wealthy. It meant deregulating business and cutting business taxes, reducing the rate of growth of government spending, and "getting the government off the backs of the American people." From this, the administration promised, we could expect increased productivity, more investment, more savings, lower rates of inflation, higher real average incomes, and a growing economy.

The record on all this is mixed. It is clear that the economy did grow, albeit at sluggish rates, and the continuous recession-free recovery between 1983 and 1988 set new records. Therefore,

Table 9–1
U.S. Economic Data, 1973–1987

	Real GNP *a*	Unemployment	Inflation*b*	Budget Deficit (billions)	Trade Balance (billions)
1973	5.2%	4.9%	8.8%	–$14.8	+$.9
1974	–0.5	5.6	12.2	–4.6	–5.5
1975	–1.3	8.5	7.0	–45.1	+8.9
1976	4.9	7.7	4.8	–66.4	–9.4
1977	4.7	7.0	6.8	–44.9	–31.1
1978	5.3	6.0	9.0	–48.8	–34.0
1979	2.5	5.8	13.3	–27.6	–27.5
1980	–0.2	7.1	12.3	–59.5	–25.5
1981	1.9	7.5	10.2	–57.9	–27.9
1982	–2.5	9.5	6.0	–110.6	–36.4
1983	3.5	9.5	3.6	–195.4	–67.2
1984	6.5	7.7	3.5	–183.6	–114.1
1985	2.3	7.1	3.6	–212.3	–122.0
1986	2.9	7.0	1.7	–220.0	–150.0
1987	2.9	6.2	3.8	–150.0	–160.0

Source: *Economic Report of the President* (Washington, D.C.: Government Printing Office, February 1988).

*a*Change in gross national product based on 1982 dollars.

*b*Measured by increases in the consumer price index.

the proponents of supply-side economics can argue with some legitimacy that the experiment *did* work. However, Keynesian opponents can make a convincing argument that it wasn't supply-side prescriptions that were responsible for the recovery but the simple application of countercyclical Keynesian monetary and fiscal policy tools. In a recession, Keynesian economics says, to stimulate the economy the government and the monetary authorities should do some combination of four things: increase government spending, decrease taxes, lower interest rates, and increase the money supply. In a period of inflation, when the economy is running too fast, you do the opposite.

During the first six years of the Reagan administration, the rhetoric aside, federal government spending *increased* from $600 billion to over $1 trillion dollars. (See table 9–1.) Interest rates were pushed down from a prime rate of 22 percent in 1981 to 9.5 percent by 1988. The money supply was increased at an annual rate of 7.8 percent and, of course, taxes were cut drastically. (See table 9–2.) This is the standard Keynesian prescription, and therefore, Keynesians argue, it should be no surprise that the patient recovered.

So, depending on your political proclivities, you can take your choice. Either way, what matters is that one thing is clear: the tax reduction coupled with the increase in government spending *did* produce historically unprecedented structural federal deficits and

Table 9–2
The Tax Burden: Before and After Reagan

| | As a Percentage of Family Income | | | |
| | Income Tax Alone | | Income and Social Security Taxes | |
Family Income, 1980	1980	1984	1980	1984
$10,000	3.7	5.2	9.9	12.2
$20,000	11.3	11.1	17.5	18.1
$35,000	18.9	18.4	25.0	25.4
$50,000	24.2	22.1	30.4	29.1
$100,000	35.7	30.8	38.9	35.0
$250,000	49.5	39.2	50.8	40.9

Source: Center for Popular Economics, *A Field Guide to the U.S. Economy* (Nancy Folbre, ed.) (New York: Random House, 1987).

a national debt of $2.8 trillion, which in turn put the U.S. economy in an extremely precarious and fragile position —dependent on infusions of foreign savings for survival. It was the evolving recognition of this simple fact that led to the stock market crash of October 19, 1987, which in turn forced both the government and the people of the United States to rethink the situation.

The October 1987 Stock Market Crash

The short-run lessons from the crash were that the stock market had been overvalued for some time, fueled by speculative frenzy. When that bubble burst it became obvious that the market was a very volatile place to invest and many small investors pulled out. However, the Dow-Jones average closed the year 3 percent higher at the end of 1987 than it had been at the beginning.

Perhaps even more important was the now-universal recognition that the stock market is more closely intertwined with the international economy than it is the domestic economy. After the crash it became clear that what happens on the Tokyo stock exchange or in Bonn may be more important that what happens in New York.

In the longer run the crash caused the nation, indeed the world, to move into a period of reassessment. On the practical side Congress and the president agreed on a deficit reduction program which, while minuscule—$32 billion, in the overall scheme of things—did serve to calm the financial markets, and did meet the guidelines of the newly revived Gramm-Rudman Deficit Reduction Law. Also, interestingly, the trade deficit hit a record high of $17.6 billion in November, but the market shrugged it off as if nothing had happened. To all appearances the October crash had been a "correction," albeit a big one. The specter of recession remained, as did the underlying structural problems, but the most important part of the crash was that it caused the country to realize that the party was over. It was, as *Business Week* put it in a cover story, time to "Wake Up, America."[1]

One of the more significant things to come out of the October stock market crash and its aftermath was that it spawned an unprecedented amount of literature on a topic that few had been thinking much about: Where is the U.S. economy heading, and what role will it be able to play in the resolution of the increasingly serious world economic crisis?

Interestingly, a number of highly respected journalists, economists, and other commentators had been warning for some time that the day of reckoning was coming.

Just before the crash former Secretary of Commerce Peter G. Peterson wrote a provocative article in the *Atlantic Monthly* that America was beginning to suffer a serious hangover from its spending and borrowing binge—"the morning after," he called it. Also, in the summer of 1987 in *The New York Review of Books*, investment banker Felix Rohatyn warned that the Western world was "on the brink" of economic collapse; and *Wall Street Journal* economic editor Alfred Malabre penned a book detailing why the United States was living "beyond its means."[2]

What's interesting about all this is that *before the crash* no one paid much attention to these supposed doomsday soothsayers. Now, however, everybody was paying attention. Early in 1988 *Newsweek* summed up the national mood in a lead story, "The 1980s Are Over, Greed Goes Out of Style."[3]

Out of this mounting collection of literature there seemed to be an emerging consensus that *five* major economic issues would eventually bring the U.S. economy to its knees unless some fundamental changes were made.

First, conservatives and liberals alike agree that the United States had, indeed, been spending far beyond its means. It is now clear that can't continue. If it does the country faces a substantial—externally imposed—reduction in its standard of living, possibly of depression proportions.

Second, the United States can't keep borrowing from abroad to finance its lavish lifestyle. If it does it will, at the least, face the prospect of becoming a second-rate power.

Third, import consumption has to be reduced and the export sector has to become more efficient. That is, if the United States is to maintain even a semblance of world economic leadership it has to become more "competitive." Even current improvements in productivity will not be enough to keep Japan, West Germany, and many others from catching up soon.

Fourth, the Third World debt problem has to be resolved. Otherwise, these impoverished nations are going to fall into a domino-like default that will drag everyone into a quagmire. As things stand everyone is losing from the situation.

Finally, the role of the U.S. dollar as the anchor currency of the international financial system has to be reevaluated. The United States can't be the world's largest debtor and also continue acting as if it could be the lender of last resort if it were necessary.

The Emerging Agenda

Out of this recognition that over the long run these problems must be resolved has come a general consensus about what policies will need to be implemented.

First, spending has to be cut on most fronts or revenues must be increased. The major issue here is that spending can't realistically be cut until the built-in escalators in the programs that people have come to think they are entitled to (such as annual cost of living increases in social security and federal pensions) and exorbitant defense expenditures are revised to reflect modern-day realities. This is difficult and complicated and would no doubt create hardships, but so will the alternatives. In the private sector levels of consumption have to be reduced and saving increased. If this doesn't happen then the falling value of the dollar will do it instead by making imports prohibitively expensive and kicking off inflation in the process. If we consume less we will, by definition, save more.

The issue here, of course, is that such measures—as attractive as they seem in a rhetorical sense—involve tradeoffs and questions of equity and burden sharing. To say that entitlements must be reduced means that if they were it would be the poor and middle class who would sacrifice the most. This is not easy to recommend; nor is it likely to be politically feasible. The obvious solution, increasing taxes, does not appear politically feasible either, given the antitax climate of both parties.

Second, to stimulate the sluggish economy and reduce the level of borrowing from other countries, real interest rates will have to be lowered even further. This is the best chance to avert a recession and at the same time reduce the incentive for foreigners to invest here, which is what borrowing from abroad really means. That's risky and complicated but necessary.

Third, to improve "competitiveness" the United States should keep trying to improve its industrial productivity, forget about self-defeating trade protectionist legislation, and try to engineer a gradual coordinated reduction in the value of the dollar, while at the same time encouraging our allies to lower their interest rates and stimulate their economies. This means a concerted domestic industrial policy and a coordinated international economic policy.

Fourth, the United States should prevail on the trade surplus countries, especially Japan, to become more involved in resolving the Third World debt crisis while at the same time implementing one of the several debt moratorium schemes that have been proposed. Otherwise, the debtor countries, as Brazil and Peru have already done, will do it unilaterally. That would allow the developing countries to begin producing their way out of their increasingly serious predicament and, at the least, begin buying more of the U.S. exports they need. Everybody gains from that.

Finally, the United States should take the lead in organizing an international monetary conference to begin restructuring the international monetary system along more realistic lines that reflect the simple fact that the United States is now the largest debtor nation and Japan the largest creditor, and that the role of the U.S. dollar as the key reserve currency is going to have to be reevaluated.

There are those who will disagree with some of the specifics, but the emerging consensus is that this is the agenda for the next decade.

Short-run vs. Long-run Scenarios

All of this suggests some interesting but potentially dangerous scenarios. In the short run the market crash and other factors that have been building up for some time may push the U.S. economy into a recession. If that happens all problems we have delineated up to this point will be more serious than they already are and, more importantly, the longer-run scenarios will be exacerbated to crisis proportions.

While only about half the economists who participate in the Egbert Blue Chip Consensus Forecast thought the market crash would bring on a recession in 1988, most thought the U.S. economy was long overdue for a downturn and that it would probably begin sometime in 1989. One reason is that historically big market crashes have always preceded recessions. The market has fallen by 30 percent or more eleven times since 1885 and each time a recession has followed within a year or so.

A recession in itself is nothing unusual. The U.S. economy has experienced nine of them since World War II and has always managed to pull out. But this time, when it comes, things are going to be a bit more complicated. The reason is that all the things that are presently troubling the economy while it is still relatively strong are going to be exacerbated if there is recession.

The biggest problems, as we have seen, and which finally added up to investors losing confidence in the market, are the federal budget deficit, the trade deficit, the Third World debt, and high interest rates. In a recession scenario each would get worse. Consider:

- There is no indication that the U.S. budget deficit will be decreased significantly—even with Gramm-Rudman in place. If there is a recession, as unemployment increases, government revenues will fall while expenditures will increase and the deficit will skyrocket.

- A recession might temporarily improve the U.S. trade deficit as imports are reduced, but that would soon reverberate throughout the world economy. As other countries lose their

U.S. markets they would also have to cut back on their imports. Everybody comes out a loser.

• In a U.S. recession the already fragile Third World debt situation would become much more serious than it is already. The only way the Third World countries can service their debt is to sell more to the creditor countries than they buy, which is what they have been doing. In a recession, exports and imports on both sides would have to be reduced, making it virtually impossible to service foreign debt.

But what's probably most important of all is that in a recession scenario interest rates become a crucial unknown. Normally in a recession the monetary authorities would push interest rates down to stimulate the economy. But in the current fragile climate that's virtually impossible because the U.S. *needs* high real interest rates to keep foreign investors happy—that is, to keep them financing the huge federal deficits. But, in a recession, when U.S. investments begin to look less attractive, the Fed might be forced to raise interest rates above their already high levels.

A high-interest-rate recession would be disastrous for the U.S. economy and the world economy as well. But the alternative, a low-interest-rate recession and a foreign investment pullout, would be even worse because it would push the dollar into a free-fall and, at the least, take the market with it. So the Fed is caught in a dilemma that seems almost unsolvable. As long as the United States is dependent on foreign savings to finance its own deficits, it will not have control of its own economy, much less the world economy.

What seems to be happening is that all the old monetary and fiscal policy prescriptions for keeping the economy out of a recession have become neutralized by the international dimensions of the U.S. economy.

One way out of this dilemma would be for the major industrial powers, especially the United States, Japan, and West Germany, to agree to a coordinated gradual reduction in interest rates. That would stimulate their economies and ours and, at the same time, reduce the worrisome trade imbalance, but since no nation wants to relinquish significant control—or perceived control—of its own economy this seems an unlikely possibility in the foreseeable future.

But in any case it is now much more important than ever that the U.S. economy doesn't slide into a recession. Even a slight downturn could snowball into a serious crisis. That means more attention must be paid to resolving the longer-run problems. Until they are resolved the world will continue to teeter on the brink of depression.

The Longer-run Scenario

Earlier in this chapter we briefly sketched the five major issues the United States must face if it is to extricate itself from the present crisis. They were: 1) reduce spending and/or increase revenues on all fronts, 2) reduce borrowing from abroad, 3) become more competitive in the international markets, 4) resolve the Third World debt problem and, 5) reevaluate the role of the U.S. dollar as the world's key reserve currency. All of that is easy to say but not so easy to implement. But if these are not implemented, as many have pointed out, the longer-run scenarios for each are dismal, if not catastrophic.

The United States as a Debtor Nation

As we have seen, the United States in 1985 became a debtor nation for the first time since 1914. By 1988 total U.S. net foreign debt had reached $425 billion and was projected to top $1 trillion by 1990. In the short run this is not a major calamity for the world's largest economy, but the longer-run implications are quite another story.

As Peterson puts it:

> The incredible speed of America's transformation from creditor to debtor can hardly be exaggerated. Only six years ago, at the end of 1981, the United States had achieved its all-time apogee as a net creditor, with an official position of a positive $141 billion. Over the past six years, in other words, the United States has burned up more than $500 billion, net, by liquidating our

foreign assets and by borrowing from abroad. That's an immense flow of capital, even in global terms. By 1986 our net borrowing had dwarfed the fabled bank recycling of OPEC surpluses after the oil price hike of 1973 and 1979. The sum was twice the size of all foreign interest payments by all the less-developed debtor nations, and about half the approximate dollar value of total net investment in all less-developed countries combined.[4]

As we saw earlier, there are only two ways a nation can sustain a net debtor position over any period of time. One is that it maintains a balance of trade surplus, thereby earning sufficient foreign exchange in its merchandise and service trade accounts to finance its deficit in the investment account. This is one way to keep the overall current account in balance, and it is what the United States did for most of the postwar period when both the trade *and* the investment accounts were positive. The other way is to run balance of trade deficits but balance them from a surplus in the investment account—that is, let the flow of foreign investments coming into the country exceed the flow going out. Since the flows are cumulative (flows of investment become stocks of it), if the inflow exceeds the outflow eventually the recipient country becomes a debtor nation, which is what happened in 1985 when the total value of foreign-owned assets within the United States began to exceed the value of U.S. investments abroad. Part of those assets, as we have seen, are ownership of direct investments such as factories and real estate and part—the vast majority—come from purchases of portfolio investments, mostly stocks and government bonds. The latter, of course, help finance the federal deficit and allow levels of consumption that would not otherwise be possible.

Put differently, one country can enjoy high levels of con-sumption by borrowing another's savings. This, it is important to remember, is not quite the same as borrowing in the more conventional sense of the word—directly from a bank or international agency, as the Third World debtor countries have done, but the long run result is the same: the country has to service the debt with exports, which means a reduction in its own standard of living. This, of course, is what is happening in the underdeveloped debtor countries now as they struggle to service their foreign debts and it is what is beginning to happen in the United States.

As long as the trade surplus countries, notably Japan and West Germany, are willing to continue assuming U.S. debt obligations the situation is sustainable, but, clearly, there are limits to how long this can go on, and the opportunities for a smooth readjustment of this growing imbalance are, as Peterson points out, somewhat limited:

> Our opportunity for a relatively smooth readjustment is perilously narrow. On the one hand, it seems likely that the rest of the world will grow reluctant to keep lending to the United States once our net indebtedness rises much beyond 35 percent of our GNP, or a bit more than $1 trillion at today's prices. Some experts suggest that this debt may entail net U.S. debt-service payments equivalent, as a share of exports, to those of many developing nations and about on a par with Germany's reparations burden following the First World War. The experts agree that it is quite impossible for the United States to go on indefinitely borrowing principal at or near its current rate of 3.4 percent of GNP per year. Such borrowing, combined with accumulating debt-service costs, would dictate an absurd $3 trillion in net debt by the end of the century, and foreign investors would close down the pipeline long before we got there.[5]

The scenario seems improbable, if not impossible. How would we go about improving our export position? One possibility would be to increase agricultural exports, traditionally a major U.S. export. But nowadays Europe, and even India and China, have all become net farm-product exporters. The U.S. trade surplus in agricultural products has dwindled to almost zero in recent years, while agricultural subsidies still hover around $25 billion.

Another possibility would be to reduce oil imports, but after some improvement in the 1980s, U.S. oil imports have been steadily increasing and are predicted to double or triple (to $130 billion) by 1995.

That leaves services, thought by many to be the eventual savior. But, Peterson points out, the vast majority of services the United States provides the rest of the world are *debt* services—servicing its own debt. Services that would improve the trade balance are mostly shipping, insurance, and travel, which added up to only about $50 billion in 1986 and certainly can't be expected to increase much beyond that in the foreseeable future.

We are then left with the manufacturing export sector, which, although it has shown some improvement in recent years, would have to grow at a rate of 10 percent over the next ten years to even approach any semblance of balance. That hardly seems likely even under the most optimistic projections.

> In every respect the achievement would be unprecedented: we would have not only to break our earlier record but to do it with a lower average level of domestic business investment, with a complete freeze on imports, and with steadily declining living standards.
>
> Any way one looks at it, the arithmetic is cruel and inescapable. It's hard to imagine huge growth in our manufacturing output, for instance, without a very large increase in domestic business investment. But to further increase investment at home we may have to undergo a further decline in consumption, in order to hold constant our net export improvement. And, clearly, we are not going to see any decline in consumption in favor of saving unless there is a radical change in our public policy, especially our fiscal policy and in our politics as well.[6]

Competitiveness and Productivity

Much of the overall problem facing the United States is commonly attributed to the apparent inability of the country to compete effectively against the rapidly gaining Japanese and other now highly industrialized nations. "Competitiveness" is the new buzzword. We simply have to become more competitive, it is said, and all of our problems will go away.

In one sense when people are talking about competitiveness they are really talking about the balance of trade deficit. If the country becomes more competitive then it will be able to sell more abroad, which will reverse the trade deficit. But what competitiveness really means is productivity and around that issue there is a lot of confusion that must be sorted out before the long-run implications of declining U.S. productivity can be analyzed.

Simply stated, productivity is the ratio of what goes into the process of producing something to what comes out. But productivity is an elusive term. There are many ways to define it. Since there are millions of different products and services produced and they can't be weighed or measured to get a total, productivity is usually measured in terms of the market value of whatever is being produced. Typically, therefore, productivity is measured in terms of the value of the output produced by a worker in an hour, or what is known as output per hour worked.

Measuring the productivity of workers involved in manufacturing is a pretty straightforward proposition. If the average worker in the widget industry can produce ten widgets in an hour and widgets sell for a dollar a piece then the value of output per hour worked in the widget industry is ten dollars.

But measuring the productivity of workers involved in service industries gets pretty tricky pretty quickly. There's a question, in some cases, of what the worker is actually producing: what is the product of an airport security guard, a receptionist in a dentist's office, or a college professor of economics? And then there's the question of assigning some price to what has been produced. Suppose the average airport security guard averts one highjacking a day. What's that worth?

In our economy only about one worker in five is employed in manufacturing, mining, forestry, agriculture, or other areas in which they produce some measurable tangible product. So, for the other 80 percent of the labor force, productivity figures are generated by assuming that the value of what a worker produces is exactly equal to what that worker is paid. If a convenience store clerk is paid five dollars an hour, then his output per hour worked is—according to the way we keep productivity figures—five dollars and he is considered to be only half as productive as the average worker in the widget industry. And so on.

So the whole issue of "competitiveness" as it relates to productivity is at once overworked and not very well understood. Supposedly the United States is losing the trade battle because it has become a whimpering, lazy, inefficient bunch of slobs, unable to "compete" with the hard-working omnipotent Japanese, Germans, Taiwanese, and others. This notion has received so much publicity in recent years that—according to one survey we conducted—87 percent of college business students believe Japan is the most productive country in the world and that the United States runs a poor third, after West Germany. This, of course, is not true. Many studies show that in terms of output per worker the United States is still the most productive country in the world. Among them a 1986 study by the Federal Reserve Bank of Boston shows that Japanese productivity is only 93 percent of the U.S. rate of output per hour, and West Germany's is only 90 percent. There are several reasons for all the confusion over this issue.

The most important reason is that it is the relative rates of productivity growth that muddy the waters. To be sure, productivity growth rates in many other countries are increasing faster than they are in the United States. So, if current trends continue, it is possible that Japan, for one, could overtake the United States sometime in the near future.

Over the 1981–1985 period eleven countries achieved increases in output per worker that exceeded U.S. increases. Korea headed the list, with a whopping 6 percent growth rate, followed by Japan with 3 percent. The U.S. rate of productivity growth during the same period averaged 1 percent. But current trends are not continuing. According to the Labor Department, U.S. non-farm productivity was increasing at an annual rate of 1.7 percent in 1986.

Beyond that, looking at overall productivity figures provides a deceptive picture of what's going on where it really counts. According to the 1986 *Economic Report of the President,* United States output per hour has grown at an average of 3.8 percent, almost 50 percent faster than the postwar average and more than twice the annual average recorded between 1973 and 1981.

So it's pretty clear that U.S. business has gotten the message: to compete in the world market it has to be more flexible, more conscious of worker output, less concerned with short-run profits at the expense of longer-run investments in research and development, more consumer- and service-oriented, more quality conscious, and so on.

But the important thing to remember is that in the process of making manufacturing more competitive, much of U.S. employment has shifted out of manufacturing into the less-productive and therefore lower-paying service sector. That's the primary reason for the increase in manufacturing productivity. More output is being produced with fewer workers, which is what productivity is—output per hour worked.

What further complicates the issue is that productivity in the service sector—which accounts for about 50 percent of U.S. personal consumption expenditures—is, as we saw, almost impossible to measure.

And, in any case, in the context of world competitiveness it's the manufacturing sector that counts, not services. As we saw earlier, services account for only a small part of U.S. exports—about $50 billion in 1986 out of $217.3 billion total exports. So the key point here is that U.S. manufacturing is not fading away, as many would have us believe. Indeed, the share of GNP accounted for by manufacturing has remained almost constant over the postwar period. But what does count is that it is the people who are—or were—employed by it that are fading away; into lower-paying jobs in the less-productive and therefore lower-paying service sector. As a result, among other things, average incomes in the United States are falling at the same time average productivity is rising. In the longer run that is the problem of competitiveness and productivity.

While much is made of the fact that total employment has increased during the 1980s as unemployment has decreased, the data, although factually correct, are illusory. Manufacturing jobs have *declined* during the period, while some 44 percent of the new jobs created in the service sector between 1979 and 1985 paid poverty-level wages. This, according to a study by Professor Barry Bluestone and Bennett Harrison for the Joint Economic Committee, was "more than twice the rate of low-wage job creation that prevailed during the 1960s and 1970s."

The reasons for this disturbing turn of events, they argue, are mostly directly or indirectly related to international factors.

> We think these developments are explained—at least in part—by plant shutdowns, foreign imports (including imports from the offshore plants or partners of American companies), subcontracting of production to lower-paying suppliers, employer mandated wage freezes and takeaways, the proliferation of involuntary part-time work schedules and personnel cutback, associated with corporate restructuring plans. Since none of these developments is likely to change in the near future, we should probably expect the disturbing trend toward low wages to continue.[7]

The Third World Debt Question

The other issue that will continue to haunt the United States until it is resolved is the staggering and still formidable question of the $1 trillion accumulated Third World debt. There are many possible solutions but, with the exception of the Brady Plan Mexican debt agreement, which has met with only very limited success, there has been little progress. If anything, the problem has become worse since it first captured world attention when Mexico nearly defaulted in the fall of 1982.

The key factor here is that the Third World debt crisis is part of a much larger international problem of imbalanced flows of trade and capital. Until those are addressed the Third World debt issue will continue to fester.[8]

The Trade Gap and the Role of the Dollar

The devaluation of the dollar over the 1985–1986 period should have—according to economic theory—caused the U.S. trade deficit to turn around dramatically. It seems logical that a 50 percent reduction in the price of the dollar should translate into a 50 percent increase in the price of imports and a corresponding decrease in export prices. That, *ceteris paribus,* should solve the trade imbalance problem. But, in the modern world, other things are seldom equal. By 1987 the U.S. trade deficit had hit a new record high: $171 billion.

This suggests that the trade imbalance problem and the concomitant dollar problem is structural in nature. It seems highly unlikely that even a further drastic reduction in the value of the dollar, which may in any case be beyond the power of the monetary authorities to implement, would resolve the problem. Given that, the structural changes that would be required add up to a reduction in the U.S. standard of living, at least in the short run.

At the bottom line it is becoming clear that the days of U.S. hegemony are over, and that brings into question the role of the dollar as the world's key reserve currency. At issue here is the now incompatible interrelationship between domestic macro-economic policy and international economic policy.

It is often suggested that the United States must maintain a rapid rate of economic growth and *at all costs* avoid a recession. But with a recession long overdue, the tradeoffs to avoid one are untenable under the current unbalanced trade and investment climate. To keep the U.S. economy growing, interest rates would have to be lowered and other monetary and fiscal stimuli applied. Lower interest rates mean a reduction in flows of foreign investment that now finance the U.S. federal and other deficits. The United States is, therefore, faced with a balancing act that cannot be sustained over the long run. As Michael Moffitt has pointed out:

> The United States—in part because of the policies of the Reagan administration—has considerably less leverage than it once did to apply unilateral solutions to international economic disequilibrium. The decline of U.S. power, which began in the late 1960s, has been accelerated by the twin deficits, the resulting growth of U.S. foreign debt, and, in turn, the increasing vulnerability of our financial markets. It is no wonder that the leading lights of business and politics are bemoaning the fact that the United States is now a debtor nation. Debt and hegemony do not mix—at least not for very long.
>
> With both its monetary and fiscal policy constrained by current imbalances, the United States is now dependent on the

expansion of other countries' economies to keep the current recovery going. For without greater world growth, the United States will not be able to reduce its trade deficit and its accumulation of foreign obligations—indeed, they will only grow larger. Yet the United States finds it no longer has the ability to impose its will on the rest of the world and, even if it did, it is not clear that countries like West Germany and Japan could (or would) quickly take up the role of economic locomotive.[9]

It is clear, then, that any viable solution must take into account—*and involve*—the interests of Japan, Western Europe, and the increasingly important Newly Industrialized Countries on the Pacific Rim. Their interests are intertwined with U.S. interests in a way that is certain to change the character and structure of international economic relations for many years to come.

Key Concepts

Supply-side Economics
Recession Scenario
Competitiveness
Productivity
The Balancing Act

Discussion Questions

1. Common sense says that if the government lowers taxes it will receive less tax revenue. Supply-side economists don't agree. Why?

2. Suppose Japan decided to stop investing in U.S. government bonds. What would happen?

3. Which is the most productive nation in the world? Where does the United States rank in the productivity heirarchy?

4. What would *you* do to increase U.S. productivity?

5. How long can a nation sustain a net debtor position?

10
Japan, Western Europe, and the
Newly Industrialized Countries

W hile it is easy to argue that the decline of U.S. dominance of the world economy is a result of nearly stagnant productivity growth rates, low savings and investment rates, addiction to imports, and the resultant debt buildup, it is important to remember that the balance of world economic power would not have shifted so dramatically in recent years if it were not for the emergence of new economic power blocks that now seem certain to assume world economic leadership sometime early in the next century. Of these, of course, Japan provides the most dramatic example, followed closely by the European Economic Community (figure 10–1).

Japanese Miracle

Japan has only half the population of the United States and a total land area roughly the size of California. But it is now challenging the United States on all fronts. The Japanese economy is now the second largest in the world and Japanese investments abroad are, as shown in figure 10–2, now almost equal to total U.S. foreign investments, while the U.S. economy is still two times larger than Japan's.

What's behind the Japanese economic miracle? There are a number of theories and the literature on the topic is voluminous. Some argue that the Japanese are harder workers; others say their

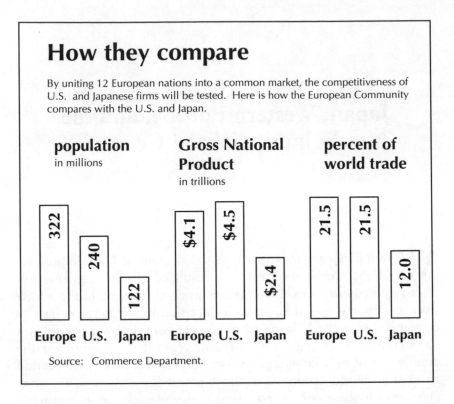

Figure 10–1. *U.S., EEC, and Japan Compared*

success comes from innovative management techniques like the widely copied Quality Circles and other methods of worker involvement in the production process. Other explanations are that they have fewer layers of management and less administrative overhead. However, the most common explanation is that Japan (and Western Europe) got a new start after World War II when they rebuilt their industrial plants with U.S. financial aid and at the same time adopted the latest U.S. technology. And the list goes on. Obviously there is some truth to all that, but it hardly tells the whole story.

The one overriding factor is simply that Japanese cultural traditions are different from those in the West and highly amenable to rapid capitalist industrial development. As compared to the stereotype, Japanese culture is flexible and open to change, rather than being bound by long-standing traditions that tend to stifle change and inhibit growth. But, more importantly, Japanese culture places a high value on saving and investment. Since 1960 total (public and private) net new investment in Japan has averaged about 15 percent of its GNP, compared to just over 5 percent for the United States. In 1986 net Japanese investment exceeded $300 billion annually, compared to $270 billion in the United States. Put differently, that means that in *absolute* terms, total Japanese investment exceeded total U.S. investment, even though Japan's economy is only half as large.

$ billions

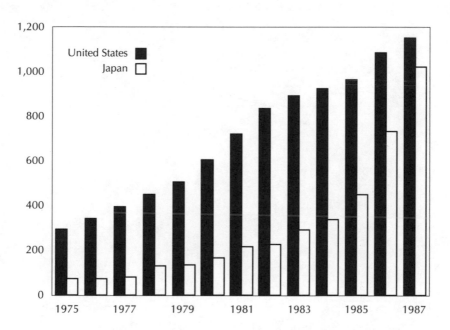

Source: U.S. Department of Commerce, *Survey of Current Business*, Vol. 68, No. 6, June 1988.

Figure 10–2. *Year-end Value of All Foreign Assets Held by U.S. and Japanese Residents, 1975–1987*

More importantly, Japanese investment is financed by *internal* savings. The Japanese save about 17 percent of their disposable income, compared to only 4 percent in the United States. With those savings they are adding more to their capital stock than the United States is and *still have enough left over* (about $80 billion) to finance one-third of the U.S. federal deficit.

When put into the context of longer-run trends, the future scenarios are startling. As shown in figure 10–3, the United States and Japan maintained rough equality in current account balance from about 1975 until 1981, but from there on the trend lines diverge dramatically. By 1987 Japan had a current account

Source: U.S. Department of Commerce, *Survey of Current Business,* Vol. 68, No. 6, June 1988.

Figure 10–3. *U.S. and Japanese Current Account, 1975–1987*

surplus with the United States of almost $100 billion, while the United States was running a deficit of nearly $200 billion in trade and financial transactions with Japan. Moreover, and more important in the long run, was the fact that in 1975 U.S. foreign investment far exceeded Japanese investments abroad—roughly $300 billion compared to $20 billion—but by 1987 Japanese assets held abroad had reached nearly $1 trillion, compared to $1.2 trillion for the United States. Continuing at that rate, Japan soon will be the world's largest foreign investor.

All this means that if present trends continue Japan will become the dominant world economic power sometime early in the next century. It is already—by a large margin—the world's largest creditor nation, with the power to throw the U.S. economy into turmoil at will. A sudden withdrawal of Japanese investment would send U.S. interest rates through the roof and push the Western world into a disastrous recession, if not worse. (See figure 10–4.)

Interestingly, such a scary scenario is not likely to happen because Japan now has a huge stake in the U.S. economy. Some 40 percent of Japanese exports (almost $50 billion annually) are sold to the United States and, beyond that, their direct investments in U.S. companies and real estate now exceed $25 billion. A U.S. recession would send their economy into a tailspin too.

In fact, these days, trying to keep the United States out of a recession is one of Japan's biggest problems. At first glance it seemed curious that Japan would cooperate in letting the value of the dollar fall as it has since the Plaza Agreement in 1985, because a cheaper dollar of course means a more expensive yen, which should have made Japanese exports more expensive and turned the trade deficit around. But, for reasons we have explored earlier, that didn't happen. What did happen, however, was that direct investments in the United States, given a dollar now depreciated by almost 50 percent against the yen, have become a dirt-cheap bargain for the Japanese while, at the same time, adjusted for the fall in the dollar, average American wage rates became less than Japanese wages.

This was most dramatically illustrated by the 1987 announcement that the Japanese automaker Honda was going to begin

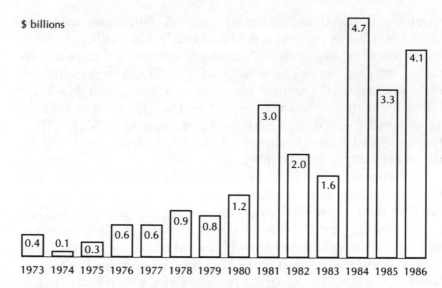

Source: U.S. Department of Commerce, *Survey of Current Business,* Vol. 68, No. 6, June 1988.

Note: Equity in and net outstanding loans to U.S. affiliates.

Figure 10–4. *Japanese Direct Investments in the United States, 1973–1986*

exporting cars made at its Marysville, Ohio, plant *to* Japan. That marked a turning point in economic history.

The explanation for the move is that Honda is now able to produce the cars—which will presumably bear the label "Made in the USA"—more cheaply in the United States than it can in Japan, even counting the considerable transportation costs. Part of the cost advantage can be explained in terms of the fall in the value of the dollar, since it now takes fewer yen to buy the dollars needed to buy cars produced in the United States. An equally important factor is that since 1970, manufacturing sector real wages in Japan have increased by 115 percent, while in the United States they have only increased by 17 percent. Adjusted for the fall in the value of the dollar, the average worker in Japan earned eighteen thousand dollars in 1987, compared to sixteen thousand dollars in the United States. So it's not surprising that the Japanese are increasingly moving their production operations to the United States to exploit the relatively cheap labor.

New Mercantilism

The Japanese economic strategy is based on two interrelated long-run policies. One is a return to the mercantilistic policies of Europe in the seventeenth and eighteenth centuries; the other a concerted effort to tie its fortunes to the United States without assuming a hegemonic leadership role.

Mercantilists believed a nation's future hinged on its ability to produce as much for export as possible while importing as little as possible to build monetary surpluses (which in those days meant gold). Put differently, export your production rather than consume it. Such policies have long been discredited as, at best, a curious way to construe a nation's economic welfare, but this has been the cornerstone of Japanese international economic policy for some time now.

The United States has, unintentionally, pursued just the opposite policy over the past decade or so. Exports have been declining while domestic consumption, fueled mostly by imports, has been increasing. What this means is that Japan is rapidly becoming the world's dominant economic power, but at the same time it is becoming increasingly dependent on the United States for markets and outlets for its rapidly accumulating investment funds.

Newly Industrialized Countries

A related and in the longer run perhaps equally important development is the emergence of the Newly Industrialized Countries of the Pacific Rim: China, Hong Kong, Singapore, South Korea, and Taiwan. By the year 2000 it is estimated that the GNP of Japan and the NICs combined will exceed that of the United States. Already, as shown in figures 10–5 and 10–6, the

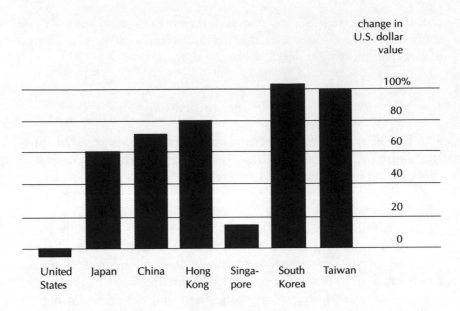

Source: International Monetary Fund, *World Economic Outlook* (Washington, D.C.: IMF, April 1988).

Figure 10–5. *Increase in Exports, 1980–1986*

rate of increase in *exports* dwarfs that of the United States and per capita incomes are rapidly gaining.

There are two significant issues here. One is that much of the economic growth in the Pacific Rim has been dependent on increasing rates of exports to the United States. So long as this continues, an interdependent relationship similar to the Japanese-U.S. symbiotic interdependence will benefit both sides. But there is an increasing trend of economic activity between Japan and the NICs that could eventually develop into a Pacific Rim "common market" that could emerge as the dominant world economic power bloc early in the next century. When that happens the rules of the game will have to be rewritten—again.

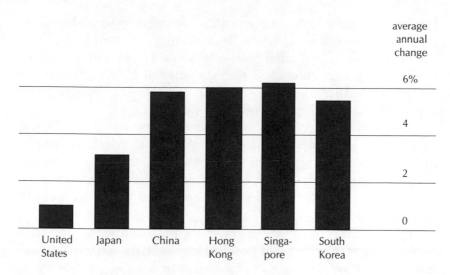

Source: International Monetary Fund, *World Economic Outlook* (Washington, D.C.: IMF, April 1988).

Figure 10–6. *Increase in Per Capita GNP, 1973–1986*

Role of Hegemony

There has been no time in modern history when the international economy was not dominated *and fueled by* a hegemonic power. Great Britain played that role during the nineteenth century until it began to lose power after World War I. The United States played the role from the end of World War II until the end of the 1970s when it began to lose the battle of competitiveness and wallow in a quagmire of debt.

Barring an alternative system of international policy coordination, a hegemonic power can take up the slack in the world economy by providing markets for less powerful economies and by allowing, indeed encouraging, its currency to be used as a standard of value for other countries' reserves and as a medium of exchange for international transactions. By doing so it provides the engine of growth for the rest of the world and, if need be, it can be the lender of last resort—the one country with the power to bail out any others who have become overextended in the international arena. The United States, to some extent, still plays that role, but it is becoming clear that the days of U.S. hegemony are dwindling, which brings us full circle to Japan and its interdependent relationship with the United States.

Japan, with an economy only one-third the size of the United States', is not yet strong enough economically to take over the role of world economic leadership. But, as we have seen, at current rates it is just a question of time until it will have little choice but to assume more responsibility for keeping the world economy in balance.

However, hegemony requires more than economic power. It requires military power and political clout. Japan has neither and, moreover, shows little sign of developing or wanting to develop its power in either of these areas. The Japanese, partly because of limitations placed on them after World War II, spend only 1 percent of their GNP on defense, while the United States spends 6 percent. That means in absolute terms the United States spends eighteen times more on defense than Japan does. This leaves the burden of "keeping the world safe for democracy" mostly on the United States and, to a lesser extent, Western Europe. Japan has shown little interest, for example, in participating in United Nations peacekeeping operations or even in maintaining the free flow of oil in the Persian Gulf, even though it has vital interests at stake there. There is, these days at least, little evidence that Japan has the "sense of empire" that is required of a hegemonic power. This leaves the noncommunist world with its former hegemonic leader, the United States, with the military power but not the economic power to sustain it, and, Japan, the emerging economic power, without military power.

Divergent Scenarios

All this means, as historian Paul Kennedy has pointed out in *The Rise and Fall of the Great Powers*,[1] that there are two possible future scenarios. One is that Japan and the United States share world leadership, with Japan providing the economic muscle and the United States providing the military power and political initiative.

Under that scenario, which seems to be a primary Japanese agenda, Japan would increase its role in funding international organizations like the World Bank and the International Monetary Fund, increase its rate of lending to the debt-ridden under-developed countries, open up its economy to U.S. exports, and, most importantly, take measures to stimulate its economy, especially domestic consumption. At the same time, the United States would continue to bear the burden of perceived mutual defense needs.

By 1988 there were signs that all this was beginning to evolve, albeit slowly. The Japanese trade surplus with the United States was beginning to narrow and Japanese domestic consumption grew by more than 10 percent over the previous year, and it has now become a major contributor to the international financial organizations. Moreover, Japan pledged some $30 billion toward resolving the Third World debt crisis. But there is little evidence that Japan has much stomach for assuming world economic leadership. Yutaka Kosai, president of the Japan Economic Research Center in Tokyo, probably expressed the Japanese feeling most aptly when he was quoted in *The New York Times* as saying: "I have mixed feelings about being a dominant economic power. . . . We hope the United States can recover and Japan will be the second fiddle. Being No. 2 is really quite pleasant."[2]

What may be more likely, unless a new system of global economic cooperation is devised, is that the noncommunist world will gradually evolve into three major trading blocs, each a world within itself, while trading with each other. One would consist of the United States and the Western hemisphere, another would be built around Japan and the Pacific Rim countries, and yet another in Europe with West Germany as its leader. This, however, is complicated by the fact that Western Europe has problems and agendas of its own that make it vulnerable to such a division of labor.

The European Question

In many ways Western Europe provides the model for economic cooperation and policy coordination that could provide the basis for a realistically coordinated world system. The European Economic Community, (EEC) which now includes twelve nations and 320 million people (table 10–1), has agreed to eliminate all trade barriers and trade-restrictive regulations between member countries by 1992. That will make Western Europe a coordinated economic entity almost as large as the United States and by far the world's largest consumer market. In 1987 the combined Gross Domestic Product of the EEC was $4.1 trillion, compared to $4.5 trillion in the United States. (See table 10–2.)

One of the things that has made the U.S. economy what it is, is the fact that the United States is the world's largest free-trade zone. U.S. citizens tend to take for granted the free movement of goods, services, and people between the fifty states without any trade barriers.

But if you had to have a passport to travel from New York to Pennsylvania and stop for a customs check every time you crossed

Table 10–1
Member Nations of the European Economic Community, 1987

Country	Gross Domestic Product (billions)	Growth Rate, 1986–1987	Population (millions)
West Germany	$1,121.2	1.50%	61.1
France	870.3	1.50	55.4
Italy	749.8	2.75	57.2
Britain	658.9	3.75	56.8
Spain	285.5	4.50	38.5
Netherlands	213.6	1.75	14.6
Belgium	139.7	1.25	9.9
Denmark	102.0	–0.75	5.1
Greece	47.1	–0.50	10.0
Portugal	35.4	5.00	10.2
Ireland	28.7	2.00	3.6
Luxembourg	6.2	1.75	0.4

Source: Organization for Economic Cooperation and Development, *European Integration*, 1988.

Table 10–2

Estimates of Potential Annual Economic Gains Resulting from a Europe without Internal Borders

Source of Gain	Amount (billions)	Percentage of Gross Domestic Product
Removing customs formalities	$11	0.3
Removing barriers affecting production	87	2.4
Exploiting economies of scale more fully	75	2.1
Intensifying competition by reducing business inefficiencies and monopoly profits	57	1.6
Total	230	6.4

Source: European Commission of the European Community, *European Integration*, OECD, 1988.

a state border you would have a better feel for what things are like in Europe. Each nation has its own set of regulations governing trade and, more importantly, its own currency, which has to be exchanged every time you cross a border.

But this, too, is changing. The EEC already has adopted a coordinated exchange rate system (the European Monetary System), which keeps member country currencies from fluctuating excessively. And it's likely that by sometime in the 1990s a European central bank will be established, which will operate much like the U.S. Federal Reserve System and allow for the adoption of a common currency.

So it's clear that the Europeans have finally awakened to the fact that if these barriers were removed their economic well-being would be greatly improved and their status as a world economic power vastly enhanced.

Indeed, a recent study by the Organization for Economic Cooperation and Development predicts that the efficiencies that will come out of the planned uniting of the European economy will increase its combined GNP by $230 billion.

In the face of what appears to be a rapidly developing trade war, sparked by the myopic new U.S. protectionist trade legislation, the uniting of Europe stands to be one of the most significant new developments—from a long list—of the decade.

This would be good news for the U.S. economy if a more efficient European economy were able to snap out of its current doldrums and buy more U.S. products.

But it will be bad news if, as seems more likely, the EEC uses its power to erect a tariff wall that excludes the United States (and Japan) and focuses on trade between its member nations. With a home market of 320 million relatively affluent people it can easily afford to do that.

Ironically, the new trade bill allows—indeed, instructs—the president's trade representative to determine what is "fair" trade and what is not. If a country is perceived to be practicing "unfair" trade policies, unilateral retaliatory measures are supposed to be put in place against the culprit nation. It's that clause in the bill—the Super-301 clause—that has outraged the Japanese and Europeans, who feel they are already doing everything possible to open their economies to U.S. exports.

Such a policy might make sense if the United States were still the dominant world economic power or if we were simply dealing with a few banana republics. But to be talking about retaliatory measures against economic powers like Japan and a united Europe is quite a different story. They can and most certainly will match any retaliatory measures we can come up with and there won't be anything we can do about it.

The new developments in Europe seem to portend the emergence of four large trading blocs that will wield tremendous economic power and make protectionist trade policies seem silly.

By the end of the century we'll probably be looking at one free-trade bloc made up of Canada, the United States, and Mexico. The second bloc will contain the EEC nations of Western Europe, and the third will consist of Japan and the rapidly industrializing countries of the Pacific Rim: Taiwan, Singapore, South Korea, and others. The communist bloc nations will round out the list.

Each will have its own tariff walls and tremendous negotiating power. In such a scenario the idea of the United States retaliating against what is perceived to be unfair trading practices won't make any sense at all—just as it doesn't now.

European Monetary System

One of the best currently functioning examples of how economic policy can be coordinated is the European Monetary System, or the EMS. Concerned about the effects of the strong dollar that peaked during the Carter administration, European monetary authorities agreed in March of 1979 to peg the value of their currencies to a common unit of account—the European Currency Unit. The ECU differs from the Bretton Woods system, which tied currencies to the value of the U.S. dollar, in that it is a weighted average of all European monies; thus it is, in essence, a "floating peg" that can vary with economic conditions. However, if any one currency diverges in value in relation to the ECU then the country's authorities are obligated to intervene in the exchange markets to correct the imbalance and/or to make appropriate monetary and fiscal policy changes.

As a practical matter, however, the dominant currency in the EMS is the West German deutsche mark, which makes up over 33 percent of the weighted average. Germany's traditional aversion to inflationary policies has, consequently, been a major force in keeping European inflation rates in check.[3]

The EMS, as Michele Fratianni and others have pointed out, is on the one hand a system to maintain short-run exchange rate stability. In that sense, it has been rather successful. On the other hand, and in a broader context, the EMS is perceived as a step toward economic policy coordination between the members of the European Common Market that would achieve parity of purchasing power for each country and provide a common standard by which their currencies could be valued against others, especially the U.S. dollar and the Japanese yen. To some extent this has been successful, but it is not clear that it has yet stimulated trade between Common Market members, or with the rest of the world.

Others, such as French Finance Minister Edouard Balladur, have argued that the EMS provides a model system of monetary coordination that should be adopted on the world level.[4] For a number of reasons, while such a possibility appears attractive in a utopian sense, it is probably not a practical reality unless current trade imbalances are corrected—in which case it also wouldn't be necessary.

One of the reasons, as noted above, that the EMS has been successful to a degree is that Western Germany has been reluctant to fuel inflation with stimulative monetary and fiscal policy. Yet one of the major thrusts of U.S. policy prescriptions to resolve trade imbalance has been to encourage Japan and West Germany to speed up their economies to absorb more U.S. exports.

If Western Europe ever were to play a major role in world economic leadership it would require the cooperation of West Germany, which has an economy roughly one-fourth the size of the U.S. economy. But only about 10 percent of German exports go to the United States, and over 40 percent go to other EEC members. To make any difference in the current world situation Germany would have to increase its growth rates far above its 1988 level of 1.5 percent. To be sure, there is room, many analysts feel, for more German cooperation in stimulating world economic growth. German unemployment rates (in 1988), for example, were running above 9 percent. But Germany already cut taxes by $8 billion (in 1988) and another $12 billion tax cut was scheduled for 1990, and the German federal domestic deficit was $16 billion in 1988.

However, there is little evidence that West Germany has any interest at all in becoming the locomotive of growth for the rest of the Western world, even if it were big enough to do so. The German population is now growing and living standards are already among the highest in the world. And the lessons of the 1920s' hyperinflation are firmly implanted in the German psyche. Any administration that let inflation get out of control would soon find itself out of office.

Expanding the EMS worldwide would mean Germany would have to give up a large degree of its control over its own destiny, and that is not a likely possibility any time soon. That means if Germany is not ready, it falls back on the United States to take leadership in initiating a system of coordinated exchange rates. But that, first of all, has already been tried during the Bretton

Woods period and failed and, second, the United States has a dismal record of maintaining inflationary stability, which is the one prerequisite for any worldwide exchange rate system to work. Therefore, while the EMS model has a certain theoretical attractiveness, it is not a model that could easily be expanded to the extent that it would make any significant difference in the current fragile international economic climate. As long as Japan and Western Europe are in the driver's seat, the United States will have to look for other ways out of the dilemma of its fractured hegemony.

Key Concepts

New Mercantilism
Newly Industrialized Countries
Hegemony
European Economic Community
European Currency Unit

Discussion Questions

1. How would you explain the rapid growth of the Japanese economy in recent years?

2. The U.S. and Japanese economies are becoming more and more closely interdependent. Why?

3. What is meant by the phrase "new mercantilism"?

4. What is the difference between the NICs of the Pacific Rim and the developing countries of Latin America?

5. Why does the world economy (apparently) need one dominant hegemonic power?

11
Policy Challenges for the 1990s

The issues facing the global economy are becoming more and more clear even as politically viable policy responses become more and more nebulous. The overriding issue is that the trend lines in almost every sector of the United States and the world economy all add up to an impending crisis.

Even if there is gradual improvement in the U.S. trade and budget deficits the situation is not sustainable. The primary problem is not found in the international sector, as one would expect, but in the U.S. economy itself. That is, solutions, if they are to be found anywhere, will come from initial U.S. macroeconomic policy adjustments, followed by consistent and supportive policies coordinated internationally.

Trade Imbalance

There is, as we have seen, little reason to expect that *any kind* of changes in U.S. trade policy or in the policies of its trading partners would be sufficient to significantly improve—much less correct—the bleak trade picture. The U.S. auto industry had by 1988 lost 31 percent of its *own* market to foreign producers. Fifty percent of U.S. machine tools and textiles are now imported. And the U.S. consumer electronics industry is almost totally dominated by foreign producers.

The Omnibus Trade Bill, after three years of negotiation and political infighting among seventeen different congressional subcommittees, finally became law in 1988. But there is little evidence that the myriad of protectionist measures in it will do any more than placate special interest groups, further confuse the issue, and invite self-defeating retaliation. Only about 15 percent of the U.S. trade deficit can be traced to tariffs and other trade restrictions that are higher than similar U.S. restrictions against what are called "unfair trade practices" when someone else does it and "tariffs" when it's done in the United States.

Other measures to correct the trade imbalance, such as depreciating the U.S. dollar, have, as we have seen, done little to improve the deteriorating U.S. position in the world markets. Efforts to improve U.S. productivity have been somewhat successful in the sense that exports have increased slightly but continue to be counterbalanced by the onslaught of imports. Moveover, the gains in productivity have mostly come from decreases in manufacturing employment that have resulted in massive shifts into the lower-paying service sector.

Debt Overhang

It is possible, as Wall Street economist Alan Sinai argued in a provocative *Challenge* magazine article, that the "twin deficits"—the federal deficit and the trade deficit—will improve slightly over the next several years, but even if they do the specter of a growing foreign debt will continue to haunt the U.S. economy.[1] Sinai states the case bluntly:

> Though the budget and trade deficits will likely improve as a percent of GNP in coming years, the growth of government and foreign debt will continue so long as the deficits remain. Eventually, the debt and interest payments on them must be paid through less spending, more savings, and restrictions in the U.S. standard of living.
>
> The so-called "twin deficits" plus trade surpluses abroad are the fundamental problems facing U.S. financial markets and eventually the economy. The large budget and huge trade deficits

that have required high interest rates to finance them now apparently require low enough stock prices as well, in order to slow the economy and release more savings.

Large deficits—outlays exceeding receipts in the case of the federal budget and imports greater than exports—beget increased debt and require borrowing, for a country just as for an individual or a company. If the borrowing continues, outstanding debt keeps rising along with interest payments.

The scenario by now is familiar. Huge budget and trade deficits and debt spew out a large supply of dollars relative to demand, tending to produce a lower dollar. Expected and actual inflation rise. Interest rates are pushed higher. Higher inflation hurts the dollar. The Federal Reserve is either forced to tighten monetary policy against inflation or keep interest rates high to support the dollar and to guard against inflation. If the budget and trade deficit do not improve, the process continues. Eventually, if nothing else intervenes or is done by policymakers here or abroad, interest rates must rise high enough to compensate foreign lenders for dollar and interest-rate risks and to reduce economic growth at home so that enough saving is released domestically to finance the U.S. deficits. The levels of interest rates necessary to do this are uncharted, since the circumstances of the twin deficits are without precedent in the postwar period. At some point, interest rates can reach levels that threaten business expansion in the United States and overseas, where strong currencies already may be threatening economic growth. The result then is lower stock prices in anticipation of a possible recession.[2]

Policy Proposals

There is no shortage of proposals to remedy the situation, but scarce are proposals that are both workable and *politically feasible*. Sinai suggests that a three-part combination of federal budget reduction and monetary policy easing both in the United States and abroad could perhaps reverse the negative trends:

A curative approach that can cut at the heart of the problem involves: 1) a massive reduction in the budget deficits, up to $50 billion or so, with further reductions of less magnitude next year and the year after; 2) a massive offsetting monetary ease in the United States; and 3) stimulative monetary policy abroad to ease any drop in the dollar. This solution must be simultaneous—a "three-legged stool," no leg without the others.

But he admits that:

The likelihood of such a solution being undertaken must be assessed as very small, however. The odds on this grand coordination of policy, even if it is the correct policy prescription, must be regarded as very low. But, at one swipe, it would tend to relieve and probably eliminate a big chunk of the problem for the financial markets that has kept nominal and real interest rates at growth-inhibiting levels for almost all of this decade.[3]

Writing in *Newsweek* two weeks after the October (1987) stock market crash, Peter Peterson proposed that four major areas must be addressed if the United States is going to avoid a total economic collapse.

First, like Sinai—and almost everyone else—he proposed that federal budget reforms be implemented. To accomplish this he suggests a combination of specific spending reductions and tax increases: reduce expenditures for "entitlements," especially built-in cost of living allowances in the various pension funds, increase taxes on Social Security benefits and other pensions, institute a gasoline tax, and so on.

Second, Peterson suggests that more macroeconomic policy coordination will be a prerequisite for any long-term solution to be viable. The current policy of propping up the dollar by intervention in the foreign exchange markets (which amount to printing money) will, he argues, only lead to more inflation and exacerbate the problem.

Third, he says, "the United States must begin to rethink how it allocates its security resources." What will be required in "a sizeable increase in the European contribution to NATO's conventional forces."

Finally, he argues, the time has come for a new pact with the Japanese that would involve trading security guarantees in the Pacific for a rechanneling of Japanese trade surplus earnings toward the Third World "through the (existing) multilateral economic institutions, aid untied to exports and incentives for private capital investments. Not only would this lead to greater Third World development, but it would calm fears that the debt bomb will explode."[4]

Then Peterson sums up the situation aptly:

> At bottom, our problems are not economic. Rather, we are stymied by our lack of political consensus. We do not even agree on the nature of our economic difficulties. In Japan and West Germany, by contrast, there is widespread accord, born of national crisis, on the necessary, long-term connection between savings and investment, between investment and productivity growth, and between productivity growth and real wage increases.
>
> Historically, the American character has emphasized optimism, unfettered energy, "win–win" choices and the direct pursuit of dreams. Circumstances are now forcing us to change our behavior in a direction that has few recent precedents: toward self-denial, collective discipline, "win–lose" choices and deferred gratification. For at least a couple of decades, both in our private and public lives, we have fixed our attention on spending and consuming. Now we will have to fix it on producing and saving. Without this change, our next economic coronary could put us under for a very long time.[5]

Macroeconomic Policy

As it has become more and more clear that externally imposed trade measures such as protectionism and exchange rate manipulation do not and will not alter the growing imbalance of trade, it has become equally clear that the root of the problem is more a question of appropriate *macroeconomic* policies rather than *ad hoc* and *ex post* international economic policy responses.

If we look back at recent history it is easy to see that the trade imbalance problem first came to public attention in the early 1980s, especially between 1981 and 1984, which was the beginning of the Reagan administration and included the 1982–1983 recession. The recession—the worst of the postwar period—was a planned part of the administration's overall economic strategy. The goal was to rein in inflation by increasing interest rates and generally tighten the money supply, while at the same time lowering taxes, which is, of course, contradictory monetary and fiscal policy, and one result was record-high unemployment rates (about 10 percent) and record-high interest rates (over 22 percent). This policy, coupled with rapid increases in debt levels, did eventually break the back of inflation and by 1983 the U.S. economy began to recover. Since then, driven by the huge debt buildup on all fronts, the economy has grown at slow but steady rates, unemployment has fallen, and inflation has remained at relatively low levels.

However, during the same period the trade situation worsened precipitously. The reason was partly that the Third World debt buildup effectively cut off U.S. exports to most of the lesser-developed areas, and partly that the U.S. economy was, by 1984, growing at very high rates (7 percent), which fueled import growth without any significant increase in exports.

In addition, it was this strange combination of unexpected events that also caused the U.S. dollar to skyrocket in the exchange markets. Normally, a U.S. trade deficit would mean a *weaker* dollar as dollar demand dwindled. But *macroeconomic* policies caused international capital flows to shift in the other direction. High interest rates in the United States, which were partly a result of the inflation reduction policies of the Fed and partly a result of the debt buildup, increased the demand for dollars, pushed the dollar up, and with it the trade deficit—to record levels.

There are two lessons in these unprecedented historical developments. One, as I.M. Destler has pointed out, is:

> [I]n a world of floating exchange rates and large-scale capital flows, trade imbalances are largely immune to treatment by

trade policy measures. They can be reached only by other means, mainly macroeconomic measures that influence total demand and affect the savings–investment balance within trading nations. Also, when circumstances are favorable, trade imbalances can be influenced by official intervention in foreign exchange markets.

Trade measures can affect the volume of trade. They can influence the composition of that trade. But unless coupled with other measures, they will have little impact on the overall surplus or deficit run by a nation.[6]

The other lesson is that as long as the United States continues to run federal budget deficits that depend on foreign financing, i.e., use foreign savings to finance domestic consumption, interest rates will of necessity remain high, the dollar will remain structurally strong, and the trade balance will continue to deteriorate. With it the international position of the United States will continue to erode. Unless something is done to reduce the federal deficit, there is little reason for optimism on any front. The net result, as the U.S. international debtor position builds, will be a gradual lowering of the U.S. standard of living as more resources are diverted abroad to service growing external debt.

Microeconomic Policy Strategies

At the microeconomic level there are numerous proposals and strategies to improve U.S. competitiveness in the international sector. Mostly they fall under the rubric of "industrial policy," which has been popularized by writers like Robert Reich and embraced in varying degrees by liberal elements of the Democratic Party. There is, as Reich and others have pointed out, some confusion and misunderstanding over what industrial policy really means. In Reich's view:

Any mention of industrial policies summons the specter of national planning, in which bureaucrats—ignorant of or indifferent to market force—shift capital from industry to industry to nurture their favorite future "winners." Our inability to distinguish between this caricature and the realities of well-designed adjustment policies—through which government seeks to promote market forces rather than to supplant them—has confounded political dialogue.[7]

There are many ways in which business, labor, and government could cooperate to the end of revitalizing the American economy, and to some extent this is being done.[8] Even under the Reagan administration, where strong ideological free-market attitudes dominated most strategies, there was an increasing recognition of a role government can play in improving long-run competitiveness. Indeed, Reich argues the Reagan administration did, in fact, already implement an industrial policy. He points out, for example, that:

1. In January 1987, the Administration approved a $4.4 billion plan for a superconducting supercollider: a 52-mile underground race track for subatomic particles. A White House official deemed the project "critical" to our future competitiveness.

2. Last July, the President announced an "11-point superconducting initiative" aimed at developing practical applications for superconducting material—special alloys that, when cooled, lose all resistance to the flow of electric current. The White House called this technology "absolutely essential to our future competitiveness." Antitrust laws will be relaxed to allow collaborative research, patent applications for superconductors will be put on a fast track, four special research centers will be established and the Freedom of Information Act will be modified to allow Government laboratories to withhold commercially valuable superconductor information.

3. In October, the Administration announced that it would fund "Sematech," a joint research venture comprising America's leading semiconductor manufacturers. "Semiconductor technology will be critical to our economic security in the years ahead," an Administration official said. "We can't afford to fall behind."

4. Last December, the White House unveiled a "high-tech program" of software and algorithms—all aimed at developing computers capable of performing trillions of operations per

second. Warning that Japanese supercomputers were already on the market, and "with better performance than expected," the Administration proposed spending $1.7 billion over five years.

5. During the same month, the Administration awarded contracts to begin building the nation's first permanent space station. Administration officials noted that the station would be a laboratory for developing new pharmaceuticals and high-tech materials used in computers, and thus "vital to enhancing the nation's international competitiveness in the decades ahead."

And there's much, much more.[9]

Such policies, whatever they are called, are an explicit recognition that governmental policies can influence the long-run competitiveness of industry.

Labor, and to a lesser extent, business, have also cooperated in the restructuring of American industry. Wage concessions by labor have permitted impressive productivity gains and held down inflation rates. For its part business has implemented worker training programs and instituted new, more flexible, production systems modeled in large part after Japanese methods. More importantly, there is an increasing awareness that more resources have to be channeled into investments in research and development that has in recent years been deemphasized at the expense of short-term profits.

The key issue in all this is that well-thought-out industrial policies are not the same as the seemingly socialistic "economic planning." They involve, instead, encouraging *adjustments* in all sectors toward the now commonly understood goal of and need for a revitalization of American industry if it is to survive the challenges it faces in the next decade. I.M. Destler summed up the situation well when he wrote:

> We therefore need policies to speed adjustment by industry and labor, to encourage movement of resources from less productive to more productive enterprises and regions. This should be jointed with efforts to increase productivity growth for the economy as a whole. There is a strong need for policies, in Charles Shultze's words, "designed to make the economy in general more flexible, more dynamic, more productive, and

more capable of adjustment to technological change." Such policies need to focus on labor markets, increasing training opportunities for workers and improving market information about job openings. They can include more support of general and specialized education and encouragement of research where the benefits to society exceed those recoverable by a firm. They can include tax code changes that favor productivity-enhancing forms of investment, and that favor the domestic savings that must ultimately finance such investment. . . . the focus on our industrial productivity can be enormously constructive. It can turn American attention away from nefarious-seeming foreigners, toward self-help at home. It can focus our energies on creating an appropriate, stimulative policy environment for our productive enterprises. It can encourage a creeping recognition that many of the problems of American producers are, in important part, "made in USA."[10]

Getting Specific

How can a politically feasible industrial policy be implemented? On a practical level it is at once complex and simple. It's simple to the extent that what has to be done is well understood; how to pay for it is quite another question. In a 1986 cover story titled "A Strategy for Revitalizing Industry" (and interestingly subtitled "America Should Start by Correcting Its Self-Imposed Disadvantages in World Competition"), *Business Week* outlined six areas in which change—adjustments—would have to be made.

First, *Business Week* financial analyst Norman Jonas suggests the federal budget deficit must be cut so that the government stops "sopping up the bulk of private savings to finance the federal debt." This would "free capital for private investment and trim real interest rates."

Second, the tax system should be reformed in such a way that it would encourage capital investment rather than discourage it, as the 1987 tax reform act did. "Congress," he proposes, "should eliminate the corporate tax entirely. This would end the double taxation of dividends and cancel the advantage of debt over equity investments. It would allow investment decisions to be made on the basis of business rather than tax considerations."

Third, Jonas says, "It's also time to repeal or at least re-write the Glass-Steagall Act to permit merchant banking in the United States. If banks or other institutions could take large equity positions in the companies they lend to, it would be in their interest to stick with projects that might take four or five years to reach a payoff."

Fourth, "The U.S. can no longer afford a large pool of under-educated and even illiterate workers. . . .The U.S. simply is not spending enough for education and job training. . . . Human capital requires at least as much nurturing as currently favored financial investments."

Fifth, he argues, "Management and unions can no longer afford old-style adversarial relations. . . . [They must agree on] a new system of labor-management relations and compensation that links new technology with a fundamental restructuring of work practices . . . [and] replace the traditional division of work into narrow tasks . . . with broader jobs, rotating assignments, and considerable self-management."

Finally, Jonas argues that something must be done to reverse the lead of U.S. trade rivals in the field of research and development. "R & D is the clearest case of subsidization making sense, since the innovations produced by private research generally yield benefits to the public and not just the companies footing the bill."[11]

Such an agenda is indeed impressive and even in a free-market framework would be feasible except that someone has to foot the bill. In the current antitax environment it is not realistic to think that any political candidate could ever be elected on a tax-increase platform.

If taxes can't be increased then expenditures have to be cut. But, as we have seen in earlier chapters, politically untouchable entitlements make up such a large part of the federal budget that meaningful expenditure cuts are not possible. That leaves the defense budget, which is the single largest category in the federal budget. There is a voluminous literature that makes the case that defense expenditures could be cut without significantly reducing the national security, but as long as the United States remains committed to both its own defense *and* that of its allies, reductions in defense spending are not going to be feasible.[12] That has led some to suggest that the entire question of U.S. world dominance needs to be reevaluated.

Decline of U.S. Hegemony: Who Cares?

Underlying the overall issue of the decline of U.S. dominance of the world economy is the question: why does it matter? A 1987 survey found that 67 percent of those polled felt that the United States has "grown weaker relative to other countries" and 67 percent believed "Americans' industries aren't geared to keeping up with changes taking place in the world economy." Clearly, there is concern among the American people that the future is bleak. By 1988 several books outlining the "decline of the American empire" hit the best-seller lists. They represent a new intellectual movement dubbed a "school of decline" by writer Peter Schmeisser.[13]

The essence of their message, which is perhaps most forcefully stated in Yale historian Paul Kennedy's lengthy book *The Rise and Fall of the Great Powers,* is that the United States rose to a position of economic hegemony after the Second World War through economic and technological achievements that allowed it to devote larger and larger proportions of its wealth to military expenditures. But as the U.S. economy has moved into a more mature stage it has not been able to sustain its worldwide military commitments and at the same time maintain economic growth levels required to keep the balance of economic power tilting in its direction.[14]

The picture of this book and others like it is one of a nation overextended on all fronts, gradually slipping into second-rate status, and being forced to share power with emerging power blocks in Europe and the Pacific. This has sparked lively debate in Congress and spawned several new organizations devoted to "correcting the problem." Among these is the Democratic Leadership Council of the Congress, which proposes a system of democratic capitalism, i.e., an "industrial policy," to revive the sleeping giant. Another group, called Rebuild America, which is linked to 1988 Democratic presidential candidate Michael Dukakis, calls for a political consensus for a national investment strategy to improve capital formation, manufacturing technology, productivity, and job training—all within the context of the first priority: reduction of government spending. How these conflicting goals are to be reconciled with the need to reduce the federal deficit is not clear.

The bottom line is that America has to decide whether it wants to attempt to regain its position of world economic leadership and maintain military hegemony. If it does then it is clear enough that sacrifices have to be made. Consumption levels have to be reduced and investment has to be rechanneled toward nonmilitary sectors such as education, research and development, and other things that will eventually lead to increased productivity without at the same time pushing the work force into non-productive service areas. This, as we have argued, is not a likely scenario. The question of Who Cares? has so far been answered by ever higher consumer spending, ever increasing levels of imports, and ever lower savings levels.

Should the United States Be Number One?

Much of the argument we have made here depends on the assumption that free trade between nations benefits everyone. Virtually all economists support the venerable theory of comparative advantage to the extent that is has become the corner-stone of international economic theory and the rationale by which all arguments for protection are summarily dismissed. But free trade has a way of bestowing advantages on the strong at the expense of the weak.[15]

Free trade benefited Great Britain during the mid-nineteenth-century period of its dominance of the world economy when it could rely on the British Empire to absorb its surpluses and supply its raw material needs. As the empire crumbled so did the advantages of free trade and Britain settled into a period of slower growth and lower relative standards of living. But it didn't wither and fade away.

Some economists, albeit a minority, now argue that the United States has reached a similar stage in its development and that by clinging to outmoded theories of comparative advantage it is merely ensuring its further demise. Everyone in America bemoans the loss of U.S. dominance because it is assumed that free trade benefits America and that what is good for the United States is good for everyone else. Every policy proposal we have examined in this book presupposes that assumption. The problem is, of course, that even if every single tariff or other trade protection *in the world* were somehow magically eliminated overnight or even if all tariffs were doubled overnight the same problems would still be there. Japan would still be the world's largest creditor nation, the United States the largest debtor, and so on.

That fact has led some to suggest that all policy proposals designed to resolve the trade imbalance question are misdirected. Why, they ask, does everybody think we have to be Number One? Why do we have to restructure our economy to emulate the mercantilistic policies of Japan, or the low-wage-driven export strategy of the Newly Industrialized Countries of the Pacific Rim? Why not, as economist David Gordon and others have asked, just tend to our own front yard? Such a strategy, Gordon argues,

> would promote a transition away from domestic dependence on the global economy and toward cooperation with our friends and allies abroad. . . . [Why not] . . . pursue more effective domestic production of necessities—such as energy, clothing, and transportation—not indulgent succor of backward industries.[16]

In the internationally interdependent world of the 1990s, such a proposal seems like pie-in-the-sky Pollyannaish utopianism at best, or a thinly disguised argument for protectionism at worst, but *given the alternatives*—decline in living standards and loss of economic sovereignty—any proposal that would reduce the level of U.S. import consumption makes sense if it can be accomplished without triggering retaliatory responses from the rest of the world.

Actually, import substitution schemes are not new. In various forms they have been tried by many developing countries, Mexico's Import Substitution Industrialization program of the 1970s being the most notable example (and a most notable failure). In many ways, the debtor status of the United States is not much different than that of most of the heavily indebted Third World countries, but the major difference is that the United States has the economic power and, more importantly, the internal resources, to implement an import substitution program if it really wanted to *and* was ready to make the necessary sacrifices.

As short-term measures, it would be possible, David Gordon suggests, to:

1. Chart the sectors of the economy that are experiencing the most rapid increases in foreign imports, and explore concrete domestic alternatives to those imports—for example, federal subsidies for developing conservation and renewable-energy alternatives to imported oil.

2. Negotiate trade agreements that not only aim at reductions in tariffs but also seek multilateral treaties allocating imports and exports for each nation participating. At the moment we have few such agreements, and those we have are largely obsolete. We need, in effect, to update the General Agreement on Tariffs and Trade (GATT), first negotiated nearly forty years ago, through either a new general treaty or a set of bilateral or multilateral agreements.

3. Establish programs during the transition to a Front Yard economy that are aimed at cushioning the costs of adjustment for U.S. workers in affected industries, emulating (for example) the Japanese program for "structurally depressed industries."

4. Adopt specific proposals such as recently debated legislation for a domestic-content requirement for automobiles. Such measures are less protectionist than quotas, because they both encourage production in the United States—under domestic-content legislation foreign firms would be mandated to invest and produce in the United States—and expose U.S. enterprises to the best of foreign technical and managerial practice.

5. Institute plant-closing legislation that would to some degree protect workers against the sudden flight of capital abroad, by making advance notification and indemnification provisions for plant shutdowns and sudden shifts of investment abroad, and by removing current tax incentives for domestic firms to invest abroad.

In the longer run Gordon suggests that the United States may be thinking backward when it comes to restoring international competitiveness. In theory as well as practice everyone has assumed that one key to being competitive was holding down wages and paring down the size of the work force. Fewer workers producing the same or more amount of goods at lower wages does, to be sure, add up to higher productivity, i.e., higher output per man-hour. But, Gordon asks, couldn't the reverse also be true? Would not *higher* wages and better job security increase productivity as workers were able "to identify their stake in the future of the enterprise. . . .When offered job security and promises of stable wage growth in the proper management climate . . . [workers] can actually take the initiative in spurring productivity growth."[17]

Under current and "normal" conditions workers generally *oppose* productivity-oriented technological changes because they fear losing their jobs. Under a wage-led productivity plan the opposite would be the case. Such a radical proposal seems unlikely to infiltrate corporate board rooms any time soon, but experiments at Procter & Gamble, General Motors, General Electric, Goodyear, and many other companies have caught the attention—if not the imagination—of many corporate leaders. It is, in any case, one example of how a Front Yard strategy would differ from a strategy of Staying on Top. Workers not only produce goods but also buy them. Higher-paid workers buy more of them.

Gordon also suggests that a different way of thinking about international trade in general would greatly reduce U.S. dependence on imports *and* exports. The conventional strategy is to close the trade deficit by increasing exports while "tolerating" imports. But, he says, a Front Yard strategy, in contrast, calls for reducing both the export and the import share over the long term, while reducing the import share by a somewhat wider margin.

The increasing U.S. dependence on imported oil, which peaked in the 1970s but is now growing again, is probably the most clear example of how the different strategies would work:

> Take the case of imported oil and the aftermath of the OPEC price hikes of 1973 and 1979. One response to the immediately higher costs of imports was to seek compensating increases in our exports—searching vigorously for commodities such as grain, arms, and computers for which we could find new markets abroad. Another approach could have placed a higher priority than the government did during the 1970s on reducing our dependence on imported oil—through invigorated energy-conservation programs and an emphasis on locally available and renewable sources of energy like solar and geothermal power. The former strategy might work over the short term but is likely to lose effectiveness over the longer term, because international markets and prices periodically shift. The latter strategy has clear promise for both the short and long term, because it would more or less permanently lessen our demand for a substance that is a significant component of our import bill. The former would require that we continually adjust to unexpected shocks from beyond our borders. The latter would gradually reduce our exposure to such shocks.[18]

Clearly such a strategy seems protectionist, if not Pollyannaish, but when considering the broader context of increasing world economic interdependence functioning on the rationale of perceived comparative advantages, one has to remember that one result of letting free markets function internationally is that wages tend to level worldwide. Therefore, while in the short run the United States may benefit from the "cheap labor" abroad, the end result is that U.S. wage levels will fall as others rise. To a certain extent that has been happening already, which is one reason the Japanese can produce Hondas in Ohio and export them *to* Japan. Average manufacturing wages in

Japan now exceed similar wages in the United States. Ultimately, Gordon argues, it is a question of national sovereignty.

> The final major goal of international economic policy involves the question of national sovereignty. . . . While realism requires flexibility in the face of international competition, the U.S. cannot agree to abandon its standard of living or its traditional commitment to restrain exploitation of child labor, preserve the health of its workforce, protect its environment, [or] provide retired, unemployed, or handicapped citizens with an adequate level [of] income. . . . If we permit ourselves to become locked into the competitive "race to the bottom" we will inevitably lose control over the most basic social and political aspects of our national life.[19]

End of an Era

Whatever the theoretical subtleties, the short-term–long-term trade-offs, or the political consequences, no one can argue that we have not reached the end of the era of U.S. hegemony. This was inevitable any way you look at it but it was clearly speeded by the globalization of production, which, as Michael Moffit and many others have pointed out, is probably the single most important development of the postwar era. And it is irreversible. Moffitt makes the point clearly:

> The rise of the multinational corporation, I am increasingly convinced, represents the central macroeconomic event of the postwar world, the significance of which neither academic analysis nor policy has fully grasped. While most economists and politicians discuss world trade as if individual nations were engaged in shipping products to and from one another, the rise of multinational corporations has made these conventional concepts of world trade obsolete. Consider the facts: one-third or more of all "trade" in manufactured goods now consists of intracompany transactions by multinationals. In the last five years, foreign direct investment by U.S.-based multinationals has expanded by about 25 percent, a very respectable increase given worldwide gluts in many products. There has also been a real

shift away from investment in petroleum and mining toward manufacturing, finance, and banking. Direct investment in manufacturing facilities is up nearly 30 percent since 1983. In certain industries, like machinery, it has soared more than 60 percent.

In manufacturing today, foreign jobs account for about a third of U.S. multinationals' total employment. And, according to business consultant Peter Drucker, around 20 percent of all manufacturing by U.S. multinationals is done outside of the United States. It has been estimated that multinationals import up to 40 to 50 percent of all U.S. imports, with a third of these coming in the form of intracompany transactions.[20]

During the 1960s and early 1970s, Moffitt argues, the situation was quite different. Then "the U.S. economy clearly benefited from the spread of U.S. multinationals, and the U.S. standard of living was higher as a result of their activities. [And then] . . . overseas investment by U.S.-based multinationals boosted U.S. exports of capital goods. . . . These exports . . . dwarfed U.S. capital goods imports . . . [and] offset growing imports of televisions, radios, and other consumer goods."

But that era is over. The multinationalization of production is a result of the fact that capital is mobile and labor, by and large, is not. With the growth of worldwide sourcing, telecommunications, and money transfers, there is no pecuniary reason for U.S. firms to pay Americans to do what Mexicans or Koreans will do at a fraction of the cost. This is why "elite" U.S. working-class jobs are being sent abroad and "outsourcing" is the current rage in manufacturing. As a result, American multinationals remain highly competitive and their profits are booming, while the United States itself is becoming less and less competitive. In the 1980s, U.S. capital goods exports have collapsed while imports of both consumer and producer goods have surged, no doubt in part because U.S. firms are not importing these products from foreign lands. In other words, we once exported the capital goods used to manufacture our consumer imports; now we are also importing the capital goods to run what remains of our domestic industry.[21]

Add that to the debt explosion and the now almost-total U.S. dependence on foreign capital to finance its deficits and, Moffitt argues, we have come full circle:

> Thus, we have the outlines of a true vicious circle: the world economy is dependent on growth in the U.S. economy but the U.S. domestic economy is skewed more toward consumption than production and investment, and this consumption is in turn sustained by borrowing—at home and abroad. An economy sustained by debt, especially foreign debt, is always vulnerable to an interest rate shock, whether it is administered by the Fed or by the markets. Given foreign dependence on the U.S. market, a rate shock that is great enough to send the U.S. economy into a new recession thus virtually guarantees a worldwide economic collapse with all that that implies for bankruptcies, defaults, and the widespread liquidation of debt. [22]

From a slightly different perspective, W. Michael Blumenthal, who was Secretary of the Treasury during the Carter administration and is now chairman and CEO of the Unisys Corporation, writing in the prestigious *Foreign Affairs,* reaches similar conclusions. The problem, he argues, is that technological change has far outpaced the ability of political and economic institutions to cope with it.

> I believe there is one circumstance which overshadows all else and has set the current period apart: unprecedented, deep, and continual technological change. In the 1970s and 1980s extraordinarily rapid technological change has thrust upon us new and as yet unresolved problems of governance in the national and international spheres.
>
> There appears to be a fundamental lag between the current rate of technological change and the rate of adjustment to these changes among decision makers. Technology that evolves much more rapidly than the body politic can absorb creates strains and stresses which lead to dislocations, instabilities, and paralysis of action—and sometimes perverse responses. This is what characterizes our situation today. The problem is further complicated because the private sector accepts technological change more rapidly than the government.

Today's situation differs in one fundamental aspect from earlier periods of rapid technological change (e.g., during the invention of the steam engine or the telephone). The current period of revolutionary change is occurring in a much more interdependent world in which purely or largely national efforts to adapt to change have ceased to suffice. Furthermore, existing international institutions have been rendered obsolete by technological change, and the capacity for making international reforms is even less developed than that for making domestic reforms. In the absence of adequate institutions, progress on adjusting to the new technology is reduced to a slow crawl.[23]

The advances in microelectronics, Blumenthal argues, have revolutionized the production process to the point that the shift of employment to the service sector has become the issue of the decade and, as well, the challenge of the world economy.

Service trade was not a problem in the Kennedy Round twenty years ago. Today, it is the issue. In an advanced country such as the United States, 75 percent of the work force is now employed in the service sector overall, and two-thirds of that number are connected in one way or another with information or with the knowledge industry itself. The estimate is that by the year 2000 only 15 percent of all employment in the United States will be devoted to the manufacture of goods.

Increasingly, then, a country's comparative advantage lies in its ability to utilize effectively the new information technology, in the speed of its absorption into the productive process, and in the relative efficiency with which it is applied. Less and less it is the other factor endowments, the availability of raw materials or the cost of labor, that determine which country has the advantage and which has the lowest total cost.[24]

At bottom line the issue has become one of national sovereignty, which, he argues, has become obsolete in all but the most philosophical sense:

Technology is rapidly making the basic notion of national sovereignty obsolete in many areas of economic affairs—at least for some of the major nations of the world, and ultimately for most:

- There is now one world capital market. How then can any major nation hope to conduct a truly effective national monetary policy all on its own?
- Exchange rates quickly transmit the effects of key tax, spending, and budget decisions from one major country to another. How then can there be a truly independent national fiscal policy?
- Factors of production are less fixed and knowledge flows freely across borders. How then can strictly national rules and regulations remain effective if they are out of step with the rest of the world?
- And if technology can rapidly override the effects, how can national import restrictions and protectionism possibly still achieve their stated aims?

The conclusion is inescapable that technology has created a world no longer effectively composed of individual national economic entities. Thus, if we continue to act as if nothing has changed, our persistence in applying strictly national policies is bound to prove frustrating, and often counterproductive as well.[25]

The problem facing the world is: what role will the United States play in adjusting to this new reality? One possibility is to slide into a secondary role and forfeit leadership to Japan or Europe. And this, as we have argued, is the more likely scenario. But, as Blumenthal points out, this may not be possible.

No real progress is likely or possible without the leadership of the United States. We are no longer the dominating world economic power, but we are still the largest and most powerful nation. Ours is the world's largest single market and our currency remains at the center of international finance. We remain the political and strategic leader of the West. And we have the greatest military strength, with worldwide interests and commitments that span the globe. What happens in the United States affects world economic events profoundly. We were the principal architect of the existing framework created in the wake of the Second World War, and none of these international economic institutions can evolve without our active initiative and support.[26]

Therefore, Blumenthal suggests, we need "to define a bold and comprehensive new philosophical underpinning for the management of domestic and international affairs . . . a new strategy," based on five key principles.

The effort to define a new strategy must be based, first, on realism, on a willingness to think about the world as it is and not as it once was, and second, on a recognition that U.S. hegemony in economic affairs has come to an end; the triangular power bloc of the United States, Japan, and the European Economic Community, and the three-currency grouping of the dollar, mark, and yen has taken its place.

The third principle will be particularly difficult to put across, but strikes me as a prerequisite for intelligent progress on almost any front. We need to lead the way in redefining, for others and for ourselves, the meaning of "national interest" in broader terms than in the past. Implied here is the proposition that national interest now dictates for all a limiting of unilateral moves in economic affairs, and that for all the key actors it must encompass greater concern over the impact of major domestic measures on others. It implies acceptance of the principle of common responsibility for internationally compatible solutions to domestic needs, and for the creation of and support for the institutions necessary to coordinate these efforts on a broader scale.

The fourth principle is a corollary of the third. It involves the commitment to renounce, or at least to limit wherever possible, those measures that are particularly incompatible with the expanded definition of what the true national interest now means. Protectionist policies immediately come to mind. The unwillingness to collaborate on environmental issues, it can be argued, is another case in point.

Fifth and finally, the principle of nonexclusivity, that is, the need to take account of the broader interdependencies of economic problems affecting the many, should also be recognized and understood. Technology will tie all of us together on this Earth. And more than before, broad interrelationships will have to be taken into account, whether they concern the communist bloc or the wider range of LDCs, and whether they deal with currency problems or the connection between market access and economic aid.[27]

Translating such challenges into concrete policies without at the same time bringing the world economy to its knees is a tall order. It is easy to point out problems. Critics of capitalism were doing that long before the trade and debt crisis, and long before the stock market crash made everyone realize that the bubble had, indeed, burst. Ironically, what seems to underlie most of the problems and the developing crisis we have outlined in this book is not the failure of capitalism to deliver the goods, but its tendency to deliver too many. The system, as Marx thought it would, produces but hasn't been able to distribute. Excess capacity and insufficient demand, as Keynes demonstrated, is a sure formula for recession. Mix that with record trade imbalances and an unprecedented debt explosion and you have written the program for another Great Depression. If that is to be avoided changes must be made. If they are not made voluntarily they will be imposed on us at a cost much higher than we can currently imagine.

As the thoughtful reader will no doubt point out, there are many contradictions in the varied lines of argument we have examined here. On the one hand, it seems logical, if not sagacious, to argue that the current imbalance problems could—and should—be solved if the United States would—and could—put its own house in order. Making the U.S. economy more productive and competitive to reverse the current disturbing trade balance trends, might, perhaps, restore the world economy to levels it enjoyed during the 1960s and 1970s, when it was dominated by U.S. economic power and fed by increasing levels of consumption amid rising incomes.

But, on the other hand, to argue for that highly unlikely scenario while at the same time stressing the need for increased international coordination between the United States and the rapidly emerging economic power blocs doesn't fit well with the spectre of reality that haunts the world economy today. International policy coordination requires externally imposed discipline and, more importantly, it requires that *someone give up something*. Until someone is willing to do that the trend lines that already have crossed into an abyss of imbalance will continue to diverge.

At some point they will go off the charts. When that happens it will be time to talk.

Meanwhile, as a beginning, the time has come for the major players to sit down at the same table and consider ways in which the international financial system can be restructured to reflect the realities of the modern world. Some would call it a New Bretton Woods Conference. We would call it a poker game in which the United States is no longer the dealer *and* the banker. Whatever it is called, it will be a very high-stakes game.

Key Concepts

Debt Overhang
Twin Deficits
Industrial Policy
Multinational Intracompany Transactions
National Sovereignty

Discussion Questions

1. What is meant by the term "debt overhang"?

2. How does macroeconomic policy affect international economic policy, and vice versa?

3. Some people feel industrial economic policy can be equated with socialist economic planning. Why?

4. Why should the United States try to maintain its position as Number One?

5. What, in your mind, is the major challenge facing the U.S. economy in the next decade?

Appendix:
International Statistics

Table A–1

U.S. International Transactions, 1946–88

[millions of dollars; quarterly data seasonally adjusted, except as noted. Credits (+), debits (–)]

Year or quarter	Merchandise [1][2]			Investment income [3]			Net military transactions	Net travel and transportation receipts	Other services, net [3]	Balance on goods and services [4]	Remittances, pensions, and other unilateral transfers [1]	Balance on current account [4]
	Exports	Imports	Net	Receipts	Payments	Net						
1946	11,764	−5,067	6,697	772	−212	560	−493	733	310	7,807	−2,922	4,885
1947	16,097	−5,973	10,124	1,102	−245	857	−455	946	145	11,617	−2,625	8,992
1948	13,265	−7,557	5,708	1,921	−437	1,484	−799	374	175	6,942	−4,525	2,417
1949	12,213	−6,874	5,339	1,831	−476	1,355	−621	230	208	6,511	−5,638	873
1950	10,203	−9,081	1,122	2,068	−559	1,509	−576	−120	242	2,177	−4,017	−1,840
1951	14,243	−11,176	3,067	2,633	583	2,050	−1,270	298	254	4,399	−3,515	884
1952	13,449	−10,838	2,611	2,751	−555	2,196	−2,054	83	309	3,145	−2,531	614
1953	12,412	−10,975	1,437	2,736	−624	2,112	−2,423	−238	307	1,195	−2,481	−1,286
1954	12,929	−10,353	2,576	2,929	−582	2,347	−2,460	−269	305	2,499	−2,280	219
1955	14,424	−11,527	2,897	3,406	−676	2,730	−2,701	−297	299	2,928	−2,498	430
1956	17,556	−12,803	4,753	3,837	−735	3,102	−2,788	−361	447	5,153	−2,423	2,730
1957	19,562	−13,291	6,271	4,180	−796	3,384	−2,841	−189	482	7,107	−2,345	4,762
1958	16,414	−12,952	3,462	3,790	−825	2,965	−3,135	−633	486	3,145	−2,361	784
1959	16,458	−15,310	1,148	4,132	−1,061	3,071	−2,805	−821	573	1,166	−2,448	−1,282
1960	19,650	−14,758	4,892	4,616	−1,237	3,379	−2,752	−964	638	5,191	−2,367	2,824
1961	20,108	−14,537	5,571	4,999	−1,245	3,754	−2,596	−978	732	6,484	−2,662	3,822
1962	20,781	−16,260	4,521	5,618	−1,324	4,294	−2,449	−1,152	911	6,127	−2,740	3,387
1963	22,272	−17,048	5,224	6,157	−1,561	4,596	−2,304	−1,309	1,037	7,244	−2,831	4,414
1964	25,501	−18,700	6,801	6,824	−1,784	5,040	−2,133	−1,146	1,161	9,724	−2,901	6,823
1965	26,461	−21,510	4,951	7,437	−2,088	5,349	−2,122	−1,280	1,480	8,378	−2,948	5,431
1966	29,310	−25,493	3,817	7,528	−2,481	5,047	−2,935	−1,331	1,496	6,095	−3,064	3,031
1967	30,666	−26,866	3,800	8,020	−2,747	5,273	−3,226	−1,750	1,742	5,838	−3,255	2,583
1968	33,626	−32,991	635	9,368	−3,378	5,990	−3,143	−1,548	1,759	3,693	−3,082	611
1969	36,414	−35,807	607	10,912	−4,869	6,043	−3,328	−1,763	1,964	3,524	−3,125	399
1970	42,469	−39,866	2,603	11,747	−5,516	6,231	−3,354	−2,038	2,329	5,773	−3,443	2,331
1971	43,319	−45,579	−2,260	12,707	−5,436	7,271	−2,893	−2,345	2,649	2,423	−3,856	−1,433
1972	49,381	−55,797	−6,416	14,764	−6,572	8,192	−3,420	−3,063	2,965	−1,742	−4,052	−5,795
1973	71,410	−70,499	911	21,808	−9,655	12,153	−2,070	−3,158	3,406	11,244	−4,103	7,140
1974	98,306	−103,811	−5,505	27,587	−12,084	15,503	−1,653	−3,184	4,231	9,392	[5] −7,431	1,962
1975	107,088	−98,185	8,903	25,351	−12,564	12,787	−746	−2,812	4,853	22,984	−4,868	18,116
1976	114,745	−124,228	−9,483	29,286	−13,311	15,975	559	−2,558	5,027	9,521	−5,314	4,207
1977	120,816	−151,907	−31,091	32,179	−14,217	17,962	1,528	−3,565	5,679	−9,488	−5,023	−14,511
1978	142,054	−176,001	−33,947	42,245	−21,680	20,565	621	−3,573	6,459	−9,875	−5,552	−15,427
1979	184,473	−212,009	−27,536	64,132	−32,960	31,172	−1,778	−2,935	6,214	5,138	−6,128	−991
1980	224,269	−249,749	−25,480	72,506	−42,120	30,386	−2,237	−997	7,793	9,466	−7,593	1,873
1981	237,085	−265,063	−27,978	86,411	−52,329	34,082	−1,183	144	9,278	14,344	−7,460	6,884
1982	211,198	−247,642	−36,444	83,549	−54,883	28,666	−274	−992	9,320	278	−8,956	−8,679
1983	201,820	−268,900	−67,080	77,251	−52,376	24,875	−243	−4,227	9,908	−36,766	−9,480	−46,246
1984	219,900	−332,422	−112,522	85,908	−67,419	18,489	−2,099	−8,604	9,760	−94,975	−12,102	−107,077
1985	215,935	−338,083	−122,148	88,837	−62,901	25,936	−3,431	−10,049	9,600	−100,093	−15,010	−115,103
1986	223,969	−368,516	−144,547	90,110	−66,968	23,142	−4,372	−9,344	11,600	−123,520	−15,308	−138,828
1987	249,570	−409,850	−160,280	103,756	−83,381	20,375	−2,368	−10,281	12,035	−140,519	−13,445	−153,964

[1] Excludes military.

[2] Adjusted from Census data for differences in valuation, coverage, and timing.

[3] Fees and royalties from U.S. direct investments abroad or from foreign direct investments in the United States are excluded from investment income and included in other services, net.

[4] In concept, balance on goods and services is equal to net exports and imports in the national income and product accounts (and the sum of balance on current account and allocations of special drawing rights is equal to net foreign investment in the accounts), although the series differ because of different handling of certain items (gold, capital gains and losses, etc.), revisions, etc.

[5] Includes extraordinary U.S. Government transactions with India.

See next page for continuation of table.

Table A-1—Continued
U.S. International Transactions, 1946–88
[millions of dollars; quarterly data seasonally adjusted, except as noted]

Year or quarter	U.S. assets abroad, net [increase/capital outflow (−)]				Foreign assets in the U.S., net [increase/capital inflow (+)]			Allocations of special drawing rights (SDRs)	Statistical discrepancy	
	Total	U.S. official reserve assets⁶	Other U.S. Government assets	U.S. private assets	Total	Foreign official assets	Other foreign assets		Total (sum of the items with sign reversed)	Of which: Seasonal adjustment discrepancy
1946		−623								
1947		−3,315								
1948		−1,736								
1949		−266								
1950		1,758								
1951		−33								
1952		−415								
1953		1,256								
1954		480								
1955		182								
1956		−869								
1957		−1,165								
1958		2,292								
1959		1,035								
1960	−4,099	2,145	−1,100	−5,144	2,294	1,473	821		−1,019	
1961	−5,538	607	−910	−5,235	2,705	765	1,939		−989	
1962	−4,174	1,535	−1,085	−4,623	1,911	1,270	641		−1,124	
1963	−7,270	378	−1,662	−5,986	3,217	1,986	1,231		−360	
1964	−9,560	171	−1,680	−8,050	3,643	1,660	1,983		−907	
1965	−5,716	1,225	−1,605	−5,336	742	134	607		−457	
1966	−7,321	570	−1,543	−6,347	3,661	−672	4,333		629	
1967	−9,757	53	−2,423	−7,386	7,379	3,451	3,928		−205	
1968	−10,977	−870	−2,274	−7,833	9,928	−774	10,703		438	
1969	−11,585	−1,179	−2,200	−8,206	12,702	−1,301	14,002		−1,516	
1970	−9,337	2,481	−1,589	−10,229	6,359	6,908	−550	867	−219	
1971	−12,475	2,349	−1,884	−12,940	22,970	26,879	−3,909	717	−9,779	
1972	−14,497	−4	−1,568	−12,925	21,461	10,475	10,986	710	−1,879	
1973	−22,874	158	−2,644	−20,388	18,388	6,026	12,362		−2,654	
1974	−34,745	−1,467	⁵366	−33,643	34,241	10,546	23,696		−1,458	
1975	−39,703	−849	−3,474	−35,380	15,670	7,027	8,643		5,917	
1976	−51,269	−2,558	−4,214	−44,498	36,518	17,693	18,826		10,544	
1977	−34,785	−375	−3,693	−30,717	51,319	36,816	14,503		−2,023	
1978	−61,130	732	−4,660	−57,202	64,036	33,678	30,358		12,521	
1979	−64,331	−1,133	−3,746	−59,453	38,752	−13,665	52,416	1,139	25,431	
1980	−86,118	−8,155	−5,162	−72,802	58,112	15,497	42,615	1,152	24,982	
1981	−110,951	−5,175	−5,097	−100,679	83,032	4,960	78,072	1,093	19,942	
1982	−121,153	−4,965	−6,131	−110,058	93,746	3,593	90,154		36,085	
1983	−49,777	−1,196	−5,006	−43,576	84,869	5,845	79,023		11,154	
1984	−22,304	−3,131	−5,489	−13,685	102,621	3,140	99,481		26,760	
1985	−32,636	−3,858	−2,829	−25,950	129,900	−1,196	131,096		17,839	
1986	−97,991	312	−2,000	−96,303	221,253	35,507	185,746		15,566	
1987	−75,987	9,149	1,162	−86,297	211,490	44,968	166,522		18,461	

Source: *Economic Report of the President*, together with the *Annual Report of the Council of Economic Advisors* (Washington, D.C.: U.S. Government Printing Office, January 1989).

Note: Quarterly data for U.S. official reserve assets and foreign assets in the United States are not seasonally adjusted.

⁶ Consists of gold, special drawing rights, foreign currencies, and the U.S. reserve position in the International Monetary Fund (IMF).

Table A-2
U.S. Merchandise Exports and Imports by Principal End-use Category, 1965–88

[billions of dollars; quarterly data seasonally adjusted]

Year or quarter	Exports							Imports						
	Total	Agricultural products	Nonagricultural products					Total	Petroleum and products	Nonpetroleum products				
			Total	Industrial supplies and materials	Capital goods except automotive	Automotive	Other			Total	Industrial supplies and materials	Capital goods except automotive	Automotive	Other
1965	26.5	6.3	20.2	7.6	8.1	1.9	2.6	21.5	2.0	19.5	9.1	1.5	0.9	8.0
1966	29.3	6.9	22.4	8.2	8.9	2.4	2.9	25.5	2.1	23.4	10.2	2.2	1.8	9.2
1967	30.7	6.5	24.2	8.5	9.9	2.8	3.0	26.9	2.1	24.8	10.0	2.5	2.4	9.9
1968	33.6	6.3	27.3	9.6	11.1	3.5	3.2	33.0	2.4	30.6	12.0	2.8	4.0	11.8
1969	36.4	6.1	30.3	10.4	12.4	3.9	3.7	35.8	2.6	33.2	11.7	3.4	5.1	13.0
1970	42.5	7.4	35.1	12.3	14.7	3.9	4.3	39.9	2.9	36.9	12.3	4.0	5.7	15.0
1971	43.3	7.8	35.5	10.9	15.4	4.7	4.5	45.6	3.6	41.9	13.6	4.3	7.6	16.5
1972	49.4	9.5	39.9	11.8	16.9	5.5	5.6	55.8	4.7	51.1	16.0	5.9	9.0	20.2
1973	71.4	18.0	53.4	16.9	22.0	7.0	7.6	70.5	8.4	62.1	19.2	8.3	10.7	23.9
1974	98.3	22.4	75.9	26.2	30.9	8.8	10.0	103.8	26.6	77.2	27.4	9.8	12.4	27.5
1975	107.1	22.2	84.8	26.7	36.6	10.8	10.7	98.2	27.0	71.2	23.6	10.2	12.1	25.3
1976	114.7	23.4	91.4	28.3	39.1	12.2	11.7	124.2	34.6	89.7	29.1	12.3	16.8	31.4
1977	120.8	24.3	96.5	29.7	39.8	13.5	13.5	151.9	45.0	106.9	35.0	14.0	19.4	38.6
1978 ¹	142.1	29.9	112.2	33.5	46.7	15.5	16.4	176.0	42.6	133.4	40.6	19.4	25.0	48.4
1979	184.5	35.6	148.9	51.6	59.2	18.1	20.1	212.0	61.0	151.1	47.5	24.5	26.5	52.6
1980	224.3	42.2	182.1	64.6	75.1	17.1	25.3	249.8	79.4	170.4	52.9	31.4	28.1	58.0
1981	237.1	44.0	193.1	63.2	82.4	19.3	28.1	265.1	78.6	186.5	56.4	36.9	30.9	62.3
1982	211.2	37.2	174.0	57.4	74.3	17.0	25.3	247.6	62.0	185.6	48.9	38.4	34.0	64.3
1983	201.8	37.1	164.7	52.3	69.2	18.3	24.9	268.9	55.3	213.6	53.9	43.2	43.2	73.3
1984	219.9	38.4	181.5	56.0	74.3	22.1	29.1	332.4	58.0	274.4	66.0	60.5	56.6	91.4
1985	215.9	29.6	186.4	54.0	76.5	24.7	31.1	338.1	51.3	286.8	62.4	61.4	65.1	97.9
1986	224.0	27.4	196.6	58.7	79.3	24.9	33.7	368.5	34.4	334.1	69.9	72.1	78.1	114.0
1987	249.6	29.5	220.1	62.8	88.1	26.3	42.9	409.9	42.9	367.0	71.2	84.8	85.2	125.8

Source: Department of Commerce, Bureau of Economic Analysis.

Note: Data are on an international transactions basis and exclude military.

¹ End-use categories beginning in 1978 are not strictly comparable with data for earlier periods. See *Survey of Current Business*, June 1988.

Table A–3
U.S. Merchandise Exports and Imports by Area, 1979–88
[millions of dollars]

Item	1979	1980	1981	1982	1983	1984	1985	1986	1987	1988 first 3 quarters at annual rate [1]
Exports..................	184,473	224,269	237,085	211,198	201,820	219,900	215,935	223,969	249,570	316,283
Industrial countries	115,930	137,152	141,900	127,254	128,353	140,994	140,517	150,690	164,857	204,158
Canada...............	38,690	41,626	46,016	39,203	44,512	53,037	55,390	56,601	61,092	72,347
Japan.................	17,629	20,806	21,796	20,694	21,789	23,241	22,145	26,344	27,604	37,428
Western Europe	54,177	67,603	65,108	59,701	55,448	56,867	56,015	60,630	68,758	85,559
Australia, New Zealand, and South Africa...........	5,434	7,117	8,980	7,656	6,604	7,849	6,967	7,115	7,403	8,824
Other countries, except Eastern Europe	62,630	82,941	90,657	80,130	70,426	74,583	71,968	71,235	82,475	108,386
OPEC [2].................	14,556	17,368	21,097	20,651	15,256	13,771	11,409	10,470	10,709	13,685
Other [3]...............	48,074	65,573	69,560	59,479	55,170	60,812	60,559	60,765	71,766	94,701
Eastern Europe	5,913	4,143	4,440	3,749	2,976	4,290	3,258	2,044	2,238	3,739
International organizations and unallocated......		33	88	65	65	33	192			
Imports...................	212,009	249,750	265,063	247,642	268,900	332,422	338,083	368,516	409,850	441,440
Industrial countries	112,797	127,884	144,322	144,139	159,893	205,526	219,102	245,374	259,764	278,124
Canada...............	39,227	42,901	48,253	48,523	55,982	67,630	70,394	69,621	73,647	84,432
Japan.................	26,260	31,216	37,597	37,683	42,844	60,210	65,653	80,766	84,548	86,629
Western Europe	41,817	47,235	52,864	52,900	55,623	72,054	77,454	89,039	96,215	100,698
Australia, New Zealand, and South Africa...........	5,493	6,532	5,608	5,033	5,443	5,632	5,601	5,948	5,354	6,365
Other countries, except Eastern Europe	96,131	119,135	119,188	102,414	107,593	124,679	117,134	121,163	148,167	161,152
OPEC [2].................	45,039	55,602	49,934	31,517	25,282	26,852	22,680	18,894	24,367	23,441
Other [3]...............	51,092	63,533	69,254	70,897	82,311	97,827	94,454	102,269	123,800	137,711
Eastern Europe	1,896	1,444	1,553	1,066	1,413	2,217	1,847	1,979	1,919	2,164
International organizations and unallocated......	1,185	1,287		23	1					
Balance (excess of exports +)	−27,536	−25,481	−27,978	−36,444	−67,080	−112,522	−122,148	−144,547	−160,280	−125,157
Industrial countries	3,133	9,268	−2,422	−16,885	−31,540	−64,532	−78,585	−94,684	−94,907	−73,966
Canada...............	−537	−1,275	−2,237	−9,320	−11,470	−14,593	−15,004	−13,020	−12,555	−12,085
Japan.................	−8,631	−10,410	−15,801	−16,989	−21,055	−36,969	−43,508	−54,422	−56,944	−49,201
Western Europe	12,360	20,368	12,244	6,801	−175	−15,187	−21,439	−28,409	−27,457	−15,139
Australia, New Zealand, and South Africa...........	−59	585	3,372	2,623	1,161	2,217	1,366	1,167	2,049	2,459
Other countries, except Eastern Europe	−33,501	−36,194	−28,531	−22,284	−37,167	−50,096	−45,166	−49,928	−65,692	−52,766
OPEC [2].................	−30,483	−38,234	−28,837	−10,866	−10,026	−13,081	−11,271	−8,424	−13,658	−9,756
Other [3]...............	−3,018	2,040	306	−11,418	−27,142	−37,015	−33,895	−41,504	−52,034	−43,010
Eastern Europe	4,017	2,699	2,887	2,683	1,563	2,073	1,411	65	319	1,575
International organizations and unallocated......	−1,185	−1,254	88	42	64	33	192			

Source: Department of Commerce, Bureau of Economic Analysis.

Note: Data are on an international transactions basis and exclude military.

[1] Preliminary; seasonally adjusted.

[2] Algeria, Ecuador, Gabon, Indonesia, Iraq, Kuwait, Libya, Nigeria, Qatar, Saudi Arabia, United Arab Emirates, and Venezuela.

[3] Latin America Republics, other Western Hemisphere, and other countries in Asia and Africa, less members of OPEC.

Table A–4
International Investment Position of the United States at Year-End, 1980–97
[billions of dollars]

Type of investment	1980	1981	1982	1983	1984	1985	1986	1987
Net international investment position of the United States...	106.3	141.1	136.9	89.4	3.5	−110.7	−269.2	−368.2
U.S. assets abroad	607.1	719.8	824.9	873.9	896.1	950.3	1,071.4	1,167.8
U.S. official reserve assets	26.8	30.1	34.0	33.7	34.9	43.2	48.5	45.8
Gold	11.2	11.2	11.1	11.1	11.1	11.1	11.1	11.1
Special drawing rights	2.6	4.1	5.3	5.0	5.6	7.3	8.4	10.3
Reserve position in the International Monetary Fund	2.9	5.1	7.3	11.3	11.5	11.9	11.7	11.3
Foreign currencies	10.1	9.8	10.2	6.3	6.7	12.9	17.3	13.1
U.S. Government assets, other than official reserve assets	63.8	68.7	74.6	79.5	84.8	87.6	89.5	88.4
U.S. loans and other long-term assets	62.0	67.2	72.9	77.8	82.9	85.8	88.7	87.6
Repayable in dollars	59.8	65.0	70.9	76.0	81.1	84.1	87.1	86.0
Other	2.2	2.2	1.9	1.8	1.8	1.7	1.6	1.6
U.S. foreign currency holdings and U.S. short-term assets	1.7	1.5	1.7	1.7	2.0	1.8	.8	.8
U.S. private assets	516.6	621.1	716.4	760.7	776.3	819.5	933.4	1,033.6
Direct investment abroad	215.4	228.3	207.8	207.2	211.5	230.3	259.6	308.9
Foreign securities	62.7	63.4	75.5	83.8	89.1	112.8	133.2	146.7
Bonds	43.5	45.8	56.7	57.7	61.8	73.0	81.8	91.0
Corporate stocks	19.2	17.6	18.8	26.1	27.3	39.8	51.4	55.7
U.S. claims on unaffiliated foreigners reported by U.S. nonbanking concerns	34.7	35.9	28.6	35.1	30.1	29.1	33.3	30.1
U.S. claims reported by U.S. banks, not included elsewhere	203.9	293.5	404.6	434.5	445.6	447.4	507.3	547.9
Foreign assets in the United States	500.8	578.7	688.1	784.5	892.6	1,061.0	1,340.7	1,536.0
Foreign official assets in the United States	176.1	180.4	189.1	194.5	199.3	202.6	241.7	283.1
U.S. Government securities	118.2	125.1	132.6	137.0	143.0	143.4	177.3	219.1
U.S. Treasury securities	111.3	117.0	124.9	129.7	135.5	135.7	170.6	211.2
Other	6.9	8.1	7.7	7.3	7.5	7.7	6.7	7.9
Other U.S. Government liabilities	13.4	13.0	13.6	14.2	15.0	15.7	17.8	15.0
U.S. liabilities reported by U.S. banks, not included elsewhere	30.4	26.7	25.0	25.5	26.1	26.7	27.9	31.8
Other foreign official assets	14.1	15.5	17.9	17.7	15.2	16.7	18.8	17.3
Other foreign assets in the United States	324.8	398.3	498.9	590.0	693.3	858.4	1,098.9	1,252.9
Direct investment in the United States	83.0	108.7	124.7	137.1	164.6	184.6	220.4	261.9
U.S. Treasury securities	16.1	18.5	25.8	33.8	58.2	83.6	91.5	78.4
U.S. securities other than U.S. Treasury securities	74.1	75.1	93.0	113.8	127.3	206.2	308.8	344.4
Corporate and other bonds	9.5	10.7	16.7	17.5	32.7	82.5	142.1	171.0
Corporate stocks	64.6	64.4	76.3	94.5	94.6	123.7	166.7	173.4
U.S. liabilities to unaffiliated foreigners reported by U.S. nonbanking concerns	30.4	30.6	27.5	26.9	31.0	29.5	26.6	28.8
U.S. liabilities reported by U.S. banks, not included elsewhere	121.1	165.4	228.0	278.3	312.2	354.5	451.6	539.4

Source: Department of Commerce, Bureau of Economic Analysis.

Table A–5
Civilian Unemployment Rate, and Hourly Compensation, Major Industrial Countries, 1960–1988
[quarterly data seasonally adjusted]

Year or quarter	United States	Canada	Japan	France	West Germany	Italy	United Kingdom
	Civilian unemployment rate (percent)[1]						
1960	5.5	6.5	1.7	1.5	1.1	3.7	2.2
1961	6.7	6.7	1.5	1.2	.6	3.2	2.0
1962	5.5	5.5	1.3	1.4	.6	2.8	2.7
1963	5.7	5.2	1.3	1.6	.5	2.4	3.3
1964	5.2	4.4	1.2	1.2	.4	2.7	2.5
1965	4.5	3.6	1.2	1.6	.3	3.5	2.1
1966	3.8	3.4	1.4	1.6	.3	3.7	2.3
1967	3.8	3.8	1.3	2.1	1.3	3.4	3.3
1968	3.6	4.5	1.2	2.7	1.1	3.5	3.2
1969	3.5	4.4	1.1	2.3	.6	3.5	3.1
1970	4.9	5.7	1.2	2.5	.5	3.2	3.1
1971	5.9	6.2	1.3	2.8	.6	3.3	3.9
1972	5.6	6.2	1.4	2.9	.7	3.8	4.2
1973	4.9	5.5	1.3	2.8	.7	3.7	3.2
1974	5.6	5.3	1.4	2.9	1.6	3.1	3.1
1975	8.5	6.9	1.9	4.1	3.4	3.4	4.6
1976	7.7	7.1	2.0	4.5	3.4	3.9	5.9
1977	7.1	8.1	2.0	5.1	3.5	4.1	6.4
1978	6.1	8.3	2.3	5.3	3.3	4.1	6.3
1979	5.8	7.4	2.1	6.0	3.0	4.4	5.4
1980	7.1	7.5	2.0	6.4	2.9	4.4	7.0
1981	7.6	7.5	2.2	7.6	4.1	4.9	10.5
1982	9.7	11.0	2.4	8.3	5.8	5.4	11.3
1983	9.6	11.9	2.7	8.5	7.1	5.9	11.9
1984	7.5	11.3	2.8	10.0	7.4	5.9	11.7
1985	7.2	10.5	2.6	10.4	7.5	6.0	11.2
1986	7.0	9.6	2.8	10.6	7.0	7.5	11.2
1987	6.2	8.9	2.9	10.8	6.9	7.9	10.3

Source: Department of Labor, Bureau of Labor Statistics.

[1] Civilian unemployment rates, approximating U.S. concepts. Quarterly data for France, West Germany, and United Kingdom should be viewed as less precise indicators of unemployment under U.S. concepts than the annual data. Many Italians reported as unemployed did not actively seek work in the past 30 days, and they have been excluded for comparability with U.S. concepts. Inclusion of such persons would about double the unemployment rate for Italy through 1985, and increase it to 11–12 percent for 1986–88. There are breaks in the series for Italy and West Germany. Based on the former series, the rate for West Germany for 1983 was 7.4 percent and the rate for Italy for 1986 was 6.3 percent.

Table A–5—Continued
Civilian Unemployment Rate, and Hourly Compensation, Major Industrial Countries, 1960–1988
[quarterly data seasonally adjusted]

Year or quarter	United States	Canada	Japan	France	West Germany	Italy	United Kingdom
	Manufacturing hourly compensation in U.S. dollars (1977 = 100) [2]						
1960	36.5	30.1	6.6	15.1	10.5	11.9	24.5
1961	37.6	29.6	7.7	16.6	12.2	13.2	26.1
1962	39.0	28.9	8.8	18.4	13.9	15.6	27.5
1963	40.2	29.8	9.8	20.0	14.8	18.5	28.7
1964	41.9	31.0	11.0	21.8	16.1	20.6	30.5
1965	42.7	32.8	12.4	23.6	17.6	21.9	33.4
1966	44.6	35.5	13.6	25.0	19.1	22.9	36.1
1967	46.9	37.6	15.3	26.8	20.2	25.4	36.7
1968	50.2	40.5	17.8	30.2	21.7	27.1	34.2
1969	53.7	43.8	21.3	30.7	24.1	30.8	37.3
1970	57.4	48.8	25.3	32.3	30.5	36.8	43.2
1971	60.9	54.3	30.2	36.5	35.9	43.1	50.9
1972	64.2	59.4	39.8	44.1	43.4	52.3	60.2
1973	68.8	63.7	54.5	57.5	59.1	66.4	67.3
1974	76.2	75.0	66.4	63.4	69.1	74.0	77.0
1975	85.1	82.5	76.0	87.4	79.9	95.0	97.3
1976	92.1	97.3	81.9	90.4	84.2	89.5	91.4
1977	100.0	100.0	100.0	100.0	100.0	100.0	100.0
1978	108.2	100.3	137.0	123.4	124.8	119.1	128.3
1979	118.6	107.6	139.2	148.3	147.0	143.1	169.0
1980	132.4	119.3	143.2	172.9	160.7	165.3	224.7
1981	145.2	133.9	157.6	155.4	138.5	153.8	224.4
1982	157.5	143.8	146.9	152.4	134.8	155.4	212.0
1983	162.4	152.8	158.6	145.2	134.8	164.4	196.9
1984	168.0	152.3	163.5	137.8	126.9	159.1	185.6
1985	176.4	151.3	170.1	145.3	129.9	160.9	192.4
1986	183.0	155.6	252.7	196.7	183.7	212.7	233.7
1987	186.9	171.5	298.3	233.6	230.6	259.0	279.6

[2] Hourly compensation in manufacturing, U.S. dollar basis. Data relate to all employed persons (wage and salary earners and the self-employed) in the United States and Canada, and to all employees (wage and salary earners) in the other countries. For France and United Kingdom, compensation adjusted to include changes in employment taxes that are not compensation to employees, but are labor costs to employers.

Table A–6
Growth Rates in Real Gross National Product, 1961–88
[percent change]

Area and country	1961–65 annual average	1966–70 annual average	1971–75 annual average	1976–82 annual average	1983	1984	1985	1986	1987	1988 [1]
OECD countries [2]	5.3	4.6	3.0	3.3	2.7	4.7	3.2	2.8	3.1	3.0
United States	4.6	3.0	2.2	2.3	3.6	6.8	3.4	2.8	3.4	3.8
Canada	5.3	4.6	5.2	2.6	3.2	6.3	4.6	3.2	4.0	4.1
Japan	12.4	11.0	4.3	4.5	3.2	5.1	4.7	2.5	4.4	5.4
European Community [3]	4.9	4.6	2.9	3.0	1.5	2.4	2.4	2.6	2.7	2.5
France	5.9	5.4	4.0	3.1	.7	1.3	1.7	2.1	2.3	2.8
West Germany	4.7	4.2	2.1	2.3	1.9	3.3	1.9	2.3	1.8	2.9
Italy	4.8	6.6	2.4	2.9	1.0	3.2	2.8	2.9	3.1	3.1
United Kingdom	3.2	2.5	2.1	1.3	3.5	2.1	3.9	2.9	3.6	3.5
Communist countries [4]	4.4	5.0	4.2	2.7	2.7	2.3	2.3	4.1	1.1	([5])
U.S.S.R.	4.8	5.0	3.1	2.1	3.3	1.4	.8	3.9	.7	2.0
Eastern Europe	3.9	3.8	4.9	1.2	1.8	3.6	.8	3.0	.6	2.1
China	−.2	8.3	5.5	6.2	9.1	12.0	12.0	7.5	9.5	9.0

Sources: Department of Commerce, International Monetary Fund, Organization for Economic Cooperation and Development, and Council of Economic Advisers.

[1] Estimates.
[2] OECD (Organization for Economic Cooperation and Development) includes Australia, Austria, Belgium, Denmark, Finland, France, West Germany, Greece, Iceland, Ireland, Italy, Luxembourg, Netherlands, New Zealand, Norway, Portugal, Spain, Sweden, Switzerland, Turkey, and United Kingdom, not shown separately.
[3] Includes Belgium, Denmark, Greece, Ireland, Luxembourg, Netherlands, Portugal, and Spain, not shown separately.
[4] Includes North Korea and Yugoslavia, not shown separately.
[5] Not available.

Notes

Chapter 2

1. Adam Smith, *The Wealth of Nations* (Modern Library: New York, Random House, 1987), p. 275.

Chapter 3

1. *Dollars and Sense,* March 1986, p. 14.
2. Ibid., p. 15.
3. *The New York Times,* August 3, 1986.
4. *U.S.A. Today,* February 14, 1986.
5. *U.S.A. Today,* November 7, 1986.
6. *The Wall Street Journal,* June 19, 1986.

Chapter 5

1. Robert Gilpin, *The Political Economy of International Relations* (Princeton: Princeton University Press, 1987), p. 231.
2. Michael P. Todaro, *Economic Development in the Third World* (White Plains: Longman, 1989), fourth edition, p. 471.
3. Jean Jacque Servan-Schriber, *The American Challenge* (New York: Avon Books, 1967).
4. Raymond Vernon, "International Investment and International Trade in the Product Cycle," *Quarterly Journal of Economics,* 1966, No. 80, pp. 190–207.

5. "The Hollowing Corporation," *Business Week*, March 3, 1986, pp. 57–85.

6. "Shaking Up Detroit," *Business Week*, August 14, 1989, pp. 74–79.

7. Denis Goulet, *The Cruel Choice* (New York: Antheum, 1971).

8. Theotonio Dos Santos, "The Structure of Dependence," *American Economic Review,* 1970, No. 60, pp. 231–236.

Chapter 6

1. Jacques de Larosiere, former managing director of the IMF. Text of address given at the joint meetings of the IMF and World Bank, Washington, D.C., September 1986.

2. From text of the United Nations Economic Declaration, *The New York Times,* June 11, 1987, p. 16A.

3. *The New York Times,* November 6, 1987.

Chapter 7

1. Alfred Malabre, *Beyond Our Means* (New York: Basic Books, 1987).

2. Ibid., p. 75.

3. Ernest Conine, *The Los Angeles Times,* June 15, 1988.

4. Donald Regan, testimony before the House Bank Finance and Urban Affairs Committee, Washington, D.C., December 21, 1982.

Chapter 8

1. Morris Miller, *Coping is Not Enough: The International Debt Crisis and the Roles of the World Bank and the IMF* (Homewood, IL: Irwin, 1987), pp. 169–170.

2. Henry Kissinger, "The Future of the Global Economy," *The Washington Post,* November 22, 1984; and Miller, ibid., p. 143.

3. Miller, op. cit., p. 146.

4. Irving S. Friedman, *Toward World Prosperity* (Lexington, MA: Lexington Books, 1986), pp. 291–293.

5. Martin Feldstein, "The End of Policy Coordination," *The New York Times,* November 9, 1987.

6. Robert Kuttner, "The Theory Gap," *The New York Times,* January 17, 1988.

7. Deborah Allen Oliver, "Few Industries Benefit from the Weaker Dollar," *The Wall Street Journal,* January 30, 1987.

8. Michael Hudson, "A Cheap Dollar Won't Cure the Deficit," *The New York Times,* January 24, 1988.

9. Paul Farba, "Hidden Dangers of Currency Cooperation," *The Wall Street Journal,* November 23, 1987.

10. Ronald I. McKinnon, "A Model for Currency Cooperation," *The Wall Street Journal,* September 21, 1987; McKinnon, "When Capital Flowed and Exchange Rates Held," *The Wall Street Journal,* March 28, 1988; McKinnon, "Monetary and Exchange Rate Policies for International Financial Stability: A Proposal," *Journal of Economic Perspectives,* Vol. 2, No. 1, Winter 1988, pp. 83–103; McKinnon, *An International Standard for Monetary Stabilization,* Institute for International Economics, Washington, D.C., 1984. See also Rudiger Dornbusch, "Doubts About the McKinnon Standard," and John Williamson, "Comment on McKinnon's Monetary Rule," *Journal of Economic Perspectives,* Vol. 2, No. 1, Winter 1988, pp. 105–112 and pp. 113–119, respectively.

11. John Williamson and Marcus E. Miller, *Targets and Indicators: A Blueprint for the International Coordination of Economic Policy.* Institute for International Economics, Washington, D.C., No. 22, September 1987.

12. Edouard Balladur, "Rebuilding an International Monetary System," *The Wall Street Journal,* February 23, 1988.

13. Miller, op. cit., ch. 8. "Banks Step Up Third World Debt Disposal," *The Wall Street Journal,* July 26, 1988.

14. John Loxley, *Debt and Disorder: External Financing for Development* (Boulder, CO: Westview Press, 1986), pp. 44–50.

15. Stanley Fischer, "Sharing the Burden of the International Debt Crisis," *American Economic Review,* Vol. 77, No. 2, May 1985, pp. 165–170.

16. Jeffrey D. Sachs, "It's the Right Time to Offer Real Relief," *The New York Times,* August 9, 1987.

17. William R. Cline, *Mobilizing Bank Lending to Debtor Countries* (Washington, D.C.: Institute for International Economics, June 1987), pp. 80–92.

18. Clyde Farnsworth, "IMF Studying Plan to Ease Debt Burden," *The New York Times,* March 8, 1988.

19. World Bank, *World Development Report, 1987,* chapter 2; and International Monetary Fund, *World Outlook,* April 1988.

20. Harry Magdoff and Paul Sweezy, "International Cooperation: A Way Out?" *Monthly Review,* November 1987, pp. 18–19.

Chapter 9

1. "Wake Up, America," *Business Week,* November 16, 1987.

2. Alfred Malabre, *Beyond Our Means* (New York: Basic Books, 1987).

3. "The 1980s are Over, Greed Goes Out of Style," *Newsweek,* January 4, 1988.

4. Peter Peterson, "The Morning After," *Atlantic Monthly,* October 1987, p. 50.

5. Ibid., p. 50.

6. Ibid., p. 52.

7. Barry Bluestone and Bennett Harrison, "The Grim Truth About the Job Miracle," *The New York Times,* February 1, 1987.

8. E. Gerald Corrigan, "A Balanced Approach to the LDC Debt Problem," Federal Reserve Bank of New York, *Quarterly Review,* Spring 1988, pp. 1–6.

9. Michael Moffitt, "Economic Decline, Reagan Style: Dollar, Debt and Deflation," *World Policy,* Vol. 2, No. 3, Summer 1985.

Chapter 10

1. Paul Kennedy, *The Rise and Fall of the Great Powers* (New York: Random House, 1988); Louis Uchitelle, "When the World Lacks a Leader," *The New York Times*, January 31, 1988.

2. Uchitelle, op. cit., p. F6.

3. Michele Fratianni, "Europe's Non-Model for Stable World Money," *The Wall Street Journal*, April 4, 1988.

4. Edouard Balladur, "Rebuilding an International Monetary System," *The Wall Street Journal*, February 23, 1988.

Chapter 11

1. Alan Sinai, "The Crash of 1987 and the Economy of 1988," *Challenge,* January–February, 1988, pp. 11–21; also Sinai, "The Question Is Not If, But When?" *The New York Times*, April 3, 1988.

2. Ibid., pp. 12–13.

3. Ibid., p. 16.

4. Peter Peterson, "After an Economic Heart Attack," *Newsweek*, November 2, 1987; also Peterson, "No Pain, No Gain: How America Can Grow Again," *Business Week*, April 20, 1988.

5. Ibid., p. 53.

6. I.M. Destler, *American Trade Politics: System Under Stress* (Washington, D.C.: Institute for International Economics, 1986), p. 184.

7. Robert Reich, *The Next American Frontier* (New York: Times Books, 1983), p. 238.

8. Martin K. Starr, ed., *Global Competitiveness: Getting the U.S. Back on Track* (New York: Norton, 1988); and Michael J. Piore and Charles F. Sabel, *The Second Industrial Divide: Possibilities for Prosperity* (New York: Basic Books, 1984).

9. Robert Reich, *Tales of a New America* (New York: Times Books, 1987); and Reich, "Behold! We Do Have an Industrial Policy," *The New York Times*, May 22, 1988.

10. I.M. Destler, op. cit., p. 196.

11. Norman Jonas, "A Strategy for Revitalizing Industry," *Business Week*, March 3, 1988, p. 85.

12. Thomas Riddell, "Military Buildup, Economic Decline," *Dollars and Sense*, September 1987, pp. 6–9; and Rich West, "Military Mania," *Sane World*, Summer 1987, pp. 10–13.

13. Peter Schmeisser, "Is America in Decline?" *The New York Times*, April 17, 1988, Sunday Magazine, p. 24.

14. Paul Kennedy, *The Rise and Fall of the Great Powers* (New York: Random House, 1987).

15. John C. Pool and Stephen C. Stamos, Jr., *The ABCs of International Finance* (Lexington, MA: Lexington Books, 1987), pp. 17–24.

16. David Gordon, "Do We Need to Be No. 1?" *Atlantic Monthly*, April 1986, p. 103; see also Samuel Bowles, David Gordon, and Thomas Weisskopf, *Beyond the Wasteland* (New York: Basic Books, 1983).

17. Ibid., p. 105.

18. Ibid., p. 105.

19. Ibid., p. 106.

20. Michael Moffitt, "Shocks, Deadlocks, and Scorched Earth: Reaganomics and the Decline of U.S. Hegemony," *World Policy*, Spring 1987, p. 557.

21. Ibid., p. 559.

22. Ibid., p. 560.

23. W. Michael Blumenthal, "The World Economy and Technological Change," *Foreign Affairs*, Spring 1988, p. 531.

24. Ibid., p. 543.

25. Ibid., p. 545.

26. Ibid., p. 546.

27. Ibid., p. 547.

Suggested Reading

Jahangir Amuzegar, "Dealing with Debt," *Foreign Policy*, Fall 1987, No. 68.

C. Fred Bergsten, *America in the World Economy: A Strategy for the 1990s* (Washington, D.C.: Institute for International Economics, 1988).

C. Fred Bergsten and William R. Cline, *The United States–Japan Economic Problem* (Washington, D.C.: Institute for International Economics, October 1985).

Fred Block, *The Origins of International Economic Disorder* (Berkeley: University of California Press, 1977).

Don Bonker, *America's Trade Crisis: The Making of the U.S. Trade Deficit* (Boston: Houghton Mifflin, 1988).

Anthony Brewer, *Marxist Theories of Imperialism: A Critical Survey* (London: Routledge and Kegan Paul, 1980).

Ralph C. Bryant, Gerald Holtham, and Peter Hooper, eds., *External Deficits and the Dollar: The Pit and the Pendulum* (Washington, D.C.: The Brookings Institution, 1988).

Samuel Bowles, David Gordon, and Thomas Weisskopf, *Beyond the Wasteland* (New York: Anchor/Doubleday, 1982).

David P. Calleo, *The Imperious Economy* (Cambridge: Harvard University Press, 1982).

James A. Caporaso, ed., "Dependence and Dependency in the Global System," *International Organization*, No. 32, pp. 1–300, 1978.

Mark Casson, ed., *The Growth of International Business* (London: George Allen and Unwin, 1983).

Richard E. Caves, *Multinational Enterprise and Economic Analysis* (New York: Cambridge University Press, 1982).

Benjamin Cohen, *The Question of Imperialism: The Political Economy of Dominance and Dependence* (New York: Basic Books, 1973).

William R. Cline, *United States External Adjustment and the World Economy* (Washington, D.C.: Institute for International Economics, 1989).

———, *American Trade Adjustment: The Global Impact* (Washington, D.C.: Institute for International Economics, 1989).

——, *International Debt and the Stability of the World Economy* (Washington , D.C.: Institute for International Economics, 1983).

——, *Mobilizing Bank Lending to Debtor Countries* (Washington, D.C: Institute for International Economics, 1987).

Michael L. Dertouzos, Richard K. Lester, Robert M. Solow, and the MIT Commission on Industrial Productivity, *Made in America: Regaining the Productive Edge* (Cambridge: MIT Press, 1989).

I.M. Destler, *American Trade Politics: System under Stress* (Washington, D.C.: Institute for International Economics, 1986).

Theotonio Dos Santos, "The Structure of Dependence," *American Economic Review*, No. 60, pp. 231–236, 1970.

Gerald Epstein, "The Triple Debt Crisis," *World Policy*, Vol. 2, No. 4, Fall 1985.

Peter Evans, *Dependent Development: The Alliance of Multinational, State, and Local Capital in Brazil* (Princeton: Princeton University Press, 1979).

Martin Feldstein, "American Economic Policy and the World Economy," *Foreign Affairs*, No. 63, pp. 995–1008, 1985.

Andre Gunder Frank, *Latin America: Underdevelopment or Revolution?* (New York: Monthly Review Press, 1970).

Jeffrey Frieden, "Third World Indebted Industrialization: International Finance and State Capitalism in Mexico, Brazil, Algeria, and South Korea," *International Organization*, No. 35, pp. 407–431, 1981.

Irving S. Friedman, *Toward World Prosperity* (Lexington, MA: Lexington Books, 1986).

Robert Gilpin, *The Political Economy of International Relations* (Princeton: Princeton University Press, 1987).

Theodore Geiger, *The Future of the International System: The United States and the World Political Economy* (Boston: Allen and Unwin, 1988).

Joseph Grunwald and Kenneth Flamm, *The Global Factory: Foreign Assembly in International Trade* (Washington, D.C.: The Brookings Institution, 1985).

David Gordon, "Do We Need To Be No. 1" *Atlantic Monthly*, April 1986.

Stephanie Griffith-Jones, ed., *Managing World Debt* (New York: St. Martin's Press, 1988).

Stephanie Griffith-Jones and Osvaldo Sunkel, *Debt and Development in Latin America: The End of an Illusion* (New York: Oxford University Press, 1986).

Keith Griffin, *Alternative Strategies for Economic Development* (New York: St. Martin's Press, 1988).

H. Peter Gray, *International Economic Problems and Policies* (New York: St. Martin's Press, 1987).

Gary Clyde Hufbauer and Jeffrey J. Schott, *Economic Sanctions Reconsidered: History and Current Policy* (Washington, D.C.: Institute for International Economics, 1985).

Stephen Hymer, *The International Operations of National Firms: A Study of Foreign Direct Investment*, Ph.D. dissertation, Dept. of Economics, MIT, 1960; published by MIT Press, 1976.

"Human Capital: The Decline of America's Work Force," *Business Week*, Sept. 19, 1988, Special Report.

Inter-American Development Bank, *Economic and Social Progress Report* (Washington, D.C.: IADB, 1987).

International Monetary Fund, *World Economic Outlook* (Washington, D.C.: IMF, April 1988).

Anatole Kaletsky, *The Costs of Default* (New York: Priority Press, 1985).

Paul Kennedy, *The Rise and Fall of the Great Powers* (New York: Random House, 1988).

Joyce Kolko, *Restructuring the World Economy* (New York: Pantheon, 1988).

Pedro-Pablo Kuczynski, *Latin American Debt* (Baltimore: Johns Hopkins University Press, 1988).

Paul R. Krugman, ed., *Strategic Trade Policy and the New International Economics* (Cambridge, MA: MIT Press, 1987).

Robert Z. Lawrence, *Can America Compete?* (Washington, D.C.: The Brookings Institution, 1984).

Donald R. Lessard and John Williamson, *Financial Intermediation Beyond the Debt Crisis* (Washington, D.C.: Institute for International Economics, 1985)

———, *Capital Flight and Third World Debt* (Washington, D.C.: Institute for International Economics, 1987).

Harold Lever and Christopher Huhne, *Debt and Danger: The World Financial Crisis* (New York: Atlantic Monthly Press, 1985).

John Loxley, *Debt and Disorder: External Financing for Development* (Boulder: Westview Press, 1986).

Ira Magaziner and Mark Patinkin, *The Silent War: Inside the Global Business Battles Shaping America's Future* (New York: Random House, 1989).

John H. Makin, *The Global Debt Crisis: America's Growing Involvement* (New York: Basic Books, 1984).

Stephen Marris, *Deficits and the Dollar: The World Economy at Risk* (Washington, D.C.: Institute for International Economics, 1985). Updated in 1988.

Alfred Malabre, *Beyond Our Means* (New York: Basic Books, 1987).

Ronald I. McKinnon, *An International Standard for Monetary Stabilization* (Washington, D.C.: Institute for International Economics, 1984).

Morris Miller, *Coping Is Not Enough: The International Debt Crisis and the Roles of the World Bank and the International Monetary Fund* (Homewood, IL: Dow Jones-Irwin, 1986).

Peter Peterson, "The Morning After," *Atlantic Monthly*, October 1987.

Michael J. Piore and Charles F. Sabel, *The Second Industrial Divide* (New York: Basic Books, 1984).

Robert Pirog and Stephen C. Stamos, *Energy Economics: Theory and Policy* (Englewood Cliffs: Prentice-Hall, 1987).

John Charles Pool and Stephen C. Stamos, *The ABCs of International Finance* (Lexington, MA: Lexington Books, 1987).

————, *International Economic Policy: Beyond the Trade and Debt Crisis* (Lexington, MA: Lexington Books, 1989).

John Charles Pool and Ross M. LaRoe, *Default* (New York: St. Martin's Press, 1987).

————, *The Instant Economist* (Reading, MA: Addison-Wesley, 1985).

Robert B. Reich, *The Next American Frontier* (New York: Times Books, 1983).

————, *Tales of a New America* (New York: Times Books, 1987).

Resolving the Global Economic Crisis: After Wall Street. A Statement by Thirty-three Economists from Thirteen Countries (Washington, D.C.: Institute for International Economics, Special Report 6, December 1987).

Thomas Riddell, Jean Shackelford, and Stephen C. Stamos, *Economics: A Tool for Understanding Society* (Reading, MA: Addison-Wesley, 1987). Third Edition.

Martin K. Starr, ed., *Global Competitiveness: Getting the U.S. Back on Track* (New York: Norton, 1988).

Howard Wachtel, *The Money Mandarins: The Making of a Supranational Economic Order* (New York: Pantheon, 1986).

Murray Weidenbaum, *Rendezvous with Reality: The American Economy after Reagan* (New York: Basic Books, 1988).

John Williamson, *The Exchange Rate System* (Washington, D.C.: Institute for International Economics, 1983).

John Williamson and Marcus H. Miller, *Targets and Indicators: A Blueprint for the International Coordination of Economic Policy* (Washington, D.C.: Institute for International Economics, 1987).

World Bank, *World Debt Tables: External Debt of Developing Countries*, Vol. I. Analysis and Summary Tables (Washington, D.C.: World Bank, 1988).

Index

About the Authors

John Charles Pool received his B.A. and M.B.A. from the University of Missouri and his Ph.D. in economics from the University of Colorado. He is coauthor of *Economia: Enfoque America Latina*, *The Instant Economist*, *The ABCs of International Finance* (Lexington Books 1987), *Default!*, *International Economic Policy* (Lexington Books 1988), and author of *Studying and Thinking About Economics and Society*, and has published numerous articles on various economics topics.

He also writes (with Ross M. LaRoe) a syndicated newspaper column, "The Instant Economist," which treats current issues in economics.

Dr. Pool is a professional economist–writer based in Rochester, New York. He has taught at Bucknell University and the Universities of Iowa and Missouri; for two years he was a Fulbright Professor in Mexico, and is an adjunct professor of economics at St. John Fisher College.

Stephen C. Stamos, Jr. received a B.A. from San Diego State University, an M.S. in economics from Wright State University, and a Ph.D. in political economy from the Union Graduate School. He is coauthor of *Economics: A Tool for Understanding Society*, *Energy Economics: Theory and Policy*, *The ABCs of International Finance* (Lexington Books 1987), and *International Economic Policy* (Lexington Books 1988), and has published widely in professional journals on the topics of energy and international economics.

Dr. Stamos is professor of economics and international relations at Bucknell University. He has been a visiting professor at Evergreen State College and at the University of Massachusetts–Amherst, and a visiting fellow at the Center for U.S.–Mexican Studies, University of California at San Diego.

Pool and Stamos have collaborated on several studies of Latin American economics issues and problems, including a major study of the role of tourism in the Mexican economy and another on Mexican external debt. They have both lived and taught in Mexico.